Migration and Economy

SOCIETY FOR ECONOMIC ANTHROPOLOGY (SEA) MONOGRAPHS

Deborah Winslow, University of New Hampshire
General Editor, Society for Economic Anthropology

Monographs for the Society for Economic Anthropology contain original essays that explore the connections between economics and social life. Each year's volume focuses on a different theme in economic anthropology. Earlier volumes were published with the University Press of America, Inc. (#1-15, 17), Rowman & Littlefield, Inc. (#16). The monographs are now published jointly by AltaMira Press and the Society for Economic Anthropology (http://nautarch.tamu.edu/anth/SEA/).

Migration and Economy

Global and Local Dynamics

LILLIAN TRAGER, EDITOR

Published in cooperation with the
Society for Economic Anthropology

A Division of
ROWMAN & LITTLEFIELD PUBLISHERS, INC.
Walnut Creek • Lanham • New York • Oxford

AltaMira Press
A division of Rowman & Littlefield Publishers, Inc.
A wholly owned subsidiary of The Rowman & Littlefield Publishing Group, Inc.
4501 Forbes Boulevard, Suite 200
Lanham, MD 20706
www.altamirapress.com

PO Box 317, Oxford, OX2 9RU, UK

British Library Cataloguing in Publication Information Available

Library of Congress Cataloging-in-Publication Data

Migration and economy : global and local dynamics / edited by Lillian Trager.
   p.   cm. — (Society for Economic Anthropology monographs ; v. 22.)
   Includes bibliographical references and index.
   ISBN 0-7591-0774-2 (cloth : alk. paper) — ISBN 0-7591-0775-0 (pbk. : alk. paper)
   1. Emigration and immigration—Economic aspects. 2. Migration, Internal—Economic
aspects. 3. Emigration and immigration—Case studies. 4. Migration, Internal—
Case studies. I. Trager, Lillian, 1947– II. Series.
JV6217.M54 2005
331.5'44—dc22

                                                       2005009247

Printed in the United States of America

♾™ The paper used in this publication meets the minimum requirements of American
National Standard for Information Sciences—Permanence of Paper for Printed Library
Materials, ANSI/NISO Z39.48-1992.

Contents

List of Figures and Tables

Acknowledgments

The Society for Economic Anthropology's 2003 conference on migration and economy took place in Monterrey, Mexico, an ideal location for discussion of this subject. With one exception, the chapters in this volume were first presented at that conference. I am grateful to all of the presenters at the conference, including those who participated in the poster session, and to all those who attended, for the wide-ranging discussion that took place, which helped to address and clarify key issues. The hosts for the conference at the Universidad de Monterrey, especially Victor Zuniga and William Breen Murray, provided a welcoming and stimulating environment.

The Committee on Research and Creative Activity and the Professional Opportunities Fund at University of Wisconsin–Parkside provided support for costs associated with organizing the program. I would like to thank Kim Boyajian for assistance in the selection and initial editing of the chapters. I am grateful to the two anonymous reviewers, who provided detailed and helpful comments on the volume as a whole and on the individual chapters, as well as to Deborah Winslow, the society's general editor, and Bob Hunt, the society's senior editor, for their supportive and constructive suggestions.

Introduction

The Dynamics of Migration

Lillian Trager

In a news article with the headline "Born on the Bayou and Barely Feeling Any Urge to Roam" (Blaine Harden, *New York Times*, September 30, 2002), a resident of Vacherie, Louisiana, is quoted as saying, "Living here is like a security blanket. I stay in Vacherie because my mama's here, my grandmama's here and I just never thought of living anywhere else." The story contrasts the stay-at-home character of people in the Bayou, described as the "most rooted" part of the United States, with the high-population mobility characteristic of American society in general. It emphasizes how "Cajun culture," including food and other traditions, encourages young people to stay at home.

This view of a traditional, stable, and stationary society is similar to the way in which anthropologists and other social scientists have often viewed "traditional" societies. In traditional society, people are assumed to stay in one place, with little mobility; migration and mobility accompany modernization and the transition to urban society. Migration has been framed as an unusual activity, one that needs to be explained: why does an individual move rather than stay at home? The assumption is that any reasonable person would prefer to stay at home, if at all possible.

But is migration unusual? Or is it a normal part of human activity and human history? Clearly, the degree to which people are mobile or stationary

1

varies from one context to another, as do the reasons why people move or stay. Today, the extent of migration is vast, with people moving from one place to another within a country, people moving across international boundaries, and forced movements of people because of civil conflicts and environmental degradation. Yet, this is not necessarily a new phenomenon. In many world regions, people have long moved from one place to another, as they sought out livelihoods in new locales, moved among a set of places within a geographical region, or established new communities as kin groups expanded. The anthropological literature provides many examples of population mobility. The ethnography of West Africa, for example, includes several types of evidence of movement, ranging from pastoral transhumance to the expansionary practices of lineage societies such as the Tiv to origin stories of communities among the Yoruba, which are usually stories of migration. In Southeast Asia, the history of the Philippines provides an example of movements of people from coastal and riverine regions to the interior and, later, movement to towns that was encouraged by the Spanish colonial power (Trager 1988, 56). Recent archeological research has also begun to examine evidence of migration more closely (Burmeister 2000; see Hoerder 2002 for a world history of migration from the eleventh century to the late twentieth century).

If we take migration to be a key process not only at present but also throughout history, then the types of questions that we ask about it change. Rather than focus only or primarily on why people move, we can ask questions about the dynamics of migration in relation to other central phenomena, such as family and kinship groups, resources and livelihoods, and political and other forces. Rather than assume that most people prefer not to move, we may consider contexts where people seek out and expect to find opportunities for mobility, as well as those contexts where people decide to stay in one place. After all, the Cajun people of the Louisiana Bayou are the result of at least two earlier, very different patterns of migration—the movement of French-speaking Acadians from Nova Scotia and that of the African Americans whose ancestors were brought to the United States as slaves. We may also find that views of migration vary over the life cycle within any specific community; the young men in Mali described by Dolores Koenig (chapter 2, this volume) seek "travel" and "adventure," but elders in the same communities are expected to be back at home.

This volume examines contemporary migration in a number of contexts and from a variety of perspectives. It indicates the range of current research in migration might operate on multiple levels simultaneously, and that sorting out which of the explanations are useful is an empirical and not only a logical task" (50).

Recent research on international migration has shifted focus from simply the movement of individuals from one country to another to the study of the continuing links that are formed and maintained among those who leave and those who stay at home. The shift to the study of transnational migrants has made clear that migration is not a onetime event but rather an ongoing process, with migrants remaining connected to family and community in the home country while becoming part of networks and communities in the new country. Individual migrants move back and forth between locales. As Linda Basch, Nina Glick Schiller, and Cristina Szanton Blanc describe in their discussion of the "discovery" of transnationalism,

> the migrants in the study sample moved so frequently and were seemingly so at home in either New York or Trinidad as well as their societies of origin, that it at times became difficult to identify where they "belonged." . . .
>
> [The researchers] recognized that the dichotomized social science categories used to analyze migration experiences could not explain the simultaneous involvements . . . of migrants in the social and political life of more than one nation-state. Rather than fragmented social and political experiences, these activities, spread across state boundaries, seemed to constitute a single field of social relations. (1994, 5)

If huge numbers of people are involved in international movements, then the numbers of those who move within their own national boundaries are far greater but even harder to estimate. In countries such as the United States, with relatively accurate census data, data are collected on movement into and out of communities. It is therefore possible to know that one place, such as the Louisiana Bayou, is the "most rooted" in that there is relatively little movement in or out, while another, such as Stateline, Nevada, is "way off the mobility scale" and that the state of Nevada in general has fewer people living there who were also born there than any other state in the country (*New York Times*, September 30, 2002). Most countries collect limited data on migration; where such data does exist, they can provide statistics on the percentages of migrants living in the same place where they were born or living in the same place where they were five or ten years earlier. Some countries do collect household survey data with questions on migration, but even then the validity and usefulness of the data are limited.

The result is that our knowledge of the extent and importance of internal migration mainly derives from surveys undertaken for a specific purpose, such as the study of rural-urban migrants. Rarely do such surveys convey the magnitude of migration. For example, a national survey in Nigeria in 1986 found that 25.8 percent of urban residents and 16.9 percent of rural residents were "life-time migrants"[2] and that in one state in the southwestern part of the country, the figures were 29.9 percent and 29.6 percent, respectively (Federal Republic of Nigeria 1989, 6, 14). But when conducting research in specific communities in southwestern Nigeria, Sara Berry found that in one village over a period of seven years, the total population remained stable but that 60 percent of the people counted the first time had left and been replaced by others (1985, 70), while I found that nearly everyone surveyed in 1991 in five communities had at some time in their lives been migrants (Trager 2001, 60, 64; see also, Trager in this volume, chapter 7).

Those studying internal migration have long recognized the importance of migration as a continuing process rather than a single event, one with implications for both sending and receiving communities. By the early 1970s, several scholars studying urban migrants in various regions of Africa focused on rural-urban linkages among households and communities (e.g., Mayer 1971 for South Africa; Gugler 1971 and Aronson 1971 and 1978 for Nigeria; Weisner 1972 and 1976 for Kenya; see also Gugler 2002 for a recent discussion of this literature). This work, as well as somewhat later research in Southeast Asia (e.g, Trager 1981 and 1988 in the Philippines; Hugo 1982 in Indonesia) and to a lesser extent that in Latin America (e.g., Paerregaard 1997), led to conclusions such as my own, that for migrants "rural and urban places are part of a single social field within which, over time, there may be considerable movement, not only between one village and a particular city, but between a number of such places" (Trager 1988, 12).

There are, of course, significant differences between international and internal migration, the most important of which is that the former involves movement across national boundaries and is therefore regulated by states (or, rather, states attempt to regulate migration across their borders). In the United States, this has meant a great deal of attention in the academic and policy communities to "illegal" or "undocumented" migrants as well as to the proliferation of various forms of visa classifications for the legal movement of temporary workers (e.g., agricultural workers from Mexico and students from Europe to work in the tourist industry) and for permanent immigration, such as the visa lottery system of recent years and visas for high-tech workers. Most other regions of the world have systems for distinguishing "legal" from "illegal" immigrants, although within regions such as Europe, movement across national borders is quite unrestricted. For the migrant, movement across borders usually involves higher costs and risks than internal migration; in many situations, the distances are greater, and in others (e.g., the Mexico–United States border) the risks of entering illegally have increased. Most countries do not regulate internal mobility, although China is an exception. Chinese policies have sought to restrict urban migration through a system of household registration; nonetheless, since the early 1980s the "floating" population has included an estimated eighty million farmers who have left their villages to work as laborers and traders in the cities (Murphy 2000).

Refugees and Forced Migration

Analysis of the situation of refugees is usually discussed separately from that of other forms of migration. While it is true that the immediate cause for refugee movement is usually some form of catastrophe, such as war or drought, over the longer term, refugee mobility has many of the features of other types of migration. Officially, refugees are considered to be people who have been forced to leave their homeland because of fear of persecution (International Organization for Migration 2003, 98): they go to another country on a temporary basis, or they seek asylum in another country. However, there is increasing recognition of those termed *economic refugees*, who respond to economic crisis such as that brought on by drought by moving elsewhere. Not all move across international boundaries; some become "internally displaced," living in another area of their own country. Statistics on these movements are poor. For example, it is well known that Africa is a region with larger numbers of refugees from wars and environmental degradation; most of these people are living either in neighboring countries or in another region of their own country. Yet, recent statistics, such as those reported in a newspaper article in July 2003, only refer to the increase in numbers of African refugees being resettled in the United States and to the total of 103,000 African refugees who have been resettled in the United States over the past twelve years (Rachel L.

Swarns, "U.S. a Place of Miracles for Somali Refugees," *New York Times*, July 20, 2003).

The overlapping categories of international and internal migration, as well as those of refugee movements, become particularly apparent when we focus on the people who move. As Janet Abu-Lughod pointed out long ago, migration cannot be studied as if "human beings, like iron filings, were impelled by forces beyond their conscious control" (1975, 201). Our attention must focus on the migrants and their families, households, and communities, as well as on the larger economic and social contexts in which they live and work. This has been brought home to me in my own research, which has focused mainly on internal migration. When I was doing research in the Philippines in the late 1970s, I interviewed a woman whose husband was working in Saudi Arabia; she became one of my major case studies, one in which I was able to examine the impact of remittances from international as well as internal migration (Trager 1988, 155–68). More recently, in two academic presentations of my research in Nigeria, Nigerian scholars asked why I focused on only migration and hometown connections within Nigeria and why I had not followed members of my research communities to Chicago or other American cities. To them, it is obvious that those living outside Nigeria are following many of the same patterns as those within the country and that research is needed on the implications of international as well as internal mobility of Nigerians.

Chapters in this volume consider both international and internal migration; they also help to demonstrate the overlap in categories and provide empirical data that demonstrate the importance of considering these categories in tandem. For example, Jeffrey H. Cohen's study (chapter 3) of nonmigrants from Oaxaca explores options other than international migration open to those in a region where migration to the United States is common; Sasha Newell's study (chapter 5) of Ivoirian youth who dream of moving to France or the United States notes the facts of rural-urban migration in Côte d'Ivoire as well as the movement of those migrants from other West African countries into the country.[3]

MOVEMENT IN TIME AND SPACE: WHO IS A MIGRANT?

There is no single accepted definition of who is considered to be a migrant. Two key issues include, one, the degree of permanence, that is, the length of time that a person has spent or will spend in a new locale; and, two, the dimension of space, that is, the distance that the person travels. Early research focused on "permanent" migrants, with the assumption being that migration involved a specific activity undertaken by an individual migrant and that once that individual had moved, he or she planned to stay in the new locale. Furthermore, many researchers assume that some kind of border, or change in type of locale, is involved so that spatial distance is not only geographical but also social. For example, there is much more emphasis on rural-urban migration than on rural-rural movements. Movement to a new residence across international boundaries is always understood as migration, even when the distance between the old residence and the new one is negligible.

Current research on migration widely recognizes that migration is not always permanent, and there has been a proliferation of related concepts, such as circular migration and return migration. Nevertheless, most surveys use a definition that involves some length of stay (e.g., six months) to distinguish migrants from visitors and travelers. There is no consistency, however; for example, Arjan de Haan and Ben Rogaly refer to research on Fulani in Burkina Faso where "73 per cent of individuals were involved in some form of migration lasting at least two weeks" (2002, 3). Given that the Fulani are a pastoral society, migration of two weeks seems to have little meaning. Efforts to define migration are often based on the stated intentions of those being studied; as Koenig points out in chapter 2, an individual may say he is just going on a visit, but then he may stay away longer and work. Her discussion points out the complexity of migration and the difficulty of defining who migrants are, at least in a West African context where cultural values support the idea of "traveling" and "going on adventure."

The development of concepts such as seasonal migration, circular migration, and return migration has led to a better understanding of migration as a process rather than as a single event. No doubt there are people who move from one place to another and then stay there permanently. But there are also many who move back and forth between a set of places or who move to one place, then to another, and ultimately return home. Each pattern needs to be considered empirically in terms of the social and economic context in which varied types of movement take place.

The same is true with regard to space. Is someone a migrant who moves from one city to a neighboring city in the United States? Or must the move involve different types of social and economic spaces? In a recent paper, Alison

Newby (2003) examines people living in the border area of El Paso, Texas, and Ciudad Juarez, Mexico; these are contiguous cities divided by an international boundary. If not for that boundary, would those who move from one to the other be considered migrants?

This suggests a third dilemma in the study of migrants and migration: there is frequently an assumption that migrants are poor people who move because they must in order to seek out improved livelihoods. The old push-pull thesis of migration continually reappears, with arguments that people migrate because they cannot survive at home or because they seek economic betterment elsewhere. Many of those who migrate are poor and are seeking improvement, if not for themselves, then for their children. But not all who move are poor; for example, those who participate in contract labor in the Middle East from countries such as the Philippines are often middle-class people with sufficient resources to undertake that type of migration.[4] Recent immigrants to the United States include many highly educated professionals.

Certainly, economic context is often a crucial part of migration activity. Thomas M. Painter has proposed a particularly useful approach in the study of West African mobility, considering livelihood activities in terms of the "action space" in which people operate:

> Action space refers to the geographical and temporal distribution of opportunities and constraints, both local and extra-local, that are identified and used (or avoided) by individuals and corporate groups (e.g., households) to obtain access to the resources they define as critical for their well-being. Action spaces are created, reproduced and modified through mobility. (1996, 83)

Rather than focus on livelihood resources available in a particular type of locale (e.g., urban as opposed to rural), Painter focuses on how people seek to gain access to a range of resources through a variety of livelihood strategies in which mobility is a key element. It is likely that West Africa is not the only environment where such an approach may be useful.

But economic strategies and livelihoods are not the only reasons why people move. For example, in some regions of the world, the only way to obtain secondary school education is to move away from home (see Koenig, chapter 2). Marriage and kinship obligations also underlie migration decisions in many cases, yet there is relatively little research on marriage migration (see

Fan and Li 2002 for an exception). More significant is the fact that there may not be a single reason for a person's decision to migrate. For example, in responses to survey questions, women in Nigeria often said that they had moved for family reasons: marriage, to return home to care for someone, and so on. But when I did extended life-history interviews, these same women talked at length about the work they did and the jobs they had in the various places where they lived; they did not always move when their husbands did but stayed on because of job or educational opportunities (see discussion in Trager, this volume, chapter 7).

MIGRATION AS A DYNAMIC PROCESS: THEORIES AND DEBATES

Consideration of the definition of migrants helps to emphasize the importance of recognizing migration as a dynamic process, one with both causes and consequences. Not only do people move from one place to another, but they also may move back or on to another locale; in addition, they have continuing ties with people in both the places they left and the places they move to. Whereas earlier theoretical discussions of migration tend to focus on explanations of why people move in the first place, more recent discussions incorporate the continuing linkages and their implications. In general, theories fall into two broad groups: those that emphasize macroeconomic forces and those that emphasize individual decisions. In response to both these broad perspectives, an emphasis on intermediate levels of social organization (family, household, community) has assumed greater importance in recent discussions of migration.

Macroeconomic Forces and Migration

Analysis of migration at the level of macroeconomic forces focuses on the broad structural and historical features of societies, especially on labor markets and demand for labor. The key feature of modern migration, according to these perspectives, is that it consists of the "migrations of labor, not of people" (Amin 1974, 66). A variety of theoretical perspectives has been developed, ranging from those of economists who argue that migration is caused by geographic differences in the supply and demand for labor (e.g. Harris and Todaro 1970) to those of world systems and dependency theorists who focus on international migration, arguing that migration takes place "as part of the international dynamics" of the world capitalist system (Portes and Walton 1981, 29).[5]

These theorists are not particularly interested in the individual who migrates or the immediate social context from which one comes or to which one moves but rather in the global societal forces that impel people to move. The focus is primarily on the causes of migration and much less on the consequences. There are some exceptions, however. For example, Claude Meillassoux analyzed migration in West Africa in terms of the intersection of the capitalist economy and that of the noncapitalist, arguing that temporary labor migration "preserves and exploits the domestic agricultural economy" (1981, 110) so that labor reserves are created, with domestic relations of production in the rural area and migration for seasonal work in the capitalist sector. Some attention has also been paid to the loss of labor in rural communities as more and more community members migrate, especially those who are better educated and more skilled (e.g., Lipton 1976, 230–32).

Interest in the consequences of migration at broad societal levels is reflected primarily in studies of ethnicity and assimilation; literature on these issues can be found in studies of both internal migration and international migration. For example, many of the early studies of migration in Africa focus on the processes of adaptation to urban environments (e.g., Little 1957; Mitchell 1956) and the formation of urban associations. Recent work on host societies and international migration expands on earlier work on assimilation (Reitz 2002). This research incorporates consideration not only of race and ethnic relations but also of changing labor markets as well as changing government policies.

Current research increasingly emphasizes migration within the context of globalization. As Stephen Castles states in a recent article,

> It is now widely recognized that cross-border population mobility is inextricably linked to the other flows that constitute globalization, and that migration is one of the key forces of social transformation in the contemporary world. (2002, 1144)

Although he focuses much of his discussion on the formation of transnational communities, an issue considered later at greater length, Castles also notes the importance of globalization as a force influencing migration, arguing that "as globalization reduces barriers to flows, it seems likely that the rate of increase in migration may accelerate" and that despite the efforts to control international migration, "it seems unlikely that attempts to radically curtail migration can succeed in the face of the powerful forces which bring about flows" (2002, 1151).

Several contributors to this volume provide detailed analysis of the ways in which specific migration patterns result from and interact with broader economic, social, and cultural processes. Their work goes beyond broad statements on the impact of "globalization" or labor market forces. Robyn Eversole (chapter 9) demonstrates the importance of a truly global phenomenon, the sending of remittances and their implications for development, while in a very different vein, Sasha Newell (chapter 5) portrays the symbolic and cultural effects of globalization on urban young people's desires to migrate.

Migration and Individuals

At the opposite end of the spectrum from theories that focus on broad structural and economic forces are those that explain migration in terms of individual motivations. The questions asked are entirely different. Rather than consider labor markets or global economic conditions, proponents of these theories ask, "Who are the migrants? Why do they move, stay or return? How and where do they move? When do they move? What are the effects of such actions on the migrants and on others?" (Chang 1981, 304–6). Human capital models dominate, using as their basic premise the presumption "that an individual migrates in the expectation of being better off by doing so" (DaVanzo 1981, 92) and then seeking to explain differing patterns of migration in terms of individual decision making. Such models are found in both the literature on internal migration and that on international migration (see Massey 1998, 19–20). As Douglas S. Massey summarizes,

> The likelihood of emigration is predicted to be reliably related to such standard human capital variables as age, experience, schooling, marital status, and skill. The propensity for international migration is also expected to vary with a household's access to income-generating resources at home. (51)

As we discuss later, migrant networks have received considerable attention. Massey and colleagues (1994) identify migrant networks as a form of social capital on which individual migrants can draw. Although the incorporation of the idea of social capital expands the explanatory framework somewhat to include aspects of intermediate levels of social structure (family, networks, community; discussed later), the theoretical explanations still focus on individual behavior, again leaving us with the question, how do we explain how and why individuals move?

Although studies of individual decision making in migration reinforce the notion of migrants as active agents, not simply cogs being moved about by global forces, they lack context. Survey data on individual migration provide little understanding of the social and economic context in which such decisions are made, and they essentially provide no information on the continuing impacts of migration decisions on families, households, and communities. Some of those interested in understanding individual behavior within social contexts have found life- and family-history approaches to be useful (e.g., Trager 1988; Brettell 2003; Pérez in this volume, chapter 1).[6] In general, all the authors in this volume, including those that use survey data, have sought to place the examination of individual migrant behavior within broader social and cultural contexts in which the migrants function. For example, Silvia Grigolini's study (chapter 6) of Oaxacan migrants' investment in houses and Stephen Lubkemann's contribution (chapter 8) on the "moral economy" of nonreturn among Portuguese and Mozambican migrants both demonstrate how what may appear to be idiosyncratic behavior on the part of individuals can be explained when viewed in context.

Family, Community, and Networks: Intermediate Levels of Social Organization[7]

Dissatisfaction with explanations at both the structural level of economic and historical forces and the level of individual decision making has led anthropologists, and others, to theorize about migration in terms of those intermediate-level institutions that link individuals and macrolevel forces: the family, household, and social networks. Larissa Lomnitz proposes the study of social networks as a way of analyzing migration, arguing that the social network "represents a middle-range level of abstraction situated between large-scale social structure and the individual" (1976, 134), while Charles H. Wood (1981, 1982) suggests the household as the intermediate unit of analysis, stating that "study of household sustenance strategies, interpreted within an analysis of the socioeconomic and political forces that affect the maintenance and reproduction of the household unit, provides a framework that potentially identifies both structural and behavioral factors that propel population movement" (1982, 300).

Using such an approach in research on internal migration in the Philippines, I have argued that migration has led to the formation of dispersed family networks:

> Dispersed family networks . . . include interaction and . . . support among people who may be residing in two or more different places. These places may be the rural home and urban residence of the migrant, or they may include people in other cities, and even overseas. (Trager 1988, 182)

I argue that such networks have implications for the sharing of resources between migrants and family elsewhere and for the formation and maintenance of households:

> The effects of migration go beyond changes in household composition; migration does not simply lead to the loss of members. Rather, migration adds to the considerable flexibility in domestic arrangements that already exists in the Philippines, leading to situations where family members are residentially absent and yet remain integral to the support of other household members. Families and households engage in a wide variety of activities at different times and in different places, as part of the effort to mobilize resources for maintaining themselves; migration is one means of obtaining access to diverse sources of income. . . . [It] is necessary to examine the total field in which household members operate, the resources available, and how family networks are used to mobilize these.[8] (1988, 183–84)

Study of family, household, and other social networks in the migration process has demonstrated that migration is often part of family and household strategies and that decisions to migrate are made in a family or household context rather than as an individual decision. For example, Henry A. Selby and Arthur D. Murphy argue that "migration is an income-generating strategy directed at family preservation" (1982, iv), while I have analyzed strategies for survival and socioeconomic mobility among Filipino families (Trager 1984a; 1988), pointing out the key role played by women in these strategies. The study of remittances and other forms of economic linkages between migrants and family elsewhere became a central focus in these analyses (see later discussion).

Anthropological studies of the importance of family in migration decision making and of the role of remittances and other continuing ties have led some economists to new theoretical propositions. Spearheaded by Oded Stark, the "new economics of migration" has influenced the debate about both the causes and the consequences of migration (see Stark 1991 for a compilation of his major articles on the subject; see also Stark 1995).[9] In this approach, "the family, rather than the individual, [is placed] at the center of the migration decision" (1991, 5). This premise

> shifts the focus of migration research from individual independence to mutual interdependence. Various implicit and explicit intra-family exchanges, such as remittances, are thus integral to migration, not unintended by-products of it. And given the overall pattern of the demand for labor, the performance of individual migrants in the absorbing labor market can largely be accounted for not just (as in standard human capital theory) by the migrants' skill levels and endowments but also by the preferences and constraints of their families who stay behind. (1991, 3)

He argues further that migration cannot be seen as simply a response to wage differentials and that other variables must be considered, especially in relation to the ways in which families approach risk and to their expectations regarding returns from children. Finally, Stark proposes that migration has continuing effects, and he examines the way in which "migratory outcomes are fed back into and modify the very market environments that stimulated migration" (1991, 4).[10]

Despite the value of such insights, the focus on the family limits these studies. The family is not the only intermediate level of social organization that affects the migration process. While family and household may be key in certain contexts (e.g., the Philippines, Mexico), in other societies broader networks of kin and community members are significant. Social networks that span a number of locales may include mainly members of the same family or household or expand to include a much wider set of kin and community members. The latter is particularly true in Africa, where linkages to home community have a major influence on the behavior of migrants; there is also evidence regarding the formation of community-based links through institutions such as hometown associations, in other regions, and among international as well as internal migrants. These linkages are discussed further in the next section.

Research on intermediate levels of social organization has contributed to the analysis and understanding of the long-term consequences of migration. Migration is not a single event, of one individual leaving a place and moving to another place. Rather, it involves ongoing connections that are formed and maintained among people located in a variety of places. Those ongoing relationships have consequences for those who move and for those who stay behind; they have implications for the home community and the destination community; they lead to the formation of social networks that span specific communities and societies.

LINKAGES, REMITTANCES, AND MULTILOCALITY—
CONTRIBUTIONS OF ECONOMIC ANTHROPOLOGY

Among the most important contributions of economic anthropologists to the study of migration has been the study of the connections that are formed and maintained between migrants and those elsewhere. Whether the focus is internal migration or international migration, anthropologists have explored the material and symbolic aspects of these linkages. In the process, they have gone beyond the study of remittances per se to place material links such as remittances into a context that recognizes social and cultural values of kin and community. They have also explored the spatial dimensions of these linkages: not only are migrants linked to a specific set of people in one specific place, but such linkages may also span a number of different locales.

Linkages

During a visit to Washington, D.C., in fall 2002, one of my taxi drivers was from Ghana. When I mentioned that I would be taking a group of students to Ghana a few weeks later, he wanted to know where we would go. In response to the usual questions from me (what part of Ghana he was from, how long he had been in the United States, if he went home, and so on), he told me that he came from Kumasi, a large city in central Ghana. He said that although he had been in the United States for more than twenty-five years, he went home regularly, nearly every year. He owned houses in both Kumasi and Accra, the capital; the one in Kumasi was for him and his family and that in Accra was an investment (rental property) as well as a place to stay on short visits. In addition, he had spent several months at home two years previously so that he could participate in the Ghanaian elections, and he spoke proudly of the new Asantehene (Asante king) in Kumasi who was installed several years ago. His wife and children were with him in Washington, but he hoped to retire to Ghana eventually.

This story exemplifies the range of links that exist and the networks that migrants may participate in. It can be repeated over and over, with immigrants from Mexico, India, China, and many other countries and with various permutations, among both internal and international migrants. These connections have social and material aspects, and they exist in a variety of contexts.

The fact of such linkages is now well established. Of greater interest now is the varying forms they take, how they are used by those involved, the ways in which they form part of migration strategies, and how they vary with material and cultural context.[11] The analysis of linkages has received the most attention in studies of African rural-urban migration (e.g., Trager 1996 and its articles; McNulty 1985; Geschiere and Gugler 1998 and its articles; Gugler 2002). Perhaps the reason is that, as Anthony O'Connor points out,

> more than in any other region people belong to a combined rural-urban system
> of social and economic relationships. Many individuals have one foot in each
> world, and many families have at any given time some members in the city and
> some in the country. This intensity of social links between city and country is
> one of the few features shared by all types of tropical African city. It is also shared
> by all classes or income groups among the urban population. (1983, 272–73)

There are multiple dimensions to these linkages—social and economic, cultural and political. The cultural importance of knowing where you are from and remaining connected to your place of origin is reflected in proverbs: "A river does not flow so far that it forgets its source" is one example among the Yoruba (Trager 2001, 37); "The son of the hawk does not remain abroad," among the Igbo (Gugler 2002). It is reflected as well in the desire of many Africans to be buried "at home"; as Josef Gugler comments, "Many are the stories of family, kin, and/or co-ethnics making great efforts and going to considerable expense to fulfill this last wish, traveling with the coffin across impossible roads or sending the casket across the Atlantic" (2002, 24; see Gugler 2002 for a review of rural-urban linkages and some of the range of contexts in which they are found within Africa).

Many of the questions that are asked about rural-urban linkages can also be raised about transnational linkages.[12] Newspaper articles portray the investments that immigrants are making in their home communities (e.g., on Ghana, Joseph Berger, "American Dream Is Ghana Home," *New York Times*, August 21, 2002; on the Caribbean, Janny Scott, "In Brooklyn Woman's Path: A Story of Caribbean Striving," *New York Times*, June 28, 2003; on Latin America, Daisy Hernandez, "Sending More Home Despite a Recession," *New York Times*, July 14, 2003), and recent policy discussions have noted the importance of remittances (e.g., a report on National Public Radio, *Morning Edition*, July 21, 2003). Gugler refers to research on Nigerians in Chicago in which over 90 percent reported remitting an average of $6,000 to home families and nearly half had invested in housing in communities of origin (2002, 39). Andrew Young, in an interview held before the Sullivan Foundation Summit in Nigeria in July 2003, stated that Ghanaians in the United States repatriate "over $1 billion dollars" to Ghana every year (quoted in Emmah Ujah, "As President Bush Visits Nigeria: How We Got Bush to Fight HIV/AIDS in Africa with N200 billion—Andrew Young," *Vanguard Online Edition*, July 10, 2003). As with rural-urban linkages, there are numerous questions about what the specific dimensions of the ties are, who is involved, how they are connected to specific migration strategies, and what the impact is over time (including whether such connections continue beyond the first generation).

Using data on migrants to New York City from the eastern Caribbean, Haiti, and the Philippines, Basch, Glick Schiller, and Szanton Blanc demonstrate the significance of family and organizational linkages in transnationalism. Defining transnationalism as "the processes by which immigrants forge and sustain multi-stranded social relations that link together their societies of origin and settlement," they examine the "multiple relationships"—"familial, economic, social, organizational, religious, and political"—in which "transmigrants" are involved (1994, 7). They show how family networks, including both close and more distantly related kin, can assist in initial migration as well as in continuing "multi-stranded involvements focused on education and family reproduction, health care, and economic and political activities" (83). Among these connections are "reciprocal transactions," including "gifts of money and goods, the minding of migrants' children and the care of their property." As they point out,

> Such "gifts" are not a one way street, but rather are part of a complex web of reciprocal transactions that are at once a survival strategy for those in St. Vincent

and Grenada, a symbolic statement about the depth of the transnational relationship, and a means for migrants to secure a base in the home society. (85)

In other words, their description of the transnational links maintained by
Caribbean immigrants to the United States is highly reminiscent of descriptions of rural-urban links and family networks in Africa and elsewhere in the
developing world.

Economic aspects of transmigrant networks are not limited to family survival. Commercial networks that link migrants and family at home involve the
development of small commercial enterprises (Basch, Glick Schiller, and
Szanton Blanc 1994, 89). A perhaps exceptional case is that of the Mourides,
a Muslim brotherhood from Senegal that has established highly successful
transnational trading networks which include men in New York, Senegal, and
elsewhere (Susan Sachs, "In Harlem, Finding a Spiritual Link to Senegal," *New
York Times*, July 28, 2003).

Women play central roles in family networks linking migrants and nonmigrants; for example, in the Philippines (Trager 1984a, 1988) and among Filipino immigrants, "transmigrant kin networks frequently center around
women who are said to have special responsibilities as 'elder daughters' for
their kin" (Basch, Glick Schiller, and Szanton Blanc 1994, 239). Expectations
about the contributions that daughters will make to family sustenance are
based in ideas about familial obligations within Filipino culture, as well as in
the opportunities for education and employment that are open to women
both within the Philippines and outside the country. Differential expectations
and roles for women migrants, in comparison with those of men, vary across
society and culture; in most African societies, it is men rather than women
who play the central roles in migrant networks (Gugler 2002; Trager, this volume, chapter 7; see also, Brettell 2003, 139–51, on gender and migration).

Remittances

Within the broad range of linkages established and maintained by migrants, those that involve economic transactions from the migrant to those at
home have attracted the greatest attention. Termed *remittances*, these transactions have become the focus not only of academic debate but also of policy
discussions. In fact, if recent media attention is an indication, remittances
seem to have been "discovered" in the policy and financial world (e.g., Elizabeth Becker, "Latin Migrants to U.S. Send Billions Home," *New York Times*,

May 18, 2004; Editorial, "Banking for the World's Poor," *New York Times*, November 19, 2003).

A great deal of evidence now exists about the extent and importance of remittances. At the same time, many questions remain, both about what "remittances" actually are and about their significance for the migrants themselves and for those to whom remittances are sent.

Estimates of remittances vary widely and are problematic. In a recent review of the size of remittances in international migration, Manuel Orozco reports estimates of annual average remittance per worker of $700 to $1,000 (2003b, 1); in the 1980s, the total value of remittances was placed at between $15 billion and $30 billion annually (Russell 1986, 680), and there is general agreement that total remittance flows have been increasing. Estimates based on official reporting vary; for example, the World Bank "reports fewer than two billion dollars in remittances to the Philippines, but the Philippines' central bank reports over six billion" (Orozco 2003b, 1). In addition, remittances are often not reported at all, and immigrants remit in a variety of ways, through informal institutions, direct deposits to accounts of relatives, and so on (3). Certain countries receive a large proportion of the total remittances sent; for example, India and the Philippines are among those receiving the largest amounts of remittances. For these countries, the export of labor and the remittances received from migrants have come to play major roles in their economies. Estimates for Latin America and the Caribbean indicate quarterly flow of about $2.5 billion in Mexico, $493 million in El Salvador, and $362 million in Jamaica (Orozco 2003b, 3).

Estimates of the size of remittances in internal migration are far more problematic, as there is little data of any sort. De Haan refers to studies that estimate urban-rural remittances in Africa and Asia to be 10 percent to 13 percent of urban incomes; estimates of the relationship to rural incomes vary from 40 percent or more of rural household income to much lower percentages (1999, 23–24). Survey research in specific communities provides more details of the numbers of migrants who remit, but estimates of the actual amount of money (and other things) involved tend to be limited to ethnographic and case study data. For example, in my research in Dagupan City, Philippines, in the late 1970s, I found that about three quarters of all migrants remitted something, and about half remitted money (Trager 1984b, 324). In research in Nigeria in the 1990s, I found that more than 80 percent of those

people living in five rural communities reported receiving money from relatives who were migrants elsewhere, either at the time of visits or through other
means; the amounts reported varied from small, token amounts to larger
sums, including some reports of amounts over one thousand Naira, which
was equivalent to $50 at the time (Trager 2001, 83–85).[13]

Embedded in these analyses of remittances are a number of important questions that are not always clearly delineated and are rarely answered. As Gugler
points out with regard to the literature on remittances in African rural-urban
migration,

> the many studies of transfers by urban residents to rural areas tell us very little
> about the urban-rural connection in as much as they usually fail to ascertain the
> beneficiaries: wife and children? parents? a communal development project? or
> perhaps the sender on whose behalf an investment is to be made—farm labor
> to be hired, cattle or land to be bought, a house to be built? (2002, 28)

Similar questions can be asked about remittances in international migration.
What exactly are remittances? Are they limited to money from migrants to
family members at home? What if that money is really an investment being
made on behalf of the migrant? What about other types of gifts that are sent
home? Who are the family members who receive them, and what are their expectations (which may not be the same as the migrants' expectations)?

A central element in nearly all discussions of remittances is the question of
what their impact is. That is, how are they used by recipients? Are they simply
used for consumption, either of necessities or for consumer goods? Are they
used for productive investments and, if so, what type?

Analysis of remittances in internal migration has focused on the debate
over whether they are used for productive investments. Early on, Henry Rempel and Richard A. Lobdell argue that "it seems certain that very little is used
directly as investment for rural development" (1978, 336), whereas Oded
Stark argues that there is "sufficient evidence to suggest that rural-to-urban
migration and urban-to-rural remittances can and have actually been used to
transform agricultural modes of production" (1991, 214, originally published
1980). Using case study data on Filipino migrants, I have suggested that much
depends on the socioeconomic situation of the migrant and his or her family;
in a case of a landless, very poor household, remittances formed a crucial part

of family income and were used mainly for subsistence, whereas in households with land, some remittances were used directly for productive investments (e.g., purchase of farm animals) and others indirectly (e.g., freeing other resources for productive activities; Trager 1988, 188–89).

A second question has been whether remittances help to equalize rural income distribution or cause greater income inequality. Michael Lipton has argued that remittances are "unlikely to do much to reduce rural poverty" and that those who receive larger remittances are better off to begin with (1980, 11–13). Stark, in contrast, has suggested that by increasing the income of poor rural households, remittances help reduce overall inequality in rural areas (1978, 90). In a later analysis, Stark concludes that "the impact of migrant remittances on the rural income distribution . . . appears to depend critically on a village's migration history and on the degree to which migration opportunities are diffused across village households" (1991, 272).

Similar questions have been asked about the impact of remittances in international migration, and there seems to be a diversity of conclusions about the extent to which remittances are used for consumption, including the consumption of luxuries, and the extent to which they are used for investment in agriculture (de Haan 1999, 24–25). Stark (1991, 261–73), using data from Mexico, and R. H. Adams, using data from Pakistan, conclude that different sources of remittances have different effects. Adams argues that remittances from international migration tend to increase inequality, whereas those from internal migration have an equalizing effect (Adams 1998; de Haan 1999, 25; see also Russell 1986, 686–89).

John Connell and Dennis Conway, using comparative data from island nations in the Pacific and the Caribbean, disaggregate the ways in which remittances are used into a number of different categories:

(1) family and dependent basic needs; (2) savings strategies; (3) (flexible) human capital resource investments; (4) (fixed) location-specific capital ventures; (5) diversified micro-economic investments; (6) community support, maintenance and sustenance, and "social capital" realizations; and (7) migration and re-migration investments. (2000, 63)

They conclude that international migration has both positive and negative effects but argue that the positive effects are significant, especially for societies such as those of small island states, which have relatively limited development potential. Remittances provide migrants and their families and kin "an extended range of options for various forms of familial, personal and community development" (72). In this volume, Robyn Eversole (chapter 9) addresses the remittance debate by considering the large body of data that now exists and by arguing that remittances play an important role in rural development.

One particularly interesting type of use of remittances is investment in housing. This seems to be a near-universal way in which international migrants (and some internal migrants) demonstrate their success and commitment to remaining connected to their home area. Often seen as an example of "conspicuous consumption," such housing construction is, as Connell and Conway point out, a real investment: "In anticipation of an eventual return on retirement, many permanent migrants remit money for the construction of permanent houses for themselves, which are used by kin in their absence" (2000, 66). Similar investments are visible parts of the landscape in many regions of the world: one of the first things an urban migrant in Nigeria is expected to do is build a house "at home" (see Trager 2001). It is especially important to consider such activities from the perspective of the migrants themselves and the strategies that they and their kin pursue. Silvia Grigolini in this volume (chapter 6) focuses on housing investment as a key strategy among migrants from Oaxaca, Mexico.

Lacking from much of the debate about remittances is any discussion of the social and cultural context in which remittances are sent; at the same time, the focus on monetary remittances limits our understanding of exchanges that are one part of a broader constellation of exchanges that include visiting, gift giving, and other material exchanges. In considering remittances in the Philippines, for example, I have argued that they need to be considered in a cultural context that places high value on reciprocal obligations (*utang na loob*) that are expressed through both symbolic gifts and the giving of necessities, including money (1984b; 1988, 188). In Nigeria, I found that there were extensive two-way flows between migrants and those at home, including not only visits from both directions but also gifts and monetary remittances. However, money was mainly sent by migrants to kin at home, whereas other material goods, such as foodstuff, tended to go in the opposite direction (2001, 85–86).

Lisa Cliggett argues that, among urban migrants in Zambia, there really are no "remittances"; rather, there are "gifts." She argues that "gift-remitting" is used to express the continuing recognition and feelings of affection that exist between migrants and those at home:

> Gifts, one in two years, of a dress, a plate, or a bag of sugar, are tokens of affection that tell an old mother she is remembered, although not a remittance on which families can depend for survival. . . . Rather than offerings of support for daily life, gift-remitttances represent a gesture of recognition that will keep pathways for return to the village open. . . . Without maintaining even this symbolic relationship with the village, a migrant risks losing his option to return, should life in town become undesirable. (2003b, 23; see also Cliggett 2003a)

Similarly, Mike Evans, in a study of Tonga international migrants, argues that monetary remittances between migrants and family at home need to be viewed in the context of Tongan gift-exchange practices:

> Remittances are in fact one of several ways in which children can show their love. Fishing, farming, domestic care, and the production of women's wealth are all ways of showing love to those who benefit from one's work. Remittances are remarkable insofar as they primarily take the form of cash, while these other activities tend to result in the production of subsistence and traditional wealth. All these forms of wealth, including cash, can be and are turned toward the reproduction of social relationships through the gift exchange process. (2001, 148–49)

In this volume, Stephen Lubkemann (chapter 8) explores the phenomenon of remittances and related exchanges from the perspective of why migrants continue to send things, even in situations where they seem unlikely to ever return to their home communities.

Multilocality and Community

Most of the discussion of remittances and exchanges makes two assumptions: one, that these exchanges take place between a migrant and others in one other place, the "home"; and, two, that the majority of exchanges takes place among family or household members. It is often the case that these assumptions are correct. However, with the ever-increasing extent of mobility and the greater range of places to which people move, it is increasingly the case that connections are maintained with people in many different locales and that those connections are not just to kin elsewhere but are also with others, nonkin who identify themselves as part of the same "community."

In my contribution to this volume (chapter 7), regarding my recent work on Yoruba migrants in Nigeria, I suggest the concept of multilocality as a way of understanding connections that span more than one location, arguing that we need to examine people and their activities in terms of their "attachment to and participation in social and economic activities in a number of places" (see also Trager 2001, 60, 236–38). In my view, this concept is valuable more generally, not only for the consideration of Yoruba migrants and other internal migrants in regions of high mobility, but also for the examination of participants in transnational movements. Koenig applies it in her study of migrants in Mali (this volume, chapter 2).

Among Yoruba migrants in Nigeria, many have lived in several different places over the course of their lives, and their social and economic activities have often included connections in several different locales:

> An individual may be working in Lagos [the largest city], participating in organizations and institutions there, while also traveling home regularly to participate in hometown activities. He or she may also be involved in activities in other towns and cities . . . [including] his or her spouse's hometown. . . . Not all such connections may be of equal strength or importance, but all have potential for the individual. At a given time, the ties in one locale may have greater claim, or may provide access to resources (e.g., a job); at another time, claims and resources may be more important in a different locale. (Trager 2001, 237)

The research on transnational migration suggests similar patterns. For example, immigrants to the United States from the Caribbean may have previously moved to another island or from a small town to a city within their own country; they may also have connections with others who have moved to other countries, such as Britain. As Basch, Glick Schiller, and Szanton Blanc describe their "discovery" of transnationalism, they portray the migrants whom Basch studied in New York and Trinidad as people who "moved so frequently and were seemingly so at home in either New York or Trinidad as well as their societies of origin" that it was difficult to say where they "belonged" (1994, 5).

As migration is an increasingly important factor in the lives of people all over the world, and as transportation and communications systems make it possible for people to move and communicate over great distances, multilocality is likely to become the norm for increasing numbers of people. Perhaps paradoxically, this phenomenon seems to be accompanied by a strengthening of identity with "home" communities and of economic exchanges not only with kin but also with those communities. Rather than become "rootless," migrants are in some ways more "rooted" to those places from which they came. However, there are a number of different dimensions to this process of establishing connections with home communities, dimensions that have been explored in recent research and about which still further research is needed. In this volume, Koenig explores the relationship between multilocality and stratification.

Recent research also points to the importance of connections that are not limited to kin but rather link migrants to the home community. Philip F. W. Bartle suggests that an "extended community" formed among those in Ghana whom he studied:

> What I call the extended Obo community includes not only some people living in Obo . . . but also a much larger number . . . living in various places outside Obo. Since it includes people who identify or feel they belong to Obo, it includes many who were not born there, many who do not live there, many who have visited only a few times and even some who have not yet visited Obo. (1981, 126)

My research in several Yoruba communities in southwestern Nigeria demonstrates the multifaceted nature of these connections. It is not just that people identify with a place and with others from that place. A person is expected to act on the basis of that identity, "to fulfill obligations to the hometown, to participate in organizations and activities with others from the community, both those who live at home and others living outside. . . . It is not sufficient to claim a particular place . . . as one's hometown; rather, the hometown also places claims on those who are its 'sons and daughters'" (Trager 2001, 239–40; see also Trager, this volume). The ways in which people participate can vary considerably. Furthermore, the reasons for maintaining connections over long periods involve not only identity but also structural conditions in the broader society and economy, including lack of security and questions of access to key resources.[14]

Likewise, recent research on international migration suggests the formation of "transnational communities" in which "individuals and groups constantly negotiate choices with regard to their participation in host societies, their relationships with their homelands, and their links to co-ethnics. Their life strategies bring together elements of existence in both national and transnational social space" (Castles 2002, 1159). The specific ways in which individuals participate in activities connected to their homelands vary, but in addition to sending remittances to kin, they also include memberships to organizations and donations to philanthropic causes.

One of the problematic aspects of considering connections of this type is the question of what constitutes "home" or the "home community." Is it really a specific village or town? Or is it a larger ethnic or regional entity that has been defined as home (see, e.g., Lentz 1995; Gugler 2002; Trager 2001)?

Regardless of how migrants define their home communities, there are several common ways in which they tend to engage with those communities. Two of the major patterns are the formation of organizations and donations for the benefit of those at home.[15] Hometown organizations, and other organizations based on shared identity and membership in a community, are commonly found among migrants in Africa, and recent research describes the formation of hometown associations among immigrants from Latin America (Orozco 2003c, 13–14).

Among the activities of these associations are the raising of funds for the benefit of the home community. According to Orozco, hometown associations among Latin American immigrants in the United States are "primarily philanthropic groups whose work sometimes overlaps with economic development" (2003c, 14). The activities they undertake are similar to those undertaken by hometown organizations formed by internal migrants in West Africa (see, for example, Pratten 1996; Honey and Okafor 1998; Trager 2001). In the Ijesa Yoruba communities I studied, hometown organizations have undertaken local development projects since at least the 1920s; one of the first such organizations was the Egbe Atunluse Ile Ijesa (Ijesa Progressive Society), which established the first secondary school in the region in 1934 (Trager 2001, 103–4). They have undertaken electric and water projects in several communities and, in recent years, have been instrumental in the formation of community banks in two communities; however, other types of economic development effort have been less successful (Trager 2001, 165–203). The amounts of money collected for specific development projects and more general development funds can be substantial. Much of that money comes from the most successful migrants from the community, but nearly everyone who identifies as a member of the community is expected to contribute something (see Trager, this volume, as well as Eversole in this volume for the impact of remittances on development).

THE FUTURE: MIGRATION AND MIGRATION RESEARCH

It is evident that migration is a process in which ever-larger numbers of people are participating and, at the same time, one that has continuing ramifications for those who do not themselves migrate. In recent years, there has been more attention to the study of this process, as well as to policy issues related to it. For the most part, however, most of that attention has been to the numbers themselves and to ways to control and regulate movement, especially across international borders. Much less attention has been paid to the social and economic linkages formed through migration and to policy that recognizes those linkages, in both internal and international migration.

Recent reports (International Organization for Migration 2003) reflect the concern of international and government agencies about population mobility around the world. Within specific countries, similar concerns exist; in the United States and Europe, for example, most of the focus is on immigration, and with the recent concern about terrorism, more barriers have been established to both legal and illegal immigration. Countries such as China have also attempted to regulate the internal movements of their populations; most other countries do not have laws to restrict internal movement but are nevertheless concerned with the ever-enlarging cities and the difficulties of providing infrastructure and other basic necessities for enormous urban populations.

Most of those engaged in policy debates continue to make a number of assumptions about migration, assumptions that are contradicted by much of the recent research. It is still largely assumed that migration involves the movement of individual migrants and that most moves are permanent; there is little recognition of the role of family and kin networks in migrant decisions and activities or of the movements back and forth and continuing linkages that exist. Ironically, even when there is recognition of linkages, contradictory policies may negate those that draw on the positive aspects of those linkages. A recent example involves banking regulations and efforts to encourage more remittances through the official banking system between migrants in the United States and their relatives in Latin America. A report on National Public Radio (*Morning Edition*) in July 2003 described efforts being made to encourage

Mexican immigrants, most of whom are "unbanked," to use American banks to send remittances home (see Andres Martinez, "How a Seed-Money Loan of $60 Turned Melanie Pico into an Entrepreneur," *New York Times*, July 8, 2003; Daisy Hernandez, "Sending More Home Despite a Recession," *New York Times*, July 14, 2003; for a review of policies in various countries, see Orozco 2003b). At the same time, policies directed at terrorists are regulating more closely money sent out of the United States through banks and other institutions.

Researchers have been more successful than policymakers in moving beyond earlier assumptions about migrants and migration. Nevertheless, many research questions remain. One set of questions emerges from the recognition that large numbers of people are not only moving but also remaining connected to communities and nations of origin. As we have seen, recent research on international migration has demonstrated the existence of transnational networks that may influence economic activities, politics, and culture. What are the implications of these networks for citizenship, ethnicity, and nationality? A recent article by Castles raises some of the relevant questions in the context of international migration (2002, 1157–63). He points out, for example, that "if people move frequently between different countries, and maintain important affilations in each of them, citizenship needs to be adapted to the new realities" (1161). It may seem that these are questions most appropriate to international migration, but in fact, similar issues arise within countries, at least in those that are multiethnic (i.e., most places in the world) and where migrants do not necessarily have the same rights as others. For example, a recent study by Onigu Otite of rural-rural migrants in Nigeria points out the problem of migrants who do not have "full citizenship" in the locales to which they have migrated, even when they may have been there for several generations (2002, 153–61). Based in large part on concepts of land ownership and the claims of particular ethnic groups that are considered to be the "indigenes" of a particular locality, the lack of rights of migrant groups has widespread ramifications in economic activities and politics, leading at times to interethnic violence, not only in Nigeria, but also elsewhere in Africa (see Geschiere and Gugler 1998; Gugler 2002). How, then, can people "achieve full citizenship" in the locales to which they migrate while also retaining their connections with the places that they left? This question, and its implications for economic activities (e.g., landownership, sending of remittances), needs to be considered for both those engaged in international mobility and those who are internal migrants.

A second set of research questions concerns the broader impact and implications of kin and community networks for individuals, households, communities, and local development activities. Now that it is evident that decisions about migration are made not just by individuals but also by families and households, many questions remain. One key issue is that of who migrates and who stays; obviously, despite the increasing number of people who participate in migration, not everyone does. Why do some families and households keep all their members at home? And why are certain family members preferred as migrants? Cohen's study in this volume provides a perspective on these questions, showing a relationship between mobility and stratification.

A second set of issues involves the continuing connections that have been discussed at length here. It is clear that we must move beyond the focus on remittances to consider not just monetary exchanges but also other exchanges and the social networks in which they take place. Why do migrants continue to maintain contact with kin elsewhere, long after they have left? What are their expectations, and what are the expectations of those who remain at home? How do the monetary and other material exchanges get used, and who is making the decisions about their use? Connections that span communities also need further investigation. In what contexts do migrants make donations to home communities? Again, what are their expectations, and what do the community members at home expect from them (see Trager 1998)? When migrants make contributions for local development projects, who decides about the use of those contributions? And what is the impact of such donations on local communities?

Finally, what are the symbolic and cultural frames within which migration takes place, and how is the migration process continually reshaping those frames? In societies where migration is a normal aspect of life, how do migrants and others understand and interpret their activities? How do those understandings affect the perpetuation of the process? Koenig (this volume) quotes the Asante (Ghanaian) proverb "If the bird does not fly, it does not eat." As described by Newell in this volume, in much of West Africa today, young men seek to "travel," meaning that they hope to go to Europe or the United States for a period of time.

How are global cultural processes being affected by the activities of migrants? In March 2003, just after the Iraq war began, I saw a television news broadcast in which Tom Brokaw interviewed the mother of one of the soldiers taken as a prisoner of war in the early days of the war. When Brokaw asked Anecita Hudson, living in New Mexico, how she had heard the news about her son, she replied that she had been watching Filipino television and saw the picture of her son there (U.S. networks had not shown the images of those taken). Satellite television increasingly means not only that people in Third World countries are watching CNN but also that immigrants in the United States, from places such as the Philippines, India, and Nigeria, can watch programs from their home countries. The Internet, too, has expanded the ways in which national and ethnic communities of immigrants can communicate and mobilize, not simply on political or ethnic issues, but also for social reasons. Several years ago, for example, a notice went out on Naijanet (a Nigerian Internet list) about the death of a young Nigerian woman in Madison, Wisconsin; people were asked to contribute to the cost of sending her body home to be buried, and many who did not know her personally responded to this request.

The ability to mobilize economic resources, as in this last example, from a broader network of people than would be true in a face-to-face community suggests one of the many dimensions of the ways in which both global and local cultures are changing and the ways in which migration as a process contributes to those changes. Orozco has suggested that "remittances have become a part of the human face of globalization" (2003a, 11); and other sources point to remittances as the "second-largest source, behind foreign investment by private companies, of external funding for developing countries" (BBC 2004). But it is not just remittances; rather, it is migration itself, and all its attendant relationships and consequences, that is a central feature of contemporary globalization processes. As Newell shows in this volume, even when they do not actually migrate, young urban Ivoirian men "consume" migration; it is a feature of their dreams and desires for "modernity."

OVERVIEW OF THIS VOLUME

Authors in this volume address some of the questions outlined here and pose additional questions for further research. All of the chapters reflect a focus on migration as a dynamic process that responds to and is shaped by broader economic, cultural, and social forces. At the same time, the activities of migrants lead to new forms of social and economic institutions and processes, such as transnational and multilocal networks through which remittances and other flows take place. Those networks, involving individual migrants, families, households, and local communities, in turn have significance for larger economic and social institutions, including the potential—and, in some cases at least, the reality—to contribute to local development.

The geographic foci of these chapters include regions well-known in the migration literature, such as Mexico and West Africa, as well as regions that have been little discussed, such as Kazakstan and Mozambique (see figure Intro.1). Two authors consider migration in Oaxaca, Mexico: Cohen analyzes people who do not participate in migration, while Grigolini considers housing as a critical investment among Oaxacan migrants to the United States. Ricardo Pérez's contribution focuses on migrants from Puerto Rican fishing communities to the mainland United States and back to Puerto Rico. Three chapters utilize research in West African communities: Koenig, in a region of Mali; Trager, in a set of communities in southwestern Nigeria; and Newell, among urban youth in Abidjan, Côte d'Ivoire.

Meltem Sancak and Peter Finke deal with a complex situation of migration in one of the countries that was part of the Soviet Union, Kazakstan. Lubkemann draws on research in several ethnographic settings for his analysis; migrants from Mozambique to South Africa and from Portugal to the United States provide the basis for a comparative analysis. Finally, Eversole's study draws on data from a large number of different countries, although much of the best evidence on the use of remittances comes from Latin America.

The authors of the five chapters in part I utilize a variety of thematic and theoretical approaches to consider the relationships of individual migrants, households, and social stratification. Pérez emphasizes the ways in which Puerto Rican fisherfolk use "mobile livelihoods," moving not only between geographic locales but also among a variety of jobs. He, like Koenig and Trager, demonstrates some of the ways in which people can move between a variety of places while retaining a connection to home. Koenig and Cohen both introduce important issues of social stratification into the discussion of migration, demonstrating how local differences in social strata affect both the participation of households in the migration process and the outcomes of that process for access to resources.

Sancak and Finke, like Pérez, use life-history data as the basis for an analysis of how earlier migration and attendant exposure to other economic systems affect economic behavior, especially risk taking. In contrast, Newell is

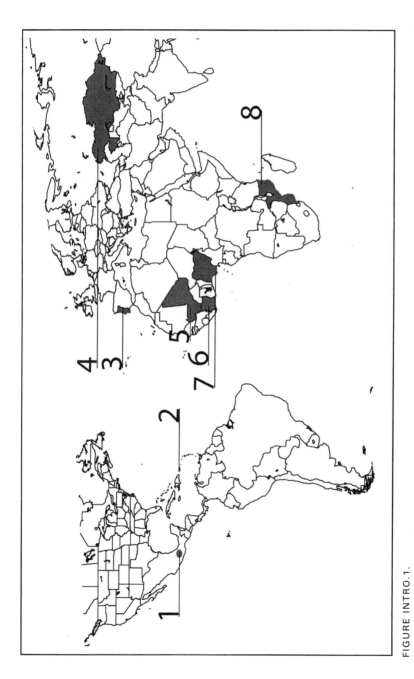

FIGURE INTRO.1.
Research locations: (1) Oaxaca, Mexico (ch. 3, 6); (2) Puerto Rico (ch. 1); (3) Portugal (ch. 8); (4) Kazakstan (ch. 4); (5) Mali (ch. 2); (6) Côte d'Ivoire (ch. 5); (7) Nigeria (ch. 7); (8) Mozambique (ch. 8)

much less interested in actual migration or in economic motivations as explanations for migration. He draws instead on consumption theory to argue that Ivoirian youth seek personal transformation. Newell's approach leads us to consider globalization and transnationalism not simply in terms of demand for labor and the responses to that demand but also in terms of the symbolic impact of global discourses, such as "modernity," and local appropriation of those discourses.

The four chapters in part II demonstrate the importance of understanding remittances within broader economic, social, and cultural contexts. Grigolini analyzes investment in housing by migrants, arguing that the construction of a house has social, symbolic, and economic significance. I consider the ways in which Yoruba women migrants contribute to their home communities, and also argue that this is one way in which those from elite backgrounds enhance their status. Lubkemann asks a key question: why do people who seem to have most of their social and economic life in the place to which they have migrated continue to send money and invest at home? He argues that there is a "moral economy" within which migrants continue to operate. In the final chapter, Eversole moves beyond a specific ethnographic setting to address the broader question of whether, and how, remittances assist in development. She argues not only that remittances contribute but also that those in the development community have largely ignored a key grassroots strategy in which people throughout the world are engaged: migration and the sending of remittances to benefit family and community at home.

The chapters in this volume demonstrate the importance of viewing migration in relation to the details of individual lives and household situations. Migration is not simply deciding to move from one place to another, nor is it simply an individual decision. Mobility is affected by the resources and assets that are available to individuals and the households of which they are a part; in turn, the process of migration affects the long-term structure of household members and their participation in local social and economic institutions. These chapters also demonstrate the importance of viewing migration and related phenomena such as remittances within broader social and cultural frameworks of kin, family, and community; local social strata; and symbolism and meaning. Finally, these chapters bring us back to questions about the global importance and impact of migration. While it is true that globalization and labor demands help shape contemporary migration patterns, it is also the case that economic activities in which migrants engage, including their investments in home communities, affect local and regional economies and development.

NOTES

1. Thomas Faist asks the question, why are there "so many international migrants out of a few places?" (2000, 7), arguing that only a small percentage of potential migrants move internationally and that most move within their own countries.

2. Lifetime migrants include people whose residence at the time of the survey differs from the place of birth, as well as those who are currently living in the birthplace but who had lived elsewhere for at least six months (Federal Republic of Nigeria 1989, 38).

3. Martha Woodson Rees (2003) and Tom O'Neill (2003) show how, respectively, Oaxacan and Nepalese migrant destinations have changed over time in response to changing opportunities and labor force demands and include both internal and international destinations.

4. When I was doing research in the Philippines, I met a woman who was home for a visit from England, where she was working as a chambermaid in a London hotel; she had been a schoolteacher before she left the Philippines. A serious aspect of the "brain drain" from African countries has been that of professionals, such as the Nigerian medical professionals who have taken jobs in Saudi Arabia.

5. Massey and colleagues (1998, 18–41) provide a comprehensive review of macroeconomic and structural historical theories as they relate to international migration.

6. I note the value of using methods based on life histories and family case studies in migration research (Trager 1988, 13–16), and Brettell (2003, 23–26) also discusses the value of life-history approaches. In general, however, there has been little discussion of methods in migration studies.

7. Three recent books use the term *meso* or *mesolevel* to refer to what I call "intermediate levels of social organization" (Brettell 2003; Faist 2000; Hoerder 2002).

8. Researchers focusing on the comparative study of households make similar points about the necessity to include nonresident members (Wilk and Netting 1984).

9. Although in most of his papers Stark does not explicitly refer to work of anthropologists, there are indications that he is familiar with at least some of the

research in which anthropologists emphasize family strategies in migration (e.g., Lauby and Stark 1988).

10. Stark's work focuses mainly on internal migration in less-developed countries, with the view that the situation there "constitutes a good migration research laboratory for studying migration in general" (1991, 23). His work has influenced scholars interested in international migration as well, however, as indicated by Massey and colleagues (1998, 21–28, 53–54).

11. Obviously, not all migrants maintain such ties; it is also interesting to examine those situations where people break their connections.

12. If I have focused on linkages in African rural-urban migration in this discussion, the reason is that Africa is the continent where this topic has received the greatest emphasis, although there is some literature elsewhere (e.g., Carrier and Carrier 1989 on Papua New Guinea; see also Paerregaard 1997, on Peru; Trager 1988, on the Philippines).

13. As discussed later, both studies examine remittances within a broader context of flows, not only of money, but also of gifts and other material exchanges.

14. There is good evidence that these connections may continue beyond the first generation of migrants (see Gugler 1991).

15. Other ways, not considered further here, are ritual and ceremonial occasions that bring people home (see Trager 2001, 15–35), which are also used for fund-raising, and political connections, such as those described among immigrants to New York (Basch, Glick Schiller, and Szanton Blanc 1994).

REFERENCES

Abu-Lughod, Janet. 1975. Comments. The end of the age of innocence in migration theory. In *Migration and Urbanization*, ed. Brian M. DuToit and Helen I. Safa, 201–6. The Hague: Mouton.

Adams, R. H. 1998. Remittances, investment, and rural asset accumulation in Pakistan. *Economic Development and Cultural Change* 47 (1): 155–73.

Amin, Samir. 1974. Modern migrations in Western Africa. In *Modern migrations in Western Africa*, ed. S. Amin, 65–124. Oxford: Oxford University Press.

Aronson, Dan R. 1971. Ijebu Yoruba urban-rural relationships and class formation. *Canadian Journal of African Studies* 5 (3): 263–79.

————. 1978. *The city is our farm: Seven migrant Ijebu families*. Cambridge, Mass.: Schenkman.

Bartle, Philip F. W. 1981. Cyclical migration and the extended community: A West African example. In *Frontiers in migration analysis*, ed. R. B. Mandal, 105–39. New Delhi, India: Concept.

Basch, Linda, Nina Glick Schiller, and Cristina Szanton Blanc. 1994. *Nations unbound: Transnational projects, postcolonial predicaments, and deterritorialized nation-states*. Langhorne, Pa.: Gordon and Breach.

BBC. 2004. Factfile: Global migration. *BBC News*, http://news.bbc.co.uk/1/shared/spl/hi/world/04/migration/html/money.stm (accessed March 24, 2004).

Berry, Sara S. 1985. *Fathers work for their sons: Accumulation, mobility, and class formation in an extended Yoruba community*. Berkeley: University of California Press.

Brettell, Caroline. 2003. *Anthropology and migration: Essays on transnationalism, ethnicity, and identity*. Walnut Creek, Calif.: AltaMira.

Burmeister, Stefan. 2000. Archaelogy and migration: Approaches to an archaeological proof of migration. *Current Anthropology* 41 (4): 539–67.

Carrier, James C., and Achsah H. Carrier. 1989. *Wage, trade, and exchange in Melanesia*. Berkeley: University of California Press.

Castles, Stephen. 2002. Migration and community formation under conditions of globalization. *International Migration Review* 36 (4): 1143–68.

Chang, Tuck Hoong Paul. 1981. A review of micromigration research in the Third World context. In *Migration decision making*, ed. Gordon F. de Jong and Robert W. Gardner, 303–27. New York: Pergamon Press.

Cliggett, Lisa. 2003a. Gift remitting and alliance building in Zambian modernity: Old answers to modern problems. *American Anthropologist* 105 (3): 543–52.

————. 2003b. Remitting the gift: Zambian mobility and anthropological insights for migration studies. Paper presented at the Society for Economic Anthropology meetings, Monterrey, Mexico, April 4–5.

Connell, John, and Dennis Conway. 2000. Migration and remittances in island microstates: A comparative perspective on the South Pacific and the Caribbean. *International Journal of Urban and Regional Research* 24 (1): 52–78.

DaVanzo, Julie. 1981. Microeconomic approaches to studying migration decisions. In *Migration decision making*, ed. Gordon F. DeJong and Robert W. Gardner, 90–129. New York: Pergamon.

de Haan, Arjan. 1999. Livelihoods and poverty: The role of migration—a critical review of the migration literature. *Journal of Development Studies* 36 (2): 1–47.

de Haan, Arjan, and Ben Rogaly. 2002. Introduction: Migrant workers and their role in rural change. *Journal of Development Studies* 38 (5): 1–14.

Evans, Mike. 2001. *Persistence of the gift: Tongan transition in transnational context.* Waterloo, Ont.: Wilfred Laurier University Press.

Faist, Thomas. 2000. *The volume and dynamics of international migration and transnational social spaces.* Oxford: Clarendon Press.

Fan, C. Cindy, and Ling Li. 2002. Marriage and migration in transitional China: A field study of Gaozhou, Western Guangdong. *Environment and Planning A* (34): 619–38.

Federal Republic of Nigeria. 1989. *Report of the survey of internal migration, December 1986.* Lagos, Nigeria: Federal Office of Statistics.

Geschiere, Peter, and Josef Gugler, eds. 1998. The politics of primary patriotism. *Africa* 68:3.

Gugler, Josef. 1971. Life in a dual system: Eastern Nigerians in town, 1961. *Cahiers d'Etudes Africaines* 11:400–421.

———. 1991. Life in a dual system revisited: Urban-rural ties in Enugu, Nigeria, 1961–1987. *World Development* 19:399–409.

———. 2002. The son of the hawk does not remain abroad: The urban-rural connection in Africa. *African Studies Review* 45 (1): 21–41.

Harris, J. R., and Michael P. Todaro. 1970. Migration, unemployment, and development: A two-sector analysis. *American Economic Review* 60:126–42.

Hoerder, Dirk. 2002. *Cultures in contact: World migrations in the second millennium.* Durham, N.C.: Duke University Press.

Honey, Rex, and Stanley Okafor, eds. 1998. *Hometown associations: Indigenous knowledge and development in Nigeria.* London: Intermediate Technology Publications.

Hugo, Graeme. 1982. Circular migration in Indonesia. *Population and Development Review* 8:59–83.

International Organization for Migration. 2003. *World migration 2003: Managing migration, challenges, and responses for people on the move.* IOM World Migration Report Series 2. Geneva: International Organization for Migration.

Lauby, Jennifer, and Oded Stark. 1988. Individual migration as a family strategy: Young women in the Philippines. *Population Studies* 42:473–86.

Lentz, Carola. 1995. "Unity for development": Youth associations in north-western Ghana. *Africa* 65 (3): 395–429.

Lipton, Michael. 1976. *Why poor people stay poor: A study of urban bias in world development.* London: Temple Smith.

———. 1980. Migration from rural areas of poor countries: The impact on rural productivity and income distribution. *World Development* 8:1–24.

Little, K. L. 1957. The role of voluntary associations in West African urbanization. *American Anthropologist* 59 (4): 579–96.

Lomnitz, Larissa. 1976. Migration and network in Latin America. In *Current perspectives in Latin American urban research,* ed. Alejandro Portes and H. L. Browning, 133–50. Austin, Tex.: Institute of Latin American Studies.

Massey, Douglas S., Joaquin Arango, Graeme Hugo, Ali Kouacouci, Adela Pelligrino, and J. Edward Taylor. 1994. An evaluation of international migration theory: The North American case. *Population and Development Review* 20:699–752.

———. 1998. *Worlds in motion: Understanding international migration at the end of the millennium.* Oxford: Clarendon Press.

Mayer, Philip. 1971. *Townsmen or tribesmen: Conservatism and the process of urbanization in a South African city.* 2d. ed. Cape Town, So. Africa: Oxford University Press.

McNulty, Michael. 1985. Urban-rural linkages and national development in Africa. Paper presented at the African Studies Association meetings, New Orleans, November.

Meillassoux, Claude. 1981. *Maidens, meal, and money: Capitalism and the domestic community.* Cambridge: Cambridge University Press.

Mitchell, J. Clyde. 1956. *The Kalela dance: Aspects of social relationships among urban Africans in Northern Rhodesia*. Rhodes-Livingstone Papers 27. Manchester: Manchester University Press.

Murphy, Rachel. 2000. Return migration, entrepreneurship and local state corporatism in rural China. *Journal of Contemporary China* 9 (24): 231–48.

Newby, Alison. 2003. A tale of two cities: Gender and migration on the U.S.-Mexico border. Paper presented at the Society for Economic Anthropology meetings, April 4–5, Monterrey, Mexico.

O'Connor, Anthony. 1983. *The African city*. New York: Africana.

O'Neill, Tom. 2003. Keeping their parent's stomachs: Intergenerational remittances and Nepalese households. Paper presented at the Society for Economic Anthropology meeting, Monterrey, Mexico, April 4–5.

Orozco, Manuel. 2003a. Worker remittances in an international scope. Inter-American Dialogue Research Series, Remittances Project. Washington, D.C.: Inter-American Dialogue.

———. 2003b. Changes in the atmosphere? Increase of remittances, price decline, and new challenges. Inter-American Dialogue Research Series, Remittances Project. Washington, D.C.: Inter-American Dialogue.

———. 2003c. Remittances, the rural sector, and policy options in Latin America. Paper presented to the World Council of Credit Unions, Washington, D.C., June 2–4.

Otite, Onigu. 2002. On the path of progress: A study of rural immigrants and development in Nigeria. Ibadan, Nigeria: University of Ibadan Press.

Paerregaard, Karsten. 1997. Linking separate worlds: Urban migrants and rural lives in Peru. Oxford: Berg.

Painter, Thomas M. 1996. Space, time, and rural-urban linkages in Africa: Notes for a geography of livelihoods. *African Rural and Urban Studies* 3 (1): 79–98.

Portes, Alejandro, and John Walton. 1981. *Labor, class, and the international system*. New York: Academic Press.

Pratten, David T. 1996. Reconstructing community: The intermediary role of Sahelian associations in processes of migration and rural development. *African Rural and Urban Studies* 3 (1): 49–77.

Rees, Martha Woodson. 2003. Zapotec women and migration in times of globalization: The central valleys of Oaxaca, Mexico, 1950–1998. Paper presented at the Society for Economic Anthropology meetings, Monterrey, Mexico, April 4–5.

Reitz, Jeffrey G. 2002. Host societies and the reception of immigrants: Research themes, emerging theories and methodological issues. *International Migration Review* 36 (4): 1005–19.

Rempel, Henry, and Richard A. Lobdell. 1978. The role of urban-to-rural remittances in rural development. *Journal of Development Studies* 14:324–41.

Russell, Sharon Stanton. 1986. Remittances from international migration: A review in perspective. *World Development* 14 (6): 677–96.

Selby, Henry A., and Arthur D. Murphy. 1982. *The Mexican urban household and the decision to migrate to the United States.* ISHI Occasional Papers 4. Philadelphia: Institute for the Study of Human Issues.

Stark, Oded. 1978. *Economic-demographic interaction in agricultural development: The case of rural-to-urban migration.* Rome: Food and Agricultural Organization of the United Nations.

———. 1991. *The migration of labor.* Cambridge, Mass.: Basil Blackwell.

———. 1995. *Altruism and beyond: An economic analysis of transfers and exchanges within families and groups.* Cambridge: Cambridge University Press.

Trager, Lillian. 1981. Urban migrants and their links with home: A case study from Dagupan City. *Philippine Studies* 29:217–29.

———. 1984a. Family strategies and the migration of women: Migrants to Dagupan City, Philippines. *International Migration Review* 18:1264–77.

———. 1984b. Migration and remittances: Urban income and rural households in the Philippines. *Journal of Developing Areas* 18:317–40.

———. 1988. *The city connection: Migration and family interdependence in the Philippines.* Ann Arbor: University of Michigan Press.

———, ed. 1996. Special issue on rural-urban linkages. *African Rural and Urban Studies* 3:1.

———. 1998. Hometown linkages and local development in southwestern Nigeria: Whose agenda? What impact? *Africa* 68 (3): 360–82.

———. 2001. *Yoruba hometowns: Community, identity and development in Nigeria.* Boulder, Colo.: Rienner.

United Nations Population Fund. 1993. *The state of the world population 1993: The individual and the world: Population, migration, and development in the 1990s.* New York: United Nations Population Fund.

Wang, Feng, and Xuejin Zuo. 1999. Inside China's cities: Institutional barriers and opportunities for urban migrants. *American Economic Review* 89 (2): 276–80.

Weisner, Thomas S. 1972. One family, two households: Rural-urban ties in Kenya. Ph.D. diss., Harvard Univ.

———. 1976. The structure of sociability: Urban migration and urban-rural ties in Kenya. *Urban Anthropology* 5:199–223.

Wilk, Richard R., and Robert McC. Netting. 1984. Households: Changing forms and functions. In *Households: Comparative and historical studies of the domestic group,* ed. Robert McC. Netting, Richard R. Wilk, and Eric J. Arnould, 1–28. Berkeley: University of California Press.

Wood, Charles H. 1981. Structural changes and household strategies: A conceptual framework for the study of rural migration. *Human Organization* 40:338–44.

———. 1982. Equilibrium and historical-structural perspectives on migration. *International Migration Review* 16:298–319.

I

MIGRATION, HOUSEHOLDS, AND STRATIFICATION

1

Unbound Households

Trajectories of Labor, Migration, and Transnational Livelihoods in (and from) Southern Puerto Rico

Ricardo Pérez

In 1955, Don Ramón Ortíz, a fisherman from La Playa de Guayanilla, a small coastal community in southern Puerto Rico, migrated to Chicago.[1] For the next three decades, he had three jobs, working mostly in low-paying, semi-skilled positions in a restaurant, for Chiquita Brands (a transnational corporation with commercial interests in the banana market of Honduras), and in a spring-mattress factory. When I asked him about his reasons for migrating to Chicago, he commented that he wanted to leave this fishing community, one of 1,317 inhabitants (U.S. Census 2000), because "the [economic] situation was getting really bad."[2] The sugarcane economy had provided him with job opportunities at various times through his young life but since the mid-1950s had been in conspicuous decline. Don Ramón used to work on the piers that Hacienda Rufina, the most important sugar mill in the region, had in this community. Fishing was the other main occupation he had at the time, but prices for fresh fish were so low that he could not earn enough money to satisfy all of his household needs. Because industrial development had not yet started in Puerto Rico when Don Ramón decided to migrate to Chicago, he did not benefit from the many employment opportunities that industrialization later created for many residents in the region. In fact, Don Ramón is one of the few residents whom I have interviewed in this community with no work experience in the industrial complex nearby that continued to expand until the early 1980s, when most industrial operations shut down or relocated off the island (see Pérez 2002).

Like Don Ramón, many rural residents from Playa de Guayanilla, Encarnación, and El Faro—three coastal communities that I have studied for the past six years—have migrated to the U.S. mainland since the early 1950s in search of jobs. Some of them have worked in factories and the service sectors of the economy in New York City and Chicago while others have worked as seasonal farmworkers in various places in the Northeastern United States and the Midwest. While the farmworkers always returned to Puerto Rico at the end of the working season, industrial workers could remain (and some did remain) in the U.S. mainland more permanently and returned to the island at the end of their productive years. In what follows, I analyze the life histories and work trajectories of Don Ramón and two other rural migrants, one from Playa de Guayanilla and another from Encarnación. I focus on these three individuals because they are representative of the migration patterns that have characterized the insertion of rural migrants from southern Puerto Rico into the labor markets of the United States since the mid-twentieth century.

In this chapter, I focus on the contributions that labor migration made from the 1950s to the 1990s to the household economies of the residents interviewed in Playa de Guayanilla and Encarnación during two periods of ethnographic research. In 1997, I studied the transformation of the rural economy in the region that resulted from government intervention, and I collected economic and demographic data in three communities that have been affected differently by government-sponsored development targeting small-scale commercial fisheries.[3] While collecting data using a household survey, I noticed that labor migration was one important economic strategy used by members of various fishing households in the three communities to supplement their incomes. In the summer of 2002, I visited the three communities again and decided to focus more closely on labor migration in order to elicit and analyze local narratives about migration to the U.S. mainland. The analysis that I present here is based on survey data collected in 1997 and structured interviews conducted in 1997 and 2002 with forty-seven fishermen. One main characteristic of small-scale fishing is that it is a male-dominated activity. Women's roles in and contributions to fishing, while important, will not be discussed in the present analysis. My goals are to describe the patterns of migration from southern Puerto Rico to the U.S. mainland from the 1950s to the 1990s and to discuss how rural migrants have developed adaptive patterns of transnational mobility that have allowed them to establish transnational labor and family networks in the two countries.

Common representations of small-scale commercial fishing point to the fact that the fisherfolk form an inherently mobile population that depends heavily on a fragile marine resource that they cannot control. Those representations also stress the fact that small-scale commercial fishermen do find employment in other economic sectors, such as agriculture, manufacturing, and the services (see Nadel-Klein 2003; Griffith and Valdés Pizzini 2002). Like the Puerto Rican fisherfolk whose life histories and work trajectories David Griffith and Manuel Valdés Pizzini (2002) have aptly documented, the three case studies presented here point to the resilience and endurance of the labor options of the small-scale commercial fishermen on the island. As an important economic option available to these fisherfolk, labor migration to the United States mainland has enabled them to participate in transnational processes of family, community, and commercial relations in both Puerto Rico and the U.S. mainland. The analysis that I present is consistent with conclusions from recent studies on transnational migration that have emphasized the "multistranded social relations that link together [the migrants'] societies of origin and settlement" (Basch, Glick Schiller, and Szanton Blanc 1994, 7; see also Pessar 1997; Trager, this volume, chapter 7).

A growing interest in the study of Caribbean (and particularly Puerto Rican) migration in the last five decades has led scholars to describe migration patterns using categories such as return migration and circular or revolving-door migration (Duany 2002; Hernández Alvarez 1967; Hernández Cruz 1985, 1994). More recently, Jorge Duany (2002) has proposed the concept of mobile livelihoods to depict the conditions of the Puerto Rican migrants who circulate from the island to the U.S. mainland and remain for relatively short periods in the two countries. He contends this is a useful concept that highlights the flexibility of household arrangements when migration becomes an important survival strategy for impoverished workers. A main contention of the recent literature on Caribbean and Puerto Rican migration is that the experiences of circular migrants challenge conventional representations of international migration as a one-way displacement to a new destination. In this chapter, I borrow from Duany's definition of mobile livelihoods as "the spatial extension of

people's means of subsistence across various local, regional and national settings" to depict the reality of migration patterns in and from the communities
I studied in southern Puerto Rico (210). I argue that industrial development in
southern Puerto Rico and migration to the U.S. mainland have contributed to
the creation and maintenance of labor strategies that allow the fishing households on the island to participate in economic activities taking place simultaneously in various locales.

The flexible insertion of the local fishing households into global processes
of capitalist development is a characteristic of the economic conditions that,
in this chapter, I call unbound households. I argue that in the context of economic development in southern Puerto Rico, the global expansion of economic opportunities since the mid-twentieth century has created conditions
for the creation and maintenance of unbound households as the fisherfolk
take advantage of employment opportunities in both Puerto Rico and the U.S.
mainland. In a recent publication on household economies in the Andean region of South America, Enrique Mayer (2002) analyzes the articulation of
capitalist and noncapitalist economic relations and explains that peasant
households are enmeshed in multiple forms of economic production that allow peasants to participate in local, regional, and national processes of economic development. The life histories and work trajectories of the three
fisherfolk whom I analyze here attest to the importance of labor migration
since the early 1950s resulting from the onset of industrial development in
Puerto Rico, which in turn reflects the transformation of the world's capitalist economy after the end of World War II (see Center for Puerto Rican Studies 1979; Hernández Cruz 1994; Meléndez 1993).

I have divided this chapter into three parts: First, I describe the region
where I conducted ethnographic research and present some background information about the main economic transformations from the 1950s to the
present. Second, I analyze quantitative data from the household survey to indicate the ways local residents have been able to draw on various economic alternatives to supplement their meager household incomes. These two sections
show that labor migration from the 1950s to the 1990s has been a response to
limited employment opportunities in the region. Third, I analyze in detail
Don Ramón's life history and work experiences and compare them to those of
Manuel Rosado and Miguel García, two local fishermen who also migrated to
the U.S. mainland in search of jobs during their youth. Finally, in the conclu-

sion I explain that the three case studies, while lending support to recent scholarly statements about the transnational spread of the migrants' commitments to communities and individuals in their "home" countries and the diaspora, also reveal that the fisherfolk remain attached to their communities in southern Puerto Rico. The migrants' narratives of return attest to the importance of this seeming contradiction that Griffith and Valdés Pizzini (2002, 242–45) have recently analyzed in relation to the fishermen's meaningful construction of place in coastal regions across Puerto Rico.

MAPPING THE REGION: ECONOMIC DEVELOPMENT IN SOUTHERN PUERTO RICO

Playa de Guayanilla and Encarnación are located approximately fifteen kilometers west of Ponce, Puerto Rico's second-largest city. Playa de Guayanilla is a rural district (or *barrio*) of the municipality of Guayanilla, and Encarnación is a rural district of the municipality of Peñuelas (see figure 1.1). The two municipalities extend north from the Caribbean Sea to the Cordillera Central— the mountainous range that runs continuously from the eastern to the western part of the island—and thus include coastal valleys, semiarid hills, and forested highlands. Because of these geographic features, the region's major economic pursuits are the cultivation of sugarcane, coffee, and fruits and the raising of livestock and cattle. The coastal landscapes in proximity to the communities under study are presently dotted with rusted chimneys and abandoned oil storage tanks that are remnants of an aborted industrial development model that the Puerto Rican government implemented in the late 1940s. This model was known as Operation Bootstrap and consisted of the promotion of industrialization by granting tax exemptions to corporations (mostly those of the United States) and reducing government investment in manufacturing.[4] According to Emilio Pantojas García (1990, 101–42), Operation Bootstrap formed the second stage of industrial development on the island and served as the backbone of the capital importation–export processing strategy that characterized the expansion of the petrochemical and oil complexes located in proximity to Playa de Guayanilla and Encarnación.

Until the early 1960s, sugarcane cultivation was the foremost economic activity in the region. Especially from the 1930s to the 1960s, the sugar economy dominated agricultural production, and two sugar mills, Hacienda Rufina and Hacienda San Francisco, were among the largest producers of sugarcane in

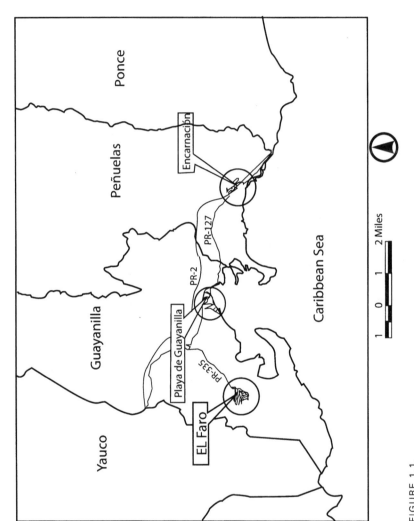

FIGURE 1.1.
The ethnographic research area

Puerto Rico (see Gayer, Homan, and James 1938, 80). Both mills provided employment opportunities to local residents in the various stages of sugar cultivation and refining. Hacienda Rufina owned the piers in Playa de Guayanilla, from which it exported refined sugar to national and international markets. According to Don Ramón, shipping refined sugar relied on different work gangs: one gang was responsible for loading the jetties (small boats used to transport sugar from the pier to the ships); another was responsible for providing water to thirsty workers; another for mending and stitching damaged bags; and another for hauling the bags into the ships using winches. Members of each gang earned a different salary because laborers were paid at piece rate depending on the number of bags that they loaded. According to some estimates, a jetty could carry between three hundred to four hundred bags of sugar, and ships had the capacity to store between twenty thousand and thirty thousand bags. Transporting sugar from Hacienda Rufina, loading the jetties in the beachfront, and hauling bags of refined sugar into the ships lasted between four and six days each summer. Therefore, a typical working year for the local residents consisted of three to four months of planting and harvesting sugarcane, two or three months of processing and refining it in Hacienda Rufina, and a week during summertime to ship the commodity to national and international markets. When the local residents were not working on any of these tasks, they engaged in productive activities, including fishing, temporary construction work, and myriad odd jobs.

According to some residents interviewed in Playa de Guayanilla, the spatial growth and development of the community depended on the availability of agricultural jobs in the coastal valleys. Local residents remembered that their parents and grandparents had migrated from the central highlands during the 1930s and 1940s to search for jobs in sugarcane fields and plantations. This pattern of rural migration from the highlands to the coasts was quite common in other areas during these decades, as indicated by earlier anthropological studies of rural development in Puerto Rico (Mintz 1956; see also Steward et al. 1956). In Playa de Guayanilla, many migrants occupied the idle lands bordering the river, the various river streams that crisscross the community, and the river estuary to build their homes. As people continued to migrate to the coastal valleys, the community kept growing and expanding. Other migrants in El Faro, however, occupied the houses built by the sugar barons, as was the case with the workers employed by the owners of Hacienda Rufina.

Hacienda Rufina closed the piers in the early 1950s. However, it continued to produce sugarcane until the late 1960s (the last harvest season was 1966–1967), at which time it began to use the port of Ponce to ship the commodity to national and international markets. By the 1950s, sugarcane production in Puerto Rico had already declined dramatically. For many residents in Playa de Guayanilla heavily involved in the sugar industry, this meant the demise of a "traditional" way of life. During the course of an interview in 1997, Don Ramón regretted the lack of job opportunities after Hacienda Rufina closed the piers. He commented that "when the piers closed, the community's well-being collapsed because fishing and sugarcane provided our economic support!" His regret was repeated by many other residents of the region that I interviewed, who compared the times when sugarcane cultivation was the mainstay of Playa de Guayanilla with the period of economic decline and resource degradation brought about by industrialization since the mid-1950s.

Industrial development in the region began in earnest in the 1950s, when the Puerto Rican government built a plant to refine oil (the Commonwealth

Table 1.1.   Industries in Proximity to Playa de Guayanilla and Encarnación

Name of Industry	Location	Years of Operation
Commonwealth Oil Refining Company (CORCO)	Peñuelas	1956–1982
Costa Sur Electric Power Plant	Guayanilla	1958–present
South Puerto Rico Towing and Boat Service	Guayanilla	1958–present
Union Carbide	Peñuelas	1959–1985
Hercor Chemical Corporation	Peñuelas	1966–1982
Peerless Oil Chemicals	Peñuelas	1968–1981
Styrochem Corporation	Peñuelas	1968–1982
Air Products and Chemicals of Puerto Rico	Guayanilla	1970–present
Orochem Enterprises	Peñuelas	1971–1978
ESSO Standard Oil	Peñuelas	1971–1978
Puerto Rico Olefins Plant	Peñuelas	1971–1978
Pittsburgh Plate and Glass Industries	Guayanilla	1972–1978
Rico Chemicals Corporation	Guayanilla	1975–1981
Caribe Isoprene Corporation	Peñuelas	1975–1982
Oxochem Enterprises	Peñuelas	1976–1978
Industrial Chemicals Corporation	Peñuelas	1977–present
DEMACO	Guayanilla	1984–present
BETTEROADS	Guayanilla	1985–present
Arochem International	Peñuelas	1988–1992
Vassallo Paints and Coatings	Guayanilla	1988–present
Peerless Oil and Chemicals	Peñuelas	1989–present
TEXACO Industries	Guayanilla	1990–present
Eco-Eléctrica	Guayanilla	2001–present

Source: Adapted from Servicios Científicos y Técnicos (1995, 64–67).

Oil Refining Company, or CORCO) and an electric power plant (Central Costa Sur Electric Power Plant) that could support further industrial developments (see table 1.1). The 1960s and 1970s were decades of heightened industrialization in the region, as the expansion of the petrochemical and oil refinery complex benefited from "the allocation to Puerto Rico of special oil import quotas between 1965–1973" (Pantojas García 1990, 106). Industrial development was so rapid and successful that in 1977, twenty-seven of fifty-one petrochemical plants in Puerto Rico were operated by CORCO or Union Carbide, the two largest corporations that supported the petrochemical and oil refining complex. According to Emilio Pantojas García (114), "both companies had been ranked among the 500 largest companies in the United States by Fortune Magazine." By 1978, "nine petrochemical plants were operating in the complex as CORCO subsidiaries or joint ventures, representing a total investment of more than $545 million" (Baver 1993, 58–59). Most of the industries were located in Peñuelas, although their economic impact extended throughout the region, even to areas far from Guayanilla and Peñuelas.

The most recent case of the region's insertion into global capitalist markets occurred in 2001, when Eco-Eléctrica—a natural gas power plant and a subsidiary of Kenetech-Enron—started operations (see Pérez 2002, 215–16). The few industries that still operate in areas close to Playa de Guayanilla and Encarnación do not provide enough employment opportunities to the local residents; they are able to obtain work in primarily low-paying and semiskilled or unskilled positions. More significant, industrial development during the last two decades has slowed down, thus reducing opportunities for regional economic development (see table 1.1).

During my fieldwork in 1997, the local population formed a mixture of full-time and part-time fishermen whose livelihood was greatly subsidized by several programs from governments of both the United States and Puerto Rico. The government support was mainly through the Nutritional Assistance Program and Social Security.[5] These fishermen combined the benefits from government transfers with benefits from small-scale fishing and other occupations, including industrial labor, odd jobs, and jobs in the informal sector. Estimates place Guayanilla's unemployment rate at close to 16 percent and Peñuelas's at 24.6 percent.[6] Today, limited employment opportunities exist in various government offices and small stores in the municipal towns, and agriculture still provides a few rural workers with seasonal jobs. For instance,

Tropical Fruit, an Israeli-owned corporation, cultivates bananas and mangoes in Barrio Boca, a few miles west of El Faro, for export to international markets. Other local residents work in agriculture north of El Faro, cultivating vegetable and fruits for distribution mostly in local markets. The agricultural fields in the latter place belong to the heirs of Mario Mercado, the sugar baron who owned Hacienda Rufina until it closed in the late 1960s.

SMALL-SCALE FISHING, INDUSTRIAL DEVELOPMENT, AND LABOR MIGRATION

Industrial Labor and Semiproletarianization of Small-Scale Commercial Fishermen

Two main outcomes of industrial development have been the semiproletarianization of the fisherfolk and migration to and from the local communities. Although industrialization diversified the economic options available locally, only a few of the fisherfolk I interviewed were able to find permanent employment in the industrial complex nearby. Many found jobs working as laborers during the early construction stages of the industrial complex and others working as janitors when the industries started full operations. Figure 1.2 shows the types of industrial jobs that local residents were able to obtain from the 1950s to the early 1980s. Quantitative data analysis indicates that twelve residents (24 percent) were employed by some petrochemical and oil-refining industries but that only one held a high-income position, as a machine operator for Union Carbide. I assume that the number of local residents employed during the years the industries were operating must have been much higher than what is indicated in the figure, especially during the construction stages, because industrial development in the region required a large labor force of primarily semiskilled and unskilled workers. Likewise, the fact that the industrial complex was constantly expanding until the early 1980s might have helped local residents to find jobs setting up the needed industrial infrastructure.

Quantitative data analysis also indicates that, with the exception of one fisherman who stated that he never worked in any economic sector besides fishing, all fishermen had combined fishing with various industrial jobs. The fact that small-scale commercial fishermen can sustain their families for long periods maintaining various jobs simultaneously is a well-known aspect of fishing households in the Caribbean. Lambros Comitas (1973) documented

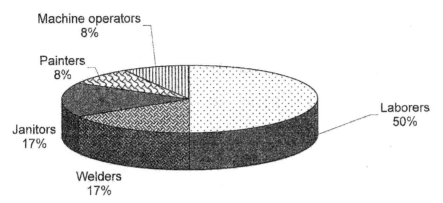

FIGURE 1.2.
Industrial jobs available to the fisherfolk from Playa de Guayanilla and Encarnación

this reality among Jamaican fishermen during the 1960s, and, more recently, Griffith and Valdés Pizzini (2002) have done so in regards to the Puerto Rican fishermen. Notably, small-scale fishing is not a profitable option for any of the households in Playa de Guayanilla and Encarnación. In fact, a typical rural household in these communities combined at least two different jobs, while many combined three. For example, a fisherman from Playa de Guayanilla mentioned that, besides working as a fisherman, he also worked as a mechanic, a taxi and truck driver, and a fruit vendor. His work experiences resemble the experiences of most residents in his community and confirm, as Charlotte Cerf (1990, 175) has correctly pointed out, that in most coastal settlements around the world "combining fishing with other occupations is more likely to occur during times of economic distress."

In a survey conducted during the late 1960s among commercial fishermen in Playa de Guayanilla and three communities in southwest Puerto Rico, Federico Blay (1972) found that advanced age and little education were factors that made it difficult for the local residents to find steady employment in the industries and factories nearby.[7] Residents from Playa de Guayanilla and Encarnación were negatively affected by these factors. For example, 50 percent of the residents from Playa de Guayanilla included in his survey had fewer than three years of schooling, while only 2.6 percent had between ten and twelve years of schooling. In addition, the average age was fifty-two, the highest of all the fishermen Blay surveyed in southwest Puerto Rico. Also, in Playa de Guayanilla, fishermen had higher average ages than those of the other laborers in agricultural and industrial tasks in all the communities surveyed (59–60). More recent data from the household survey I conducted in Playa de Guayanilla reveals that close to 50 percent of the fisherfolk are between fifty and sixty-nine years old. Age and little education negatively affect opportunities in another important way—namely, the older the fisherfolk, the more time they devote to fishing and the fewer opportunities they have to find jobs elsewhere.

The relationship between economic diversification and the semiproletarianization of the local fisherfolk can be seen more clearly if we compare it with similar processes in other regions of the island. In an analysis of the working trajectories of 102 fishermen's households across Puerto Rico, Griffith, Valdés Pizzini, and Jeffery C. Johnson (1992, 52) found that "incomplete incorporation" of small-scale commercial fishermen "into the formal economic structures and process of capitalism" is a threefold process. First, there is proletarianization, whereby fishermen may abandon fishing altogether and engage more heavily in industrial employment. Second, semiproletarianization may arise when commercial fishermen combine the income derived from fishing with earnings from industrial jobs. Third, deproletarianization may occur when fishermen abandon wage labor to pursue commercial fishing on a full-time basis. The last stage, however, should not be confused with retirement (see also Griffith and Valdés Pizzini 2002, 131–61).

Similar to the results that Griffith, Valdés Pizzini, and Johnson (1992) obtained, my data indicate that most fishermen in Playa de Guayanilla and Encarnación maintain a semiproletarian status as fishermen, continuing to fish in order to supplement the wages they earn from industrial jobs. No household was following a total proletarianization path, because fishermen did not earn enough money from other jobs to quit fishing. As I have shown elsewhere, fewer than 50 percent of the local fishermen found jobs in petrochemical plants and oil refineries (Pérez 2002, 219). But in contrast to Griffith, Valdés Pizzini, and Johnson's findings (1992), mine indicate that the majority of the fishermen's households that I surveyed in Playa de Guayanilla and Encarnación reverted to deproletarianization in the wake of industrial collapse during the late 1970s and early 1980s. The examples that Griffith, Valdés Pizzini, and Johnson (1992, 59–70) discuss show that deproletarianization resulted when small-scale commercial fishermen were injured and claimed the economic benefits of their settlement or, alternatively, when they won the lottery. Both situations allowed fishermen to invest in the acquisition of new fishing vessels and gear. Among the fishermen I surveyed in Playa de Guayanilla and Encarnación, deindustrialization meant the necessary return to part-time fishing, which they combined with agricultural labor, labor migration, and various odd jobs available in their communities.

Industrial Labor and Migration to the United States Mainland

From the 1950s, when industrial development in the region started in earnest, to the 1980s, when industrialization began to dwindle, population numbers in the communities studied shifted accordingly. For instance, in Playa de Guayanilla, the population grew from 909 in 1940, to 1,287 in 1960, to 1,704 in 1970. In Encarnación, population increased from 459 in 1950 to 1,429 in 1970. The majority of the residents that I interviewed in the three communities have families who migrated to the region from nearby regions and communities when they were able to find jobs in the petrochemical complex. With industrialization being the main economic segment, people continued to migrate, and the growth and expansion of the communities promoted commercial activities such as bars, small lodging facilities, and restaurants that increased the local demand for fish. Some fishermen took advantage of this situation and set up independent fish houses in order to purchase and sell fresh fish. Indeed, the current spatial and residential distribution in Playa de Guayanilla has been attributed to the economic and commercial boom promoted by industrial development. As a local fisherman convincingly argued, when industries were still operating in the region, the community grew, with more commercial activities being devoted to the preparation and selling of fish pastries and beverages, "just like it is now because everywhere there is a store."

When industrial development in the region began to decline during the late 1970s, many commercial fishermen continued to diversify their economic strategies in order to generate adequate household incomes. One of the most important economic alternatives available to them was migration to urban centers in Puerto Rico or to the areas in the Northeastern United States with large concentrations of Puerto Ricans, such as New York City, New Jersey, Pennsylvania, and Connecticut. The decline of industrial development in the region coincided with the period when Federico Blay (1972) conducted his survey among small-scale commercial fishermen in Playa de Guayanilla. He reports that 16 percent of the fishermen's households in Playa de Guayanilla had someone in the family who migrated to the U.S. mainland and that 7.7 percent "had worked there for a short period of time" (60). Although Blay does not provide additional information about those latter fishermen, they were likely farmworkers contracted to pick and pack fruits and vegetables in places in the Northeastern United States and the Midwest. From the late 1940s to the late 1970s, Puerto Rico's Department of Labor and the U.S. government maintained a program that allowed Puerto Rican rural laborers to work seasonally in agricultural activities in the Northeastern seaboard states (see Lapp 1990; Rivera 1979). The Puerto Rican farmworkers spent between six and eight months in the United States and returned to the island at the end of the harvest season to resume the economic activities they were doing before migrating.

Migration to the U.S. mainland has always been an important economic alternative for most Puerto Ricans. Apart from obtaining those seasonal agricultural jobs, residents of southern Puerto Rico, such as Don Ramón, obtained work in semiskilled and unskilled positions in restaurants, hotels, and factories. According to Blay (1972, 60), most residents from Playa de Guayanilla who migrated to the United States during the late 1960s were between fifteen and forty-four years old, which he defines as the most productive years of the economically active rural population. Quantitative data analysis from my research shows that thirty-two fishermen (66 percent) had migrated to the United States at some point in their lives; of this number, twenty-two migrants (61 percent) found jobs in the industrial/service sectors of the economy, four (11 percent) worked in agriculture, and ten (28 percent) worked in both agricultural and nonagricultural jobs (see figure 1.3). As the life histories and work trajectories in the next section clearly demonstrate, many local residents preferred to migrate to the U.S. mainland in search of better economic alternatives.

LABOR MIGRATION AND TRANSNATIONAL LIVELIHOODS: CASE STUDIES

Don Ramón Ortiz was twenty-one years old when he first migrated to Chicago, in 1955. Before this move, he worked in the sugar economy as a laborer on the piers of Hacienda Rufina and as a fisherman with trammel nets and gill nets. He was able to combine the two jobs successfully until the time the sugar economy ceased to be the most lucrative economic activity in the re-

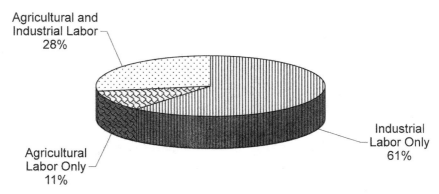

FIGURE 1.3.
Migration patterns to the United States Mainland

gion in the late 1960s. The salary he earned working for Hacienda Rufina was so low that he and his family experienced recurrent economic hardships, a situation that was not ameliorated by the money he earned from fishing, because at the time the "fish cost only thirty-five cents." During our interviews, he recalled that refined sugar was transported to the piers by train in bags weighing approximately 275 pounds. He also recalled that he helped load the bags onto small jetties, which carried them to the ships waiting a short distance from the shore.

While living in Chicago, Don Ramón maintained a pattern of holding low-skilled and low-paying jobs that helped reproduce the conditions of poverty he and his family were experiencing on the island. According to him, the first job he was able to find was as a dishwasher in a restaurant, earning $1.20 per hour. He worked at the restaurant for two years and then found a better-paying job weighing and packing bananas for Chiquita Brands. According to him, this job was much easier, but he kept this job for only six years because the company closed operations in Chicago after the business in Honduras began to decline. Don Ramón moved quickly to his third and last job in the Windy City in a spring-mattress factory, where he was responsible for operating a machine that could produce over two hundred springs per hour. It is important to note that the different jobs Don Ramón held in Chicago provided him with enough income to cover all his financial responsibilities. For example, he used to send remittances of $100 a week to his wife and two young children back on the island. A couple of years later he brought his family to live with him in Chicago, and his family group rapidly increased to six members (two more children were born in the United States). With a bigger family, Don Ramón had to find a bigger place to live.

Don Ramón spent the next fifteen years working the same factory job to support a family that kept growing in numbers. Although salary raises were difficult to obtain, he was able to save sufficient income to cover all family expenses. For example, Don Ramón did not own a car and had to walk long distances to go to work, and he had to use the public transportation system to run errands. In fact, he cited this as a main reason for the leg injury and health complications that forced him to return to Playa de Guayanilla in 1990. But he also mentioned the cold weather in Chicago, which tended to aggravate his leg injury, as another reason for his definitive return to the island. Despite the cold weather and the snow, his work experiences in Chicago were good. He commented that he liked to live in Chicago because there were plenty of job opportunities in factories and other workplaces that required little or no education or formal training. Like that of many residents from Playa de Guayanilla, his formal education did not go beyond fourth grade.

During the three decades he lived in Chicago, Don Ramón was in contact with friends and relatives in Playa de Guayanilla, and he used to visit them, for example, to attend family and community events. The salaries he earned from the jobs he obtained in Chicago provided enough income to allow him to build the house where he has been living since returning to the island in 1990. He mentioned that in 1989 he bought a plot of land for $3,000, demolished the small wooden house of the previous owner, and built a bigger house made of cement blocks, wood, and metal sheets. When I interviewed him for the first time on a hot morning in February 1997, the house was for sale because he was considering a move back to Chicago, where his sons and daughters currently live.[8] Although I asked him many times if his children send him money, he asserted that he does not need their financial assistance to cover his household expenses. Two weeks after the summer 2002 interview, two of his sons were going to visit and stay with him for fifteen days. But he was skeptical about the prospect of the visit because his oldest son is afraid of flying in airplanes.

The second case, Manuel Rosado, a resident of Encarnación, has a rather different history of labor migration. He has experiences as a farmworker through the agricultural labor program that the Migration Division instituted in 1947 (see Lapp 1990). He worked in New Jersey and Pennsylvania for two seasons in the early 1970s, a time when the agricultural program was in decline. According to Michael Lapp, "in the early 1970s, due to the attacks of critics and to increasing mechanization in the fields, the agricultural program shrank to less than a third of its size in the previous decade" (201). In 1972, at the age of eighteen, Manuel went to the agricultural program's recruitment office in Ponce and was sent to a farm in Glassboro, New Jersey, to help pick onions and tomatoes. The Glassboro Farmers Association was one of the most active recruiters of farm labor in Puerto Rico. A couple of weeks after his arrival in southern New Jersey, Manuel quit his job because it required him to kneel for a long time, and he next ended up at a farm in Pennsylvania. There, he was responsible for picking apples and peaches, which, according to him, was an easier job to do. Manuel worked eight months (from March to November) in the United States and spent the rest of the year in Puerto Rico fishing and doing odd jobs. He was living at the time with his grandparents, a couple that made ends meet with the earnings from the grandfather's artisanal broom-making job and from the sale of fish pastries that the grandmother made from Manuel's catch. While in Pennsylvania, Manuel would also send them weekly remittances of $40. His fishing methods at the time were rather simple, as he relied on fishnets and a rowboat to fish in the inshore areas near the coast of Encarnación, where he has lived almost his entire life.

Manuel never liked agricultural work, but he continued doing farmwork for the next two seasons because of the lack of employment opportunities in his native region. Upon his return to the island in 1974, he met the woman that he eventually married, and a short time later his uncle found him a job at Union Carbide, one of the petrochemical industries located in the industrial complex nearby. At Union Carbide, his work involved insulating pipes, a high-paying job that also allowed him the opportunity to pursue fishing in the afternoons and on weekends. He kept his job until 1984, when Union Carbide closed industrial operations and moved outside the region, following the trend to deindustrialization that was in full swing by the start of the decade (see table 1.1). By this time, Manuel had saved enough money to purchase a bigger boat, a powerful outboard motor, and better fishing gear, which allowed him to enhance the productivity of his fishing operations. Manuel was able to diversify his fishing techniques to include scuba diving in order to fish for lobster, the highest-priced species in the local fish markets. As a result of an accident in 1992, he contracted the bends, a serious condition that has hindered his ability to fish productively.[9] Because of this disability, he qualified to receive a twenty-five-foot fiberglass boat from Puerto Rico's Department of Labor Rehabilitation Program. Currently, Manuel goes out to fish with his *compadre* and serves as the president of the local fishermen association, Santo Cristo de la Salud, a position that he has occupied for the past seven years.[10]

The final example, Miguel García, presents a more complicated case of labor migration, in that he has worked in both the agricultural program in Michigan and upstate New York and the industrial and service sectors of the economy in New York City. Perhaps more important for the analysis I present in this chapter is his contention that he decided to migrate to the U.S. mainland "to experience a different work environment." In contrast to both Don Ramón and Manuel, Miguel was apparently not motivated by a lack of employment opportunities or a desire for a better-paying job. His life and work experiences are more typical of Duany's description (2002) of mobile livelihoods as those characterized by frequent, short-term displacements from the island to the mainland in search of jobs. With the intention "to experience a different work environment," Miguel went to Michigan in 1948 to work on a farm picking onions, blackberries, and other agricultural commodities. However, the farmer association that recruited him in Ponce did not comply with the contract stipulations (specifically, the association did not pay him the required minimum salary) and thus he ended up at a farm near Buffalo, New York.[11] He finished the harvest season in the latter place, where he returned again on two more occasions during the early 1950s. Miguel reported that he did not have a need to migrate, because he could make enough money by diving for lobsters off the coasts of Ponce and Peñuelas. He was the first fisherman on the south coast who dived for a living, originally without any equipment but since the early 1960s with tanks he was able to purchase in New York City, where he went to work intermittently for the next five years in a department store and a metal-plating factory.

Miguel never worked more than a full year in New York City, as he kept circulating between south Puerto Rico and New York City until 1992, when he finally decided to return definitively to Playa de Guayanilla. The short visits he has made to New York City since then have been to visit his children who have remained there. Miguel's case is also remarkably different from the two cases I discuss earlier in that he migrated to New York City rather late in his life (although this pattern of migration has become increasingly common among Puerto Ricans since the 1980s).[12] He was already thirty-two years old when he went to New York City, and he met his wife while living in El Barrio, the neighborhood most people know as Spanish Harlem. He first found a job at a department store, where he was responsible for loading and unloading merchandise into the warehouse in the second floor of the building. He began earning $48 a week and, after two-and-a-half years, was earning $75 a week. He liked this job very much but had to work so hard that he developed a leg injury that continued to worsen, even though he was getting accustomed to the hard job. According to him, his boss liked him very much, and during the summer his boss hired him to clean his yard in the neighborhood where he lived in Long Island.

It is not clear from the last interview, in 2002, whether Miguel quit this job as a result of his leg injury. However, it seems clear that after a short stay in Puerto Rico during 1958, Miguel returned to New York City and found a job plating metal at a jewelry factory. According to him, this was an easier job because he did not need to be seated all the time and his shift, from 8 AM to 5 PM, perfectly suited his schedule. The positive way that Miguel talked about the metal-plating work is remarkable to me because it has been noted elsewhere that, in the early 1980s, metallurgy formed one of the most vulnerable and unstable sectors of the industrial economy in New York City. For example, in a study of the "underground economy" in Spanish Harlem, Philippe Bourgois (1996, 139) has stated that metallurgy was "one of the least desirable and most unstable niches within New York City's manufacturing sector" at the time. Miguel was paid by piece rate depending on the number of jewelry pieces he was able to plate. He could produce nearly 150 rings a day, earning himself approximately $200 a day. This salary allowed him to do some repairs to the wooden house that he kept in Playa de Guayanilla until he returned to this community in 1992. Miguel continues to fish to this day; during the interview in summer 2002, he talked proudly of his fishing career and showed me the plaques and awards he has received from the municipal government, recognizing him as one of the most successful fishermen in the region.

DISCUSSION: RURAL MIGRATION AND TRANSNATIONAL LIVELIHOODS

More than an abstract academic concept, for the fisherfolk whose life histories and work trajectories I have discussed, migration was an important part of their everyday reality between the early 1950s and the early 1990s. As can be readily noted, labor migration was a convenient and important economic strategy that helped the fisherfolk supplement their meager incomes from agriculture, fishing, and temporary industrial jobs. These four decades were characterized by significant economic transformations in the region that changed the agrarian economy (based on sugarcane production) to an industrialized and, more recently, deindustrialized economy. In this chapter, I demonstrate that labor migration has been an important economic strategy that fisherfolk in southern Puerto Rico have incorporated into their already-complex repertoire of multiple occupations. The three case studies analyzed here support Duany's statement (2002) that, contrary to the perception of many Puerto Ricans, migration to the U.S. mainland can contribute significantly to rural household economies as migrants maintain successfully social networks in both countries. This popular perception of migration as a decision with potentially negative implications contrasts sharply with perceptions in several West African regions, where migration is not only encouraged but expected (see Koenig, this volume, chapter 2).

Labor migration and industrial development are elements with significant impacts on the life and work trajectories of the residents of southern Puerto Rico. Heavy industrialization in coastal areas helped modify in many ways labor strategies and economic alternatives available locally. For example, industrial development helped reduce the impact of the agrarian economy on the local households and promoted the fisherfolk's semiproletarianization. This pattern allowed some fishermen to maintain jobs in the fishing and industrial sectors for the time the petrochemical industries and oil refineries retained operations from the 1950s to the 1980s. As a result of industrial decline since the mid-1980s, employment opportunities have shrunk in recent years and have severely affected rural household incomes. Analysis of qualitative and quantitative data indicates that most rural households in Playa de Guayanilla and Encarnación experience precarious economic conditions. As a result, most local residents currently rely on a combination of multiple working strategies and economic transfers from the Puerto Rican and U.S. governments, primarily through the benefits of Social Security and the Nutritional Assistance Program.

Also as a result of changing economic conditions, more than half of the fishermen included in the household survey have migrated to the U.S. mainland. The three case studies analyzed in this chapter are representative of the patterns of migration I was able to identify in the region. For example, Don Ramón is indicative of the traditional return migrant, who decides to retire to his community after spending most of his productive life in the U.S. mainland (see Hernández Alvarez 1967). However, Don Ramón never severed contacts with community members in Puerto Rico, as he was able to visit friends and relatives on special occasions, and he still maintains kinship and family networks in Chicago. Manuel exemplifies the case of the head of the rural household, who must combine various economic alternatives at once in order to make ends meet, even though migration is not a sustainable alternative for him. It seems clear that Manuel's later success as a fisherman derived from the economic benefits of his job at Union Carbide, which allowed him to improve his fishing operations. After losing his job at Union Carbide in 1984, he intensified his fishing operations by relying on the support and labor of his *compadre*, wife, and children. In essence, Manuel's case is typical of the Caribbean situation where kinship networks are utilized to pull resources together to compensate for the industrial job that is lost and where the household becomes the "context for de-proletarianization" (see Griffith and Valdés Pizzini 2002, 172–78).

Finally, Miguel fits very well Duany's description (2002) of mobile livelihoods as a set of multiple, short-term displacements back and forth between the island and the mainland in search of jobs. Miguel's pattern of transnational mobility—where he was able to find jobs in agriculture and in factories—provided him substantial relief from insecure fishing operations in southern Puerto Rico for almost three decades. Like Don Ramón, Miguel developed family networks in New York City that have enabled him to continue visiting his children in the United States. The flexible household and labor arrangements that the fisherfolk have been able to establish simultaneously in various locales also fit Lillian Trager's definition of multilocality as "the attachment to and participation in social and economic activities in a number of places" (Trager, this volume, chapter 7). But in contrast to the case studies of the Puerto Rican fisherfolk whose work trajectories and migration experiences I have discussed in this chapter, who apart from visiting their children in the United States do not participate significantly in current labor arrangements, the Yoruba women of southwest Nigeria analyzed by Trager are active participants of hometown associations in their communities of origin.

While the three case studies of the Puerto Rican fisherfolk discussed here are examples of return migrants, all followed rather different paths to returning to south Puerto Rico. With the exception of Manuel, who migrated as a farmworker for only two years during the 1970s, Don Ramón and Miguel created and maintain to this day family networks in the U.S. mainland. Don Ramón lives on his own in the house he built in Playa de Guayanilla with the money he saved while working in Chicago, and Miguel lives with his wife and two children who are still attending high school. A fuller analysis of family networks and interactions is not possible with the data I was able to collect in Puerto Rico during 1997 and the summer of 2002 due to a lack of knowledge on the part of these two fisherfolk about the economic well-being of their children in the United States. It can be safely argued, however, that their children have opted to stay in the United States in the neighborhoods where they have lived most of their adult lives. These generational differences and preferences are certainly important but cannot be analyzed in this chapter due to a lack of systematic data on the households of the migrants' children in the U.S. mainland.

CONCLUSION: UNBOUND HOUSEHOLDS AND (THE COASTAL) PLACE

The relationship between economic transformation and labor migration is important to understanding contemporary Puerto Rico, an island that has sustained one of the largest migration flows in recent history (Duany 2002). Continuous migration from Puerto Rico to the United States since the 1950s poses many important theoretical and policy questions, but this subject is beyond the scope of this chapter. Of particular relevance to the analysis presented here is my contention that labor migration has contributed to the emergence of unbound households, as rural migrants engage in the now all-too-common practice of seeking better economic opportunities in an increasingly global economy. This is a crucial reality in rural areas in the Caribbean, southern Mexico, and the Philippines (see Basch, Glick Schiller, and Szanton Blanc 1994; Kearney 1996; Pessar 1997). As the chapters in this volume confirm, there are multiple reasons for people to migrate, as they try to find better economic options elsewhere beyond the geographical boundaries of their "home countries." In the case of Puerto Rico, it is possible to argue that labor migration will be maintained indefinitely as a main employment strategy due to the current uncertain economic situation on the island (see Baver 2000).

In the same manner that Linda Basch, Nina Glick Schiller, and Cristina Szanton Blanc (1994) have analyzed the emergence of unbound nations and deterritorialized nation-states that link immigrant communities in the United States with their "home" countries in the eastern Caribbean and the Philippines, I argue that it is necessary to construe rural fishing households in southern Puerto Rico as flexible settlements. The conventional approach to communities (and community studies) as static enclaves of individuals misrepresents rural economies in coastal regions because it overlooks the fact that the fisherfolk form a highly mobile population that normally combines successfully various economic strategies, of which labor migration is an important one. It is in this manner that the fishing economy articulates with economic transformations at the local, regional, and even transnational levels (see Mayer 2002). As the literature on West African migration confirms (see Koenig, chapter 2, and Trager, chapter 7, in this volume), it is important to consider the attachments to the "home" communities that the rural migrants are able to develop. In the case of the coastal communities in southern Puerto Rico that I analyzed in this chapter, attachment to the "home" communities is so significant that the fisherfolk have preferred to return to their places of origin while retaining kinship networks in the United States.

NOTES

I wish to acknowledge the residents of Playa de Guayanilla and Encarnación who graciously provided the data used in this chapter and Augusto F. Gandía for drawing the map included in it. I am also grateful to Lillian Trager and two anonymous reviewers for their comments and suggestions on an earlier draft. However, any omissions or misrepresentations are my sole responsibility.

1. In this chapter, I use pseudonyms to conceal and protect the residents' identities.

2. All interviews were conducted in Spanish. Excerpts and quotes from interviews are my translations.

3. See Pérez (2000) for detailed descriptions of the ethnographic research in Playa de Guayanilla, Encarnación, and El Faro. In this chapter, I rely on data from the first two communities only.

4. For detailed analyses of economic development in Puerto Rico, see Baver (1993), Dietz (1986), Maldonado (1997), and Pantojas García (1990).

5. The Nutritional Assistance Program, formerly disbursed as food coupons and currently as checks, has been in existence on the U.S. mainland since 1964. It was extended to include Puerto Rico in the mid-1970s with the intention of alleviating high poverty and unemployment rates on the island (see Weisskoff 1985, 60–64).

6. Unemployment figures were downloaded from the Internet and based on data provided by the following documents: *Unemployment Rate: Guayanilla Municipio, Puerto Rico* and *Unemployment Rate: Peñuelas Municipio, Puerto Rico* (www.economagic.com/em-cgi/data.exe/BLSLA, accessed June 1999).

7. The other communities are Puerto Real and El Combate, in the municipality of Cabo Rojo, and La Parguera, in Lajas.

8. I visited Don Ramón in December 1999 and summer 2002, and he was still living in the same house. Apparently, he changed his mind about moving because he could live in Puerto Rico with the earnings received from Social Security and fishing.

9. The bends affects divers who inhale oxygen, hydrogen, and other gases from diving tanks. It occurs when divers cannot return to the surface slowly enough to maintain an appropriate balance of gas inhalation. The condition affects the nervous system, and although many divers are successfully treated with decompression, some may still have difficulties working fully again.

10. *Compadre* derives from the fictive-kin relationships established by the *compadrazgo* system so common in Latin American countries. In the case at hand, Manuel became his fishing partner's *compadre* by becoming the godfather of one of his fishing partner's sons.

11. See Lapp (1990, 115–16) for descriptions of contract violations against Puerto Rican farmworkers in Michigan during the 1950s.

12. See Meléndez (1993, 10).

REFERENCES

Basch, Linda, Nina Glick Schiller, and Cristina Szanton Blanc. 1994. *Nations unbound: Transnational projects, postcolonial predicaments, and deterritorialized nation-states.* New York: Gordon and Breach.

Baver, Sherrie L. 1993. *The political economy of colonialism: The state and industrialization in Puerto Rico.* Westport, Conn.: Praeger.

———. 2000. The rise and fall of section 936: The historical context and possible consequences for migration. *CENTRO: Journal of the Center for Puerto Rican Studies* 11 (2): 44–55.

Blay, Federico G. 1972. *A study of the relevance of selected ecological factors related to water resources and the social organization of fishing villages in Puerto Rico.* Mayagüez, Puerto Rico: University of Puerto Rico Water Resources Research Institute.

Bourgois, Philippe. 1996. *In search of respect: Selling crack in el barrio.* Cambridge: Cambridge University Press.

Center for Puerto Rican Studies. History Task Force. 1979. *Labor migration under capitalism: The Puerto Rican experience.* New York: Monthly Review Press.

Cerf, Charlotte C. 1990. Waters of change: The impact of industrial water pollution on an artisanal fishing community in northeastern Brazil. Ph.D. diss., Dept. of Anthropology, Columbia University, New York.

Comitas, Lambros. 1973. Occupational multiplicity in rural Jamaica. In *Work and family life: West Indian perspectives*, eds. Lambros Comitas and David Lowenthal, 157–73. Garden City, N.Y.: Anchor Books.

Dietz, James L. 1986. *Economic history of Puerto Rico: Institutional change and capitalist development.* Princeton, N.J.: Princeton University Press.

Duany, Jorge. 2002. *The Puerto Rican nation on the move: Identities on the island and in the United States.* Chapel Hill, N.C.: University of North Carolina Press.

Gayer, Arthur D., Paul T. Homan, and Earle K. James. 1938. *The sugar economy of Puerto Rico.* New York: Columbia University Press.

Griffith, David, and Manuel Valdés Pizzini. 2002. *Fishers at work, workers at sea: A Puerto Rican journey through labor and refuge.* Philadelphia: Temple University Press.

Griffith, David, Manuel Valdés Pizzini, and Jeffrey C. Johnson. 1992. Injury and therapy: Proletarianization in Puerto Rico's fisheries. *American Ethnologist* 19 (1): 53–74.

Hernández Alvarez, José. 1967. *Return migration to Puerto Rico.* Berkeley, Calif.: Institute of International Studies.

Hernández Cruz, Juan E. 1985. ¿Migración de retorno o circulación de obreros? *Revista de Ciencias Sociales* 24 (1–2): 79–110.

———. 1994. *Migratory trends in Puerto Rico.* San Germán, Puerto Rico: Inter American University, Latin America and the Caribbean Research Center.

Kearney, Michael. 1996. *Reconceptualizing the peasantry: Anthropology in global perspective.* Boulder, Colo.: Westview Press.

Lapp, Michael. 1990. Managing migration: The migration division of Puerto Rico and Puerto Ricans in New York City, 1948–1968. Ph.D. diss., Dept. of Anthropology, John Hopkins University.

Maldonado, A. W. 1997. *Teodoro Moscoso and Puerto Rico's Operation Bootstrap.* Gainesville: University Press of Florida.

Mayer, Enrique. 2002. *The articulated peasant: Household economies in the Andes.* Boulder, Colo.: Westview Press.

Meléndez, Edwin. 1993. Los que se van, los que regresan: Puerto Rican migration to and from the United States, 1982–1988. Political Economy Working Paper 1, Center for Puerto Rican Studies, City University of New York.

Mintz, Sidney W. 1956. Cañamelar: The subculture of a rural sugar plantation proletariat. In *The people of Puerto Rico: A study in social anthropology,* ed. Julian Steward, Robert Manners, Sidney Mintz, Elena Padilla, Raymond Scheele, and Eric Wolf, 314–417. Urbana: University of Illinois Press.

Nadel-Klein, Jane. 2003. *Fishing for heritage: Modernity and loss along the Scottish coast.* New York: Berg.

Pantojas García, Emilio. 1990. *Development Strategies as Ideology: Puerto Rico's Export-Led Industrialization Experience.* Boulder, Colo.: Rienner.

Pérez, Ricardo. 2000. Fragments of memory: The state and small-scale fisheries modernization in southern Puerto Rico. Ph.D. diss., Dept. of Anthropology, University of Connecticut.

———. 2002. Narrating memories: Discourses of development and the environment in a Puerto Rican coastal region. *CENTRO: Journal of the Center for Puerto Rican Studies* 14 (2): 210–27.

Pessar, Patricia R., ed. 1997. *Caribbean circuits: New directions in the study of Caribbean migration.* New York: Center for Migration Studies.

Rivera, Felipe. 1979. The Puerto Rican farm worker: From exploitation to unionization. In *Labor migration under capitalism: The Puerto Rican experience,* ed. Center for Puerto Rican Studies, History Task Force, 239–61. New York: Monthly Review Press.

Servicios Científicos y Técnicos. 1995. *Proyecto de investigación de la calidad del agua en la Bahía de Guayanilla.* Hato Rey, Puerto Rico: Servicios Científicos y Técnicos.

Steward, Julian, Robert Manners, Sidney Mintz, Elena Padilla, Raymond Scheele, and Eric Wolf, eds. 1956. *The people of Puerto Rico: A study in social anthropology.* Urbana: University of Illinois Press.

U.S. Census Bureau. 2000. *Census of population.* Washington, D.C.: Government Printing Office.

Weisskoff, Richard. 1985. *Factories and food stamps: The Puerto Rico model of development.* Baltimore: Johns Hopkins University Press.

2

Multilocality and Social Stratification in Kita, Mali

Dolores Koenig

This chapter looks at the relationship between multilocality—the attachment to and participation in social and economic activities in several places (Trager 2001, 60)—and social stratification in the agricultural hinterland of Kita, a market and railway center of about forty thousand inhabitants some two hundred kilometers northwest of Mali's capital, Bamako. It addresses the question of whether there are substantially different patterns of mobility and migration among different social strata and what the implications of these differences may be for rural class formation and social mobility. Building on previous work on Kita that has shown the importance of stratified access to resources and skills (Koenig in press), I consider in this chapter the ability of the different strata to invest in and profit from activities in different localities.

In the first section, I discuss the importance of multilocality in West Africa as well as patterns of contemporary mobility and migration in the Kita zone. I then address the links between migration and inequality and describe the social strata in rural Mali. Following a section on methodology and data, I analyze the ways in which existing social networks facilitate mobility. I then turn to the ways that transfers between migrant and home enhanced resources available to local communities and affected social stratification. In the conclusion, I address the linkages between physical and social mobility, migration and stratification.

MULTILOCALITY AND LIVELIHOOD STRATEGIES IN THE WEST AFRICAN SAVANNA

Mobility has long been central to Malian social organization and environmental use. Since precolonial times, men have migrated to join armies or undertake new occupations. Moving away from home was sometimes necessary to learn a craft; for example, healers often apprenticed with distant specialists. Some "traditional" activities, such as long-distance trade and preaching, have typically been itinerant. Colonial patterns of development also encouraged and sometimes enforced labor migration to specific areas of agricultural or industrial development (Koenig, Diarra, and Sow 1998).

In rural areas, classic patterns of lineage segmentation were often linked to movement. When two brothers split, one of them would usually leave, establishing a new household. If the village was sparsely populated and the brothers got along, they might live in the same village, but both lack of land and fraternal conflict could lead a brother to migrate some distance. Even today, rural-to-rural migration is common, as people move to establish households in better-watered or more-fertile locations or those with access to better agricultural extension programs (Koenig, Diarra, and Sow 1998). These movements do not necessarily break links with other family members; instead, many maintain multilocal economic and social networks.

Mobility and multilocality are not confined to Mali but are common throughout West Africa, in the forest as well as in the savanna (Trager 2001 and this volume, chapter 7; Gugler 2002). One reason for extensive migration and movement may be to manage risks in a highly unpredictable physical or political environment (de Haan and Rogaly 2002). Yet, for West Africans, mobility is not simply an adaptation to environmental or political exigencies but a positive social value. Movement is considered essential to the ability to mature, at least for men. The Asante of Ghana have a song that reflects this maxim: "Come let's travel because you lose when you stay in one place. . . . But you don't get civilized if you do not travel." A proverb adds, "If the bird does not fly, it does not eat" (Appiah 2003, 98, 99). In western Mali, extended patrilineal and patrilocal households supported and even encouraged the absence of some members in other localities in the hope that they would profitably exploit complementary resources and contribute to the family patrimony.

As various family members moved to other places, residents expected that they would remain part of extended networks of social and economic reciprocity. The "normality" of multilocal social networks was linked to a value on cosmopolitanism. In a discussion of Zambian migration, Cliggett (2003) emphasizes the affirmation of localist identities among migrants who wished to retain connections with home. This contrasts with the cosmopolitan orientation of residents of Kita's rural hinterland. Lillian Trager (2001) found this orientation elsewhere in West Africa as well; Ijesa in Nigeria valued the new information, skills, and resources brought by community members who lived elsewhere. Ivoiriens also valued the transformational potential of migration (Newell, this volume, chapter 5).

Multilocal social networks may have helped migrants cope with the new crises brought by structural adjustment (cf. Trager 2001), but they were also a means to deal with continuing risks, such as those of the savanna environment. Mobility therefore is an old strategy to increase access to resources (cf. de Haan 1999, 2). An indicator of the more cosmopolitan orientation of Malian migrants is the extent of interethnic marriage. While Cliggett (2003) found only two cases of interethnic marriage among Gwembe migrants in Zambia, it was quite common in present-day Mali as well as in the past (Koenig, Diarra, and Sow 1998).

Contemporary Mobility and Migration in the Kita Zone

In the Kita zone, people customarily lived in large extended-family households, based on a division of responsibility by gender and age. When young men married, patrilocality meant that they brought their wives to the extended family compound; ideally, brothers would not split the household until their father had died and perhaps not even then. When fieldwork was carried out in 1999, this was still the common pattern. Despite the trend toward nuclear households found in other areas of Africa (Bryceson 2002), household size in Kita has remained relatively constant since the late 1970s (Koenig in press). The residential rural household was held together by cultivating and eating together. Resident household members, especially the men, were expected to work on household collective fields, managed by the head or his appointed replacement. Household members usually all ate together from a single cooking pot; resident women rotated cooking duties so that the more women in a household, the less time a woman dedicated to domestic duties. Beyond these obligations, each adult household member, man or woman, had the autonomy to cultivate individual fields or undertake nonagricultural activities, with the right to the production or income.

The distinction between individual and household resources and obligations was not always easy to maintain in practice. In particular, households confronted a contradiction between the rights of young men to maintain income from individual activities and their responsibility to contribute to the collective patrimony that ensured their food and housing (Grosz-Ngaté 2000). Ideally, a young man would earn enough through migration to fulfill his own desires and contribute to the rural family; in fact, this was not always the case. Yet, when a household had enough labor to cultivate its household fields, migration could provide an opportunity to exploit complementary resources.

In the Kita zone, young men were routinely expected to "go on adventure" for at least some time between late adolescence and their first marriage, although people also claimed that they ought to return home at marriage. Migration had both social and economic ends. It could demonstrate a youth's independence or serve as a temporary escape from the pressure of family responsibilities (de Haan and Rogaly 2002, 7). Migration, a period of time away from father or elder brother, allowed a young man to learn how to make his own decisions. When he became a household head one day, he would need to know how to decide and lead as well as follow. The "functionality" of this experience seemed to be recognized by the general acceptance of migration. While some elders in Kita showed concern about the timing of migration or the behavior of a particular migrant, they did not question the appropriateness of migration itself.

In Kita, the positive value on mobility, especially long-distance mobility, was limited to men. The autonomy gained through mobility and migration was not valued for women, in part because they rarely if ever became household heads.[1] Malian women had their own patterns of mobility. Patrilocal residence and lineage exogamy meant that most women moved from their natal village to another village at marriage. Moreover, Malians expected that a wife would move to her husband's place of residence when he found stable work; the patterns found in eastern or southern Africa, where men went away for years leaving wives and children in rural areas, were not common here (Gugler 2002). In addition, when husbands in Kita died or divorced their wives, women were absorbed into male-headed extended families, making female-headed households rare.

Migration, both short and long term, was one means by which Kita residents created multilocal social networks. Mobility in the Kita zone was extensive, and it came in multiple forms. Even in the relatively small sample here, people went to other rural areas in the same region, to rural and urban areas in Mali, and to other countries inside and out of Africa. Many residents from Kita went to neighboring Côte d'Ivoire, but they also migrated farther afield, to Algeria, Libya, and Spain. A few have even gone farther; as I was getting ready to leave for the field in late 1998, I met a young man from one of the study villages at a holiday party in Washington, D.C. He left Mali when he received a scholarship for university and was then working for a computer company.

People's actions did not always match their stated intentions regarding the timing and purpose of their mobility. A person might say that he was leaving for a visit (usually to relatives), yet when he returned, he recounted the money he had earned. Another would go away for a short trip, but a remunerative opportunity could keep him away longer. Some might go away for a season but find a permanent job and stay away for several years. Others carried out itinerant occupations (e.g., livestock trade) and were away from their villages regularly. This section discusses several types of mobility that were particularly important, with the focus on men, who constituted 75 percent of nonresident villagers aged ten and over.

The first type concerns young unmarried men who would go "on adventure." They would do some work to earn money, perhaps to help contribute to the bridewealth for their first wife, learn a new skill, or gather funds to invest in an off-farm activity that they could use to supplement farm income at home. Then, they were expected to return home at the marriage to their first wife, settle down, and cultivate on the household farm. Although this model was far from being universal, many men indeed conformed to it.

Some undertook seasonal migration, itself two distinct types of circular migration. A young man would leave his own family to work on somebody else's farm during the agricultural season, becoming a *navetane*.[2] This did take the young man away at precisely the time of greatest labor need, but it was attractive to the youth because he had more control over his labor and earnings than if he had stayed at home (cf. Perry 2001). Some men went relatively short distances, but many went to areas north of Kita near the Mauritanian border or to specialized farms near the capital. In contrast, in dry-season wage-labor migration, the young man worked on his household fields in the agricultural season but left after the harvest for primarily nonagricultural work, returning when cultivation began the following year. Here he remained available to his own household workforce at the time of prime labor need.

Other young men stayed away for several years at a time. They recounted a variety of reasons for returning: they had lost a job; their family needed them and called them back; they had married. The line between longer-term migration and seasonal movement was not always clear. Qualitative data suggests that when a young man left, his length of time away depended in large part on the work he was able to find.

Contemporary social and political constraints have also encouraged mobility and more permanent migration. Schooling and waged jobs have been concentrated in particular zones, often cities. In Mali, schools were more likely than jobs to be based in urban areas; remunerative employment opportunities included rural construction and mining. In the study villages, even going to middle school required moving away from home. Continuing on to high school and university meant moving even farther, as high schools were in major towns and the only university was in the capital. If someone achieved this level of education, he—or much less often, she—would almost surely move away from home indefinitely.

If a migrant, educated or not, got a stable, remunerative, or skilled job, he would work there and ideally earn a salary that allowed him to send remittances back home. In this case, the villagers expected that the man would raise his family where he lived. Depending on circumstances, he could marry either a woman from home or one he met where he lived. Some people then "retired" back home in their villages of origin. By remaining part of multilocal social networks through working years, elite kin and villagers remained identified with home but carried out their lives elsewhere.

MIGRATION AND INEQUALITY

This description of mobility patterns in Kita suggests that aspects of physical mobility and the creation of multilocal networks were linked to education and occupation, therefore to access to resources outside the village. At the same time, rural residents were developing new forms of social stratification based on access to new resources that have appeared in the countryside since the 1980s, following structural adjustment, democratization, and decentralization. For example, obtaining skills beyond "traditional" crop farming has allowed some households and individuals to diversify livelihood strategies, which in turn has helped them cope with the new risks and variability of the free-market rural economy. Evolving patterns of rural social stratification have intersected with strategies of physical mobility, including the maintenance of multilocal social networks.

Recent overviews of the migration literature suggest that migration may enhance village-level inequality in three separate ways (de Haan 1999). First, remittances may be larger among better-off households because migrants from these households may be better educated and have wider social networks, both of which can lead to better jobs. More affluent families often need remittances less, so they can use them for various kinds of investments, in contrast to poorer households who need to use remittances to make ends meet (cf. Mills 1999). Second, by getting better jobs, migrants from more affluent families may increase resources and skills; on their return, they may invest in more remunerative enterprises within the village. Third, migration by its very nature decreases labor availability in areas of origin. If there is high rural under- or unemployment, this may benefit households that can send migrants away; it may also reduce the mouths the rural household must feed. On the other hand, lack of male labor at particular times of the year may have a negative impact on rural production, especially where labor is a key resource. This chapter looks primarily at the first process within the context of Kita's specific patterns of rural stratification.

Social Stratification in Rural Mali

Concepts of class used to understand stratification in industrial societies are not always directly applicable to Africa. In Mali, for example, early post-independence governments initially chose a socialist path where control over state activities was more important than private capital in creating a national class system (cf. Meillassoux 1970). Neoliberal reforms over the past twenty years have increased the importance of private capital, but access to the state apparatus is still important. Most residents of the Kita hinterland would rank low in the national stratification system, having relatively little access to either public or private capital.

At the same time, residents of rural areas in Mali are not homogeneous. Individuals and groups have differential access to land, labor, and capital, creating local systems of stratification. Although many villagers do emphasize their own commonality as "peasants" vis-à-vis the administration, especially when talking with outsiders, it is useful to consider whether members of certain categories have better access to resources at the local level and/or better access to resources located in the national stratification system. In other words, are there different local social strata, and what are the implications of these strata for either local or national mobility, especially across generations?

To determine whether there was differential access to resources, I turned to local characteristics that reflected access to the classic factors of production: land, labor, and capital. Since Kita was still quite sparsely populated and access to farmland was relatively easy, either through lineage membership or through various lending relationships, land access depended primarily on labor available to clear it.[3] The set of characteristics used to distinguish the strata reflected access to capital and labor quantity and quality. It included household size (an indicator of gross labor power), the number of cattle owned (a major store of wealth), other assets (especially agricultural equipment and transport), and household and per capita income. Activities undertaken also indicated labor quality: human capital and skills. Although rural residents would not necessarily have delineated formal strata in exactly the same way, these characteristics were all used locally to characterize people as being better or worse off. As discussed later, differential access to these resources created varying possibilities for achieving upward social mobility in the national class system. More directly, differential access meant unequal capacity to meet immediate needs. I have chosen to use descriptive names that reflect this latter characteristic; these descriptive names also emphasize the distinction between local and national class systems.[4]

At the top were those whose standards of living were in the category of More Than Sufficiency: they could feed their families while preserving and sometimes expanding the household patrimony. Data suggest that they could also use the income from one activity to increase its efficiency or to invest in another activity. In the middle were those whose living standards were characterized as being in the Sufficiency category: they could cope well under typical conditions. They could feed their families and address the exigencies of life. They usually owned agricultural equipment, and their children often had at least some schooling. At the bottom were those whose lives were marked as being in the Insufficiency category: they often lacked labor or capital to maintain adequate living standards. Many had been unlucky in their encounter with the risks of rural life. Some suffered from demographic hazards—for example, a man who had only daughters, sons who disappeared when they left on labor migration, a young widow. Others had unresolved health problems. In the study overall, thirty-three of the sixty households fell into the Sufficiency stratum; another eighteen were categorized as being More Than Sufficiency and nine as Insufficiency.

Prior analysis (Koenig in press) has shown that More Than Sufficiency households did not so much carry out different activities than did households in the other two strata, but they carried them out on a larger scale. This enabled them to generate more income and to invest more in assets—particularly cattle but also agricultural equipment, more remunerative commercial and craft activities, more transport, and more consumer goods (modern housing and televisions). When they entered trade, the scale was also larger. These assets offered a measure of insurance against hard times, but they also rendered more productive the activities undertaken. More Than Sufficiency households remained relatively large in size, but the quality of labor counted as much as its numerical force. Individuals from Sufficiency households did undertake new remunerative activities, including craft production and commerce, but the activities undertaken were, on the whole, less remunerative and on a smaller scale than those in the More Than Sufficiency stratum. Those of the lowest stratum, the Insufficiency category, carried out many fewer and less-diverse activities, in part because of the smaller labor forces available to them. This led to lower production and incomes and more vulnerability to risk.

Some of the Insufficiency households were considered marginal by local criteria; for example, they were of minority ethnic groups or were headed by unmarried men. Yet they were also considered to be legitimate village residents. Village norms of sharing kept them from doing without food or shelter, although they sometimes had little more. As discussed in the following, the amount of remittance transfers varied substantially between strata. In contrast, this was not the case in regard to intravillage gifts between households at events such as naming ceremonies, marriages, and funerals. These varied little from one strata to another. During the study period, the average household income from these intravillage gifts was CFA francs 25,900 (approximately US$40) among both the More Than Sufficiency households and the Insufficiency households and CFAF 35,900 (US$55) among Sufficiency households.[5] Because Insufficiency households were on average smaller, the per capita income from these gifts was actually greater than that in other strata. These gifts redistributed income to poorer residents and helped them to survive, if not to get ahead.

These same norms of intravillage sharing constrained better-off villagers to show generosity to poorer kin and neighbors. Anyone who tried to cut off poorer village relatives while remaining a rural resident would run the risk of sorcery accusations. A few might move elsewhere so that they could more easily control investment of their earnings, since the demands of relatives could sometimes appear infinite. Elite Malians, such as my colleagues, have developed a variety of strategies to limit the demands of poorer rural and urban kin, yet few if any cut themselves off completely. Among more affluent Malians, links to the village provide a necessary safety net in unsettled economic and political times, much as Trager (2001) found in Nigeria. They also provide an important sense of home and belonging (cf. Trager, this volume, chapter 7). Among less-educated people, like most of the Kita residents, social security remains in the village of origin, and economic considerations reinforce cultural notions of sharing.

Elsewhere in this volume, chapters by Ricardo Pérez (chapter 1) and Jeffrey Cohen (chapter 3) show how rural residents create livelihoods based on complex mixes of activities. This was the case here as well, and earlier research has shown that these livelihood strategies were linked to processes of stratification (Koenig in press). Resident young men from More Than Sufficiency and Sufficiency households had more opportunities to carry out remunerative nonfarm activities than did those from Insufficiency households. In part, the reason was that former labor migrants often had taken jobs that increased their knowledge and skills, both technical (e.g., baking, tree grafting) and social (the contemporary Malian economy, how to forge social connections). Young men from Insufficiency households had more often done agricultural work, learning fewer new skills.

Young men from More Than Sufficiency households also appeared to have an edge on those from the Sufficiency households. The accumulated assets of their households, both human and financial, appear to have been advantageous in two ways. First, other household members often made small but key contributions to the beginnings of enterprises—for example, a small loan to start a bakery or begin trade. Second, because of their size, large More Than Sufficiency households relied less on the contribution of any single young man to agricultural work and could allow individuals the time to nourish new enterprises. Those with more human and social capital have also gained positions in the new decentralized commune governments. These findings lay the groundwork for the questions raised here: Are there also substantially different patterns of migration among these different strata, and what are their implications for rural class formation and social mobility in the Kita hinterland?

METHODOLOGY AND DATA

The research questions were addressed using data from a 1999 study of sixty rural households in two village clusters in the hinterland of Kita. The two village clusters revolved around the commune centers of Namala, approximately forty kilometers to the north of Kita town, and Senko, approximately thirty kilometers to the south. Namala residents were primarily Malinke, the dominant ethnic group in the region. Senko residents mostly identified themselves as Fulbe, distinguishing themselves from Malinke by their origins among Fulbe groups in southern Mali. However, these Fulbe were sedentary farmers, in contrast to the better-known transhumant and nomadic Fulbe of West Africa; the former no longer spoke Fulbe but the local Malinke language. The two groups, Malinke and Fulbe, are treated as a single one here because they had similar lifestyles, asset accumulation, and income-earning patterns.

The study as a whole collected a variety of information on multiple aspects of rural life. This chapter draws on income data, census data, and qualitative interviews. The research was not initially focused on migration, although it soon became clear that most households had people who were away and who residents considered part of the household. The team collected varying kinds of information about the individuals "away." Regular data collection picked up information about visits from others to the sample families, visits of family members elsewhere, remittances received, and so on. All these data depended on what people chose to volunteer and were not verified through other sources. In particular, people could choose to mention family members who were away or remittances but were not obliged to do so. To some extent, this is true of the other data that people provided as well, but interviewers living in the villages were able to verify through participant observation the information that people reported about themselves. When one relatively wealthy man reported no income, it was obvious to all that he had chosen a particular presentation of self. Information about migrants could not be cross-checked in the same way.[6]

SOCIAL NETWORKS AND ACCESS TO RESOURCES

This analysis is based on the assumption that social networks are actualized through the movement of people and resources, including money, goods, and information. This section looks at the transactions used to link people through social networks and the extent to which they differed with the three strata described earlier. The first part considers access to resources such as labor or education that might impact the decision to leave. Also of interest is the way that existing multilocal social networks might facilitate access to resources or jobs for those leaving their villages. The second part looks at the ways in which those village members living elsewhere enhanced access to resources at home. It considers both remittances and physical movement.

Using Multilocal Social Networks to Enhance Resource Access

The economic aspects of the decision to emigrate concern an evaluation about where the resources and skills of an individual might bring the greatest returns (cf. Stark 2001). The decision included evaluation of labor needs and returns at home and outside, an assessment of job opportunities elsewhere, and the skills needed to get them. Access to better returns elsewhere could be facilitated by social networks. Thus, it might be expected that existing multilocal social networks would influence the decision to migrate. However, this decision was not made by only the migrant.

Existing cultural norms required migrants to secure the agreement of their household heads, who might either encourage or discourage the move. Having too many mouths to feed was rarely a motive for encouragement. As noted, in much of the West African savanna, land was relatively abundant, and agricultural production depended primarily on the sheer size of the labor force. Wealth correlated directly with household size. More Than Sufficiency households showed the largest average size, with 15.4 persons aged ten and older; Sufficiency households were smaller, averaging 11.0 persons, and Insufficiency households were smallest, averaging 8.4 persons.[7] Thus, More Than

Sufficiency households, even though they had more mouths to feed, were less likely to confront labor insufficiencies at key agricultural times, as larger labor forces also presented economies of scale.

Overall, heads were more concerned about access to labor than they were about access to food; they often discouraged migration because of their concern about having sufficient agricultural labor. However, they also welcomed the resources that could come from migrants, so they had to evaluate trade-offs. Thus, a larger village labor force meant that household heads were more often willing to let young men leave. Although they had the most labor present, More Than Sufficiency households reported more people aged ten and over who were away, with 3.7 individuals on average (66 in 18 households), as opposed to 2.3 in Sufficiency households (75 in 33 households) and 1.3 (12 in 9 households) in the Insufficiency ones. More affluent households could then benefit more from economic transfers from migrants simply because there were more of them.

Still, young men considering their own incomes and the power to control them might have different evaluations of the profitability of migration than those of their household heads. An analysis of household residents who left during the study period shows that they did not always follow cultural ideals. Departures were considered to follow the ideal if the individual left in May or June at the beginning of the agricultural season, to work as a *navetane* or in January or February. In contrast, departures from July to September, in the middle of the agricultural season, were considered "abrupt" departures. When young men left then, not only did the head lose their contribution on household fields, but their own individual fields might be abandoned if no other household member was willing to harvest them. In fact, other household members were often quite exasperated when young men went off like this because of the labor constraints created. The largest proportion of abrupt departures was in the Sufficiency households, 9 of 18 (50 percent) who left overall. In contrast, 6 of the 16 departures (38 percent) among the More Than Sufficiency households were abrupt, as was only 1 of the 6 departures (17 percent) in Insufficiency households.

Sometimes, abrupt departures reflected strong intrafamily tensions. In one More Than Sufficiency family, a son and his father were not getting along well. Nonetheless, the family arranged the son's marriage, which occurred in early September. In late September, when his wife was still secluded in the "nuptial room," this young man left for Bamako for seasonal work, without telling his father. Because the agricultural work was not finished, the youth was persuaded to return in early October, but in early December he left, again without a word to anyone. According to his mother, the young man did not get along with his father, who was too "controlling." The young man was said to be in Bamako, perhaps with a maternal uncle, through the end of the study in February. In a Sufficiency household, one young man in the sample weeded his peanut field and then disappeared in the first weeks of September. By the beginning of October, the family learned that he had gone to Côte d'Ivoire, where his brother was; he was still there at the end of the study. His wife, who had left to visit her parents in early October, decided to prolong her visit as well, because her husband was gone.

No matter the cause for departure, these cases illustrate the importance of multilocal family links in facilitating moves out of the village. An abrupt departure was often made possible because a young man had relatives elsewhere. Requests from relatives could also provide a culturally acceptable pretext to leave the village. One man in an Insufficiency household noted that his son went to visit his uncle in Côte d'Ivoire in October; he had not returned by the end of the study in February. In another household, an uncle asked that a young man come in early December (for an unknown reason); since the uncle had sent transport money, the young man went. Later in the month, his brothers knew that he was in Kita town and said that he must have found work or he would have returned; then, by mid-January, he was said to have been sent to Bamako to do something for another relative. He evidently was still in Bamako at the end of the study period. These experiences suggest that while a young man's labor is of value to the household, it may simultaneously be made available to other members of the multilocal kin network. Social alliances sometimes cross-cut age hierarchies.

Once a young person left, he had to find a job. Education may facilitate finding remunerative employment. The occupational structure may encourage educated people to move to particular places. In fact, this was a theoretical prospect insofar as Kita migrants were concerned. Although a few had Koranic education or had taken part in local-language literacy programs, over half of the study's participants aged ten and over who were living away had no experience in the formal French-language educational system: 48 percent (32 of 66) from More Than Sufficiency households, 64 percent (48 of 75) from

Sufficiency households, and 58 percent (7 of 12) from Insufficiency house-holds. A quarter of those from Insufficiency and Sufficiency households had some primary schooling, as did slightly more (32 percent) from the More Than Sufficiency households. Ten individuals from More Than Sufficiency households had education from middle school through university, as did six from Sufficiency households and two from Insufficiency households. Some of these were students rather than workers. Overall, the level of education was not high, and there was only a slight edge among the More Than Sufficiency households.

In contrast, the future investment in education did seem to vary with so-cial strata. For many of the residents away, the primary activity was being a student; these included 23 percent (15 of 66) in the More Than Sufficiency stratum, 16 percent (12 of 75) in the Sufficiency stratum, and 8 percent (1 of 12) in the Insufficiency stratum. Ethnographic data suggest that multilocal networks facilitated the provision of housing and board for students outside the village.

Lacking formal training, adult workers depended on social networks to get good jobs. Most worked in the informal sector, either in agriculture or in trade. The possibility of a good job correlated to some extent with social strata. Agri-cultural or other rural occupations were the least remunerative possibility; in these were 50 percent (6 of 12) of individuals from Insufficiency households, 41 percent (31 of 75) from Sufficiency households, and only 29 percent (19 of 66) from More Than Sufficiency households. In contrast, trade, potentially the most remunerative informal occupation (Koenig in press), was the primary ac-tivity of 12 of 66 (18 percent) of the migrants from More Than Sufficiency households, 9 of 75 (12 percent) of those from Sufficiency households, and 2 of 12 (17 percent) of those from Insufficiency households. Workers in semi-skilled or skilled jobs, in either the informal or the formal sector, included 9 (14 percent) individuals from More Than Sufficiency households, 10 (13 percent) from Sufficiency households, and 2 (17 percent) from Insufficiency ones. Oc-cupations included carpentry, welding, baking, driving, tailoring, and working for a hotel or as a photographer, accountant, or electrician. Two civil servants and one religious practitioner were among the group. Migrants in Insufficiency households had better jobs outside of agriculture than might be expected; al-though networks may have been useful in finding a job, keeping it depended on other factors, including sheer luck.

Labor demands elsewhere allowed even less-educated men to leave their villages for extended periods, moving to other agricultural locations, to various economic centers in Mali, and even outside of Mali. Table 2.1 shows the place of residence of those who were away but included in the household census. Migrants from the poorest households were found in the smallest number of sites: half were in Bamako, Mali's capital and largest city; the rest remained in the First Region (where the study site was), or they had left Mali to go other nearby countries in West or North Africa. In contrast, the sites of migration for the other two strata were more diverse, although all showed a preponderance of residents in Bamako. The middle stratum showed more rural local migrants than did the most affluent one; the More Than Sufficiency stratum had two migrants in Spain. This suggests that the social and information networks of those in the two upper strata were broader, enabling them to find work in more places.

The data suggest that the ability to migrate and to find and keep remunerative work was somewhat linked to existing social networks in rural and urban areas. Households higher in socioeconomic status had larger labor pools, which made it easier for young men to leave. In turn, they appear to have been able to use existing multilocal networks to identify income-earning opportunities in a larger variety of places. The following section turns to the question of whether transfers from those at other sites of multilocal networks could increase rural resources.

Using Multilocal Social Networks to Maintain and Increase Resources

Households in all strata had absent members that they considered part of the household. These multilocal social networks could be strong or weak; reg-

Table 2.1. Place of Residence: Migrants Aged Ten and Over from Namala and Senko

	More Than Sufficiency		Sufficiency		Insufficiency	
	#	(%)	#	(%)	#	(%)
First Region: Kita and Kayes	17	(25.7)	13	(17.3)	1	(8.3)
Other First Region Areas	4	(6.1)	13	(17.3)	1	(8.3)
Bamako area	24	(36.4)	26	(34.7)	6	(50.0)
Southern Mali and West Africa	13	(19.7)	10	(13.3)	3	(25.0)
Other international	7	(10.6)	8	(10.7)	1	(8.3)
Other/not known	1	(1.5)	5	(6.7)	0	(0.0)
Total	66	(100.0)	75	(100.0)	12	(100.0)

Source: Study data.

ular flows of resources were needed to maintain them. This section addresses two flows: transfers of money and the movement of individuals between different parts of the network.

Economic transfers of various kinds sustained social relationships. Gifts passed between parents and children, spouses, and siblings. Emigrants sent remittances or brought gifts with them when they returned to the village. Table 2.2 compares the income gained in the study sample from economic transfers between individual family members—often, but not always, remittances.[8] This table shows a clear correlation between the income earned from economic transfers and social stratum. Insufficiency households, although they claimed to maintain links with relatives away, benefited very little in tangible fashion. Gifts from children or siblings were rare; transfer income averaged only CFAF 6,348 (US$10) per household during the study period. Sufficiency households received substantially more, CFAF 53,961 (US$83); moreover, this was 11 percent of total mean reported income. More Than Sufficiency households received even more, an average CFAF 137,189 (US$211), yet because they had much higher average incomes, this represented a lower proportion of income. These households were more likely both to produce enough to eat and to have alternative forms of village-level income earning. Unlike poorer families who needed remittance income to make ends meet, More Than Sufficiency households could often use transfers to improve living standards.

This trend was supported by information from repeat interviews. In the Insufficiency stratum, 3 of 9 households (33 percent) mentioned remittances; these ranged from CFAF 4,000 to 15,000 (US$6–$23) and came from relatives within Mali. In the Sufficiency stratum, 9 of 33 households (27 percent) mentioned receiving remittances, which ranged from CFAF 5,000 to

Table 2.2.   Mean Gift Income per Household by Stratum

	More Than Sufficiency	Sufficiency	Insufficiency
Number of households	18	33	9
Transfers	137,189	53,961	6,348
Total gifts (CFAF)[a]	163,112	89,900	32,214
Transfers as % gift income	84.1	60.0	19.7
Total income (CFAF)[a]	1,934,154	500,338	207,082
Transfers as % total income	7.1	10.8	3.1

Source: Study data.
Note: From May 15, 1999, to February 20, 2000.
[a]CFAF 650 = US$1.

50,000 (US$8–$77). In one case, the remittance was in kind, two hundred kilograms of sorghum. Most came from relatives in Mali, although two were outside, one in Mauritania and one in Gabon. In the More Than Sufficiency stratum, 6 of 18 households (33 percent) mentioned receiving remittances, which ranged from CFA 25,000 to 100,000 (US$38–$154). These households also received a wide variety of goods, including one hundred kilograms of rice, two hundred kilograms of sorghum, aluminum sheets (for roofing), soap, bed sheets, and small food items. Four households received things from relatives who lived outside of Mali. While the proportion of households receiving some kind of remittances was quite similar across the three strata, the amounts in the top strata were quite a bit larger, while those in the lowest stratum were negligible.

Ethnographic data suggest that the transfers went primarily from younger to older family members, reflecting the age hierarchy. Gifts from older to younger family members were much rarer and occurred mostly in More Than Sufficiency households, where transfers went both directions. One older man mentioned giving his daughter-in-law the money to pay for her transport back to Bamako. People from this stratum more often mentioned children in school in other places. Several mentioned paying school fees for children at school in Kita town or Bamako. One man bought a bicycle for his son who was in school in Bamako; the mother of this young man also planned on sending him money, while his father did send him ten kilograms of peanuts and some money. One man noted that he sent grain to his brother, a teacher in Bamako, while this brother sent him money.

Bidirectional economic transfers suggest more equitable and stable social networks. More Than Sufficiency households were best placed and Insufficiency households worst placed to sustain multilocal social networks that generated complementary resources to support both urban and rural households in the face of environmental and economic exigencies. This trend becomes even clearer when looking at the physical mobility of individuals.

Across all strata, household members in Kita had some contact with migrants. At the same time, in all strata, a few told us about household members who had gone off on migration and simply disappeared. Yet people knew where many of the family members were even if they did not know exactly what they were doing. People from the village sometimes visited migrant family elsewhere (especially in Mali or neighboring countries), and migrants would come back to the village to visit or send their children to spend vacations there. In all strata, life-cycle events were particularly important for linking people, and people went to and from Bamako for marriages and condolence calls.

Yet networks functioned differently across the strata. On one extreme, in the Insufficiency households, although a few claimed to have nonresident members in relatively good positions, the links between villagers and nonresidents were not important on a day-to-day basis. Sometimes, heads claimed that they received no help from migrants. As one farmer said, "My own children are not yet old enough to work. Two children of my older brother help me in my field, but the others have left on adventure and I don't know where they are or what they do.... They don't send anything." He believed that a factor in whether a man could encourage his children to stay was his level of wealth; a man needed to be rich to meet the needs of his children. Another man talked of the flight of his daughter to Bamako to avoid a rural marriage. One woman did say that her two migrant children, one gone ten years and one gone nineteen years, supported her, but she reported no remittances during the study period. This was also true for a man who claimed to get assistance from a daughter in Bamako. One recently widowed woman did get CFAF 15,000 (US$23) from a brother to provide an investment fund for undertaking trade, the largest remittance noted in this stratum. Other contacts, although there, were relatively sparse.

At the other extreme were the More Than Sufficiency households. Here households in the village and relatives in Bamako, in particular, participated in multilocal networks; there were many visits of migrants (or their children) to the village, not only from Bamako, but also from other parts of Mali and from Côte d'Ivoire. At the same time, villagers often made short trips to Bamako. One man went to Bamako because his sister who lived in Côte d'Ivoire was there; she gave him some goods, but he also managed to buy clothes there that he resold locally. Another man simply went to visit his brother (who six weeks later came to the village to visit him). Women not only went to Bamako for marriages or deaths but also to accompany and care for the sick, sustaining networks although they did not migrate specifically for income-earning opportunities.

A few people seemed to spend more time away than in the village. One young household head, relatively ambitious, spent a large amount of time in Bamako and nearby Koulikoro, where a brother lived. On June 1, he was gone to Koulikoro because there had been a death; he returned but on July 21 was there again; he returned shortly but was gone again on August 20. In mid-September, his wife went to Bamako for a marriage, and on October 9, he was again in Koulikoro. In late September, the brother from Koulikoro came to the village for a visit. In mid-October, another relative from Koulikoro came to visit. Yet, because he had other brothers who took care of the agricultural work, he could travel, even though he was a household head.

Some went to Bamako for health care, rare in the other strata. One old farmer, age eighty-nine, was accompanied to a Bamako hospital by one of his sons, a trader living in Côte d'Ivoire who had come back to the village to care for his father. Another man sent his wife to Bamako for medical treatment. Another mentioned buying medicines for a relative in Bamako.

People in the More Than Sufficiency stratum sometimes went to bring back family members who had not returned or who had "failed" migrations. One young married man was sent by his father to find his brother who was "on adventure in Côte d'Ivoire." More Than Sufficiency households could invest to encourage their children to stay as well. As one household head said, "I had a younger brother who wanted to leave; he wanted to trade. I sold some cattle to encourage him to stay [implicit: to give him commercial capital]. Since then, he is still here. He comes and goes in neighboring markets; it's now twenty years that he's been doing this. I also have a son who had left on adventure. He was in Côte d'Ivoire, but it did not work. I myself left to get him . . . and bring him back home. Since then he has begun to get involved in politics, and he became deputy to the mayor. He makes do." This was not a choice available in poorer families.[9]

This stratum also included two relatively large stores owned by married men. Both made regular trips to Bamako to purchase goods to sell in addition to making more common trips to Kita. These households had more funds to invest in activities that required them to move significantly to get good returns. On the other hand, it appears that many of them had established relatives in Bamako, with whom they could stay when they were there, decreasing expenses. As Pérez (this volume, chapter 1) suggests, people had mobile livelihood strategies, which enabled them to use resources in different places.

The Sufficiency households also had multilocal social networks that spanned different areas, but the networks through which people traveled regularly were somewhat less widespread than those of More Than Sufficiency households. People from Sufficiency households visited Bamako for social reasons, and relatives from Bamako came to visit them. Several of them even mentioned going to Bamako to ask relatives for help. They did not, however, send sick individuals to Bamako; in fact, one resident came back to the village to recuperate when he was gravely ill. Nor did those with commercial enterprises restock them from the capital. While the movement of More Than Sufficiency household members sometimes linked them into new kinds of activities (modern health care, politics, large-scale commerce), the movement of Sufficiency household members was more linked to "traditional" itinerant occupations. In this stratum were found male and female traditional healers and religious practitioners, some hunters, and a tailor. Their links were often primarily with other rural areas.

CONCLUSION

While the different strata all participated somewhat in multilocal social networks, these networks enhanced the village-level standard of living most for those who already had the most resources, the More Than Sufficiency stratum. Different social strata drew on similar cultural traditions that emphasized multilocality and mobile livelihood strategies but had differential ability to realize patterns of migration and movement that benefited them. Poorer households had fewer people to send out because they needed to preserve their smaller village labor pools; in return, they benefited less, having less-extended social networks and receiving fewer remittances. More affluent households could preserve a relatively large and diversified rural labor force while allowing members to migrate temporarily or permanently. They have made greater investments in education, only just beginning to be realized. Because their own subsistence was more secure, they often had surpluses to share with urban kin, leading to more balanced relationships between kin in different areas. Two-way transfers sustained multilocal networks more strongly than those that went in only one direction. Mobility and its associated resource transfers between different parts of multilocal networks were indeed linked to the evolving rural social strata. Large and more widespread multilocal social networks allowed their members to get access to different kinds of labor and capital in multiple places.

Other analysts writing more from the perspective of migrants have stressed the ways in which transfers from migrants to their villages maintained the possibility to return home, of increasing importance during economic crisis, structural adjustment, or the opportunities of democratization (Cliggett 2003; Trager 2001). Yet from the point of view of rural villagers, these multi-local networks also enhanced the possibility for actualizing the cosmopolitan ideal, both for the family as a whole and for the individual in his or her life trajectory. A multilocal social network gave a family access to rural, urban, and sometimes international resources and provided the individual with information about places that she or he might go.

It is less clear whether the existing relationship between physical mobility and social stratification could limit future social mobility across strata. At present, most of the transfers from those outside the village have gone to family or extended kin, thereby keeping new resources within networks and sustaining village differentiation. In other parts of Mali (Pratten 1996) and West Africa (Trager 2001), individuals or hometown associations have made contributions or played other roles at the community level. These initiatives could benefit a broader range of individuals, especially where there were strong intravillage reciprocity networks, as shown here in village-level ceremonial giving. For the moment, these kinds of contributions were only minimal in the study villages; wealthier emigrants were few, many were still young, and migrant associations were not especially active. Whether this will change in the future remains to be seen.

NOTES

This chapter is based on research funded by Fulbright Hays (PO19A80001), National Science Foundation (SBR-9870628), and USAID (LAG-A-00-96-90016-00) (BASIS CRSP). Research in 1970s Kita was funded by USAID (AFR-C-1257 and AFR-C-1258). Many Malian and U.S. agencies in Bamako facilitated this research; most important was the collaboration of Malian colleagues from the Institut des Sciences Humaines, especially Tiéman Diarra, Mama Kamaté, and Seydou Camara. I bear sole responsibility for the views presented here.

1. In other areas of Mali, young women have begun to migrate, primarily working as domestic servants (Grosz-Ngaté 2000). Other parts of Africa have also seen more female labor migration (Trager, this volume, chapter 7); in other parts of the world,

with different occupational structures and value systems, female migration may even predominate (Trager 1988; Mills 1999).

2. *Navetanes* were treated like younger men of the family. They were housed and fed in return for working on the household's collective fields. They could farm an individual field in their spare time, and the produce of this field belonged to them. Most grew a crop they could sell; the return from this crop was what they earned for their labor.

3. Rural farmland is still rarely sold or rented in this part of rural Mali. "Strangers" (people not indigenous to the village) may be given the right to clear land for farms in the village community if they accept the authority of their indigenous "hosts" and make only a token payment (e.g., a chicken).

4. For more information on these rural strata, see Koenig (in press).

5. In 1999, at the time of the study, CFAF 650 = US$1.

6. The study combined data collected from households (e.g., census data) with that from individuals. Data on topics such as activities, incomes, expenditures, and agricultural work were gathered from individuals because West African households do not usually pool incomes. Within each of the sixty sample households, up to five people were systematically interviewed, one from each of five categories that reflected major social roles: the head, one married man, one unmarried man, one older married woman, and one younger married woman. The entire sample included 229 individuals. Because people rarely kept records and because of seasonal variation, data on work, income, and expenditures were gathered at periodic intervals by Malian research assistants who lived in study villages throughout the 1999–2000 agricultural season. Quantitative data were supplemented by the knowledge gained by interviewers living in the villages, and qualitative information was obtained from eighty-two interviews and oral histories in the nine study villages. Further information on the study, as well as preliminary results on other topics, can be found in Camara and colleagues (2000) and Diarra and colleagues (2000).

7. Age provides a rough indicator of economically active individuals. Children began to assist in the fields effectively at about age ten, although few youth actually left on labor migration this young. Using this age also allowed us to document those who left the village to attend school.

8. Transfers included gifts between children and parents and between siblings, as well as gifts that were coded as remittances. Because of some variety in the way that

interviewers reported data, all three categories included economic transfers from relatives not present.

From May through early October, people were interviewed every ten days about income and expenditures during the preceding three days; after this time, they were asked only about income and expenditures during the preceding two days. To create the income table here, raw data were multiplied by the appropriate number of days to generate estimates for the entire study period. Data from the first half of the study were multiplied by 3.33 to get estimated income for the complete ten-day period and that from the second half was multiplied by five.

Aggregate household information was created by multiplying information gathered by the number of individuals in each category—that is, if there were three older women in a household, the data gathered from the married woman in the sample were multiplied by three. There was one important exception. Among the wealthiest who relied on nonagricultural incomes, three married men (a nurse and two store owners) earned high incomes from activities not carried out by other household members outside the sample. Their incomes were not multiplied by the number of married men in their households because the sample already contained the universe of those with these unique activities.

9. One man from a Sufficiency household did send someone to get his son. This man was dying; in fact, he died less than a month later. He used a gift from someone else to pay for the son's trip.

REFERENCES

Appiah, Paul. 2003. Lineage and consumption in the context of Ghana's structural adjustment program: The miners of Ghana Manganese Company, Nsuta, Ghana. Ph.D. diss., Dept. of Anthropology, Catholic University of America, Washington, D.C.

Bryceson, Deborah Fahy. 2002. Multiplex livelihoods in rural Africa: Recasting the terms and conditions of gainful employment. *Journal of Modern African Studies* 40 (1): 1–28.

Camara, Seydou, Tiéman Diarra, Mama Kamaté, Dolores Koenig, Fatimata Maiga, Amadou Tembely, and Sira Traoré. 2000. *L'Economie Rurale à Kita: Etude dans une Perspective d'Anthropologie Appliquée (Rapport Intérimaire)*. Report to USAID and Malian agencies. Bamako, Mali: Institut des Sciences Humaines.

Cliggett, Lisa. 2003. Remitting the gift: Zambian mobility and anthropological insights for migration studies. Paper presented at the annual meeting of the Society for Economic Anthropology, Monterrey, Mexico, April 4–5.

de Haan, Arjan. 1999. Livelihoods and poverty: The role of migration—a critical review of the migration literature. *Journal of Development Studies* 36 (2): 1–47.

de Haan, Arjan, and Ben Rogaly. 2002. Introduction: Migrant workers and their role in rural change. *Journal of Development Studies* 38 (5): 1–14.

Diarra, Tiéman, Ladji Siaka Doumbia, Mama Kamaté, Dolores Koenig, and Amadou Tembely. 2000. *L'Economie Rurale à Kita: Resultats de la Première Etape*. Report to USAID and Malian agencies. Bamako, Mali: Institut des Sciences Humaines.

Grosz-Ngaté, Maria. 2000. Labor migration, gender, and social transformation in rural Mali. In *Democracy and Development in Mali*, ed. R. J. Bingen, D. Robinson, and J. Staatz, 87–101. East Lansing: Michigan State University Press.

Gugler, Josef. 2002. The son of the hawk does not remain abroad: The urban-rural connection in Africa. *African Studies Review* 45 (1): 21–41.

Koenig, Dolores. In press. Social stratification and access to wealth in the rural hinterland of Kita, Mali. In *Money and modernity in West Africa: Case studies from the Mande world*, ed. S. Wooten. Berlin: Lit Verlag.

Koenig, Dolores, Tiéman Diarra, and Moussa Sow. 1998. *Innovation and individuality in African development: Changing production strategies in rural Mali*. Ann Arbor: University of Michigan Press.

Meillassoux, Claude. 1970. A class analysis of the bureaucratic process in Mali. *Journal of Development Studies* 6:97–110.

Mills, Mary Beth. 1999. *Thai women in the global labor force: Consuming desires, contested selves*. New Brunswick, N.J.: Rutgers University Press.

Perry, Donna. 2001. Strangers and sons: Trends in Senegalese time-share labor. Paper presented at the annual meeting of the Society for Economic Anthropology, Milwaukee, Wisc., April 26–28.

Pratten, David. 1996. Reconstructing community: The intermediary role of Sahelian associations in processes of migration and rural development. *African Rural and Urban Studies* 3 (1): 49–77.

Stark, Oded. 2001. Review of *On the economics of immobility*. *Economica* 68 (271): 460–61.

Trager, Lillian. 1988. *The city connection: Migration and family interdependence in the Philippines*. Ann Arbor: University of Michigan Press.

———. 2001. *Yoruba hometowns: Community, identity, and development in Nigeria*. Boulder, Colo.: Rienner.

Nonmigrant Households in Oaxaca, Mexico

Why Some People Stay While Others Leave

Jeffrey H. Cohen

Migration from communities in the central valleys of Oaxaca, Mexico, to national and international destinations is a historically significant process that increased rapidly through the final decades of the twentieth century. Nevertheless, the growth and rate of movement varied across the region, and many households elected not to migrate. Furthermore, while Oaxaca ranks as one of Mexico's most economically marginal states, its overall rate of migration ranks quite low (Consejo Nacional de Población 1987; Instituto Nacional de Estadistica Geografia e Informatica 2002).[1] Therefore, we might ask, why don't more people leave? In this chapter, I argue that we can understand nonmigrants in Oaxaca through the analysis of, first, the assets that are available to rural households and, second, the unequal distribution of those assets. I illustrate my discussion using data from the investigation of eleven communities located in the three central valleys of Oaxaca (the intermontane region surrounding the state's capital city; see figure 3.1).[2]

Understanding why members of some households elect not to migrate is as important as understanding why others choose to leave for national and international destinations. Households with members who elect not to migrate share kin ties and communal networks, social practices and community resources with most migrant households, and these resources are fundamental

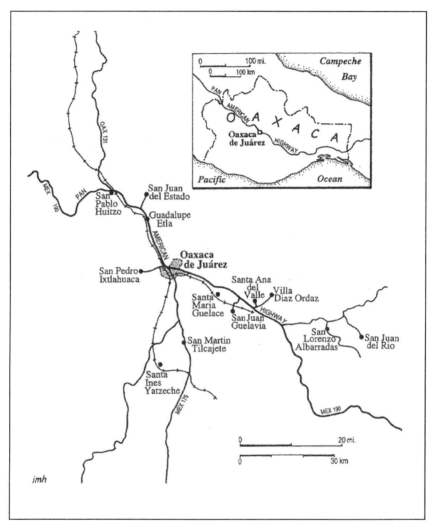

FIGURE 3.1.
Oaxaca region of Mexico

to any household's success (Conway 2000, 207). A focus on how migrant and nonmigrating households manage such resources and assets offers a material and socioeconomic foundation to understand the linkages (or articulations) that characterize transnational space in Oaxaca (see discussion in Basch, Glick Schiller, and Szanton Blanc 1994, 81; Kearney 1996).

I began my investigation of Oaxaca migration patterns assuming I would find a high rate of out-migration. I also anticipated that I would find strong transnational networks linking migrants from rural communities in the central valleys to destinations in the United States much like the patterns discovered by David Runsten and Michael Kearney (1994) for other parts of the state and for Mexico in general (Massey, Goldring, and Durand 1994). Using a systematic survey of 590 households in eleven central valley communities, I found it was clear that migration had increased rapidly since the 1970s and that thousands of Oaxacans were embedded in transnational circuits. However, it was also clear that the choice to migrate nationally or internationally was not an all-or-nothing decision. There was a range of potential outcomes, and international or transnational migrations were not consistent across the communities (see table 3.1). Rather, migration varied from 16 percent of the households in San Lorenzo Albarradas to a little more than 50 percent of the households in San Juan Guelavia (51 percent) and Santa Ines Yatzeche (53 percent). There were also alternatives to migration that included following local daily circuits to jobs in Oaxaca City and choosing to remain at home.

About 40 percent of the households sampled for this project had not sent members to migrant destinations in Mexico or the United States.[3] Nonmigrating households depended on local resources and opportunities to manage daily life; and for most households, these resources and local opportunities were adequate. However, a subgroup of nonmovers (approximately 20 percent of the total number of nonmovers) existed largely outside and marginal to growing global systems and transnational flows defined by markets and media penetration in addition to migration. These households lacked the resources to adequately cover their daily costs of living, and they could not or would not risk any losses that might come with a decision to send members to the United States or other parts of Mexico as migrants.

Peter A. Fischer, Reiner Martin, and Thomas Staubhaar (1997, 76) argue that nonmovers remain home because their households hold an "insider's advantage." In other words, nonmovers increase or at least maintain utility (social status vis-à-vis other households) through an accumulation of location-specific assets. Nonmovers (and their migrant neighbors) accumulate and rely on five kinds of resources: sociodemographic (education, household networks, family status, age of members), economic (work and careers, savings), cultural

Table 3.1. Moves and Migrations for Eleven Oaxacan Communities (590 households)

	Households Surveyed	Nonmigrant Households	Commuter Household	Internal Migrant Households	U.S. Migrant Households
Guadalupe Etla	66	24	12	12	18
Santa Ines Yatzeche	30	12	1	1	16
Santa Maria Guelace	28	11	5	7	5
San Juan del Estado	66	17	14	11	24
San Juan Guelavia	87	23	10	10	44
San Juan del Rio	47	26	1	2	18
San Lorenzo Albarradas	56	35	4	8	9
San Martin Tilcajete	58	26	2	5	25
San Pablo Huitzo	41	18	14	3	6
San Pedro Ixtlahuaca	50	14	10	8	18
Villa Diaz Ordaz	61	31	5	9	16
Total	590	237	78	76	199

(morality and practices that inform decision making), environmental and geographic (natural resources and access to those resources), and community-based resources that are available to the household and its members.

However, households do not share these assets equally, and not all households have full or open access to all resources. In fact, the internal patterns of inequality, wealth, and access to power that limit migration for some households can also limit access to resources—that is, rather than become advantaged, nonmovers may become disadvantaged, particularly in relation to migrant households and households that do not migrate because they have little need to look elsewhere for success. Thus, while local success and an insider's advantage make migration pointless for some, others are not so fortunate. In the next section, I explore how local assets and patterns of social inequality lead to different outcomes for three types of nonmigrant households: marginal households, which are disadvantaged and lack resources; common households, which hold some insider advantage in terms of local assets; and successful households, which not only hold insider advantages but use the resources and assets associated with their status to invest in familial and community growth.

MIGRATION AND "IMMOBILITY" IN THE CENTRAL VALLEYS

Contemporary Oaxacan migration to the United States has roots in mid-twentieth-century patterns of movement. Migrants from the central valleys left for national destinations as well as the United States to work in the bracero program (Cockcroft 1983; Durand, Massey, and Charvet 2000). Following the program's demise, Oaxacans sought jobs in the agricultural and service industries settling throughout California but also in less-familiar destinations such as Chicago, Illinois, and Poughkeepsie, New York (see discussion in Mountz and Wright 1996). Nevertheless, U.S.-bound migration from the region remained relatively low and was of minor importance through the 1970s.

Internal migration grew rapidly in the 1960s and 1970s, as did international movement through the last three decades of the twentieth century. Oaxacans migrating to internal destinations responded to increasing job opportunities in Mexican urban centers (Cornelius and Bustamante 1989; Downing 1979) and agrarian policies that favored large-scale agriculture (see Warman 1978). The economic crises in Mexico through the 1980s and 1990s and the economic expansion that accelerated in the United States through the

1990s worked to effectively pull Oaxacans across the border in search of jobs and higher wages (Cohen 2001; Runsten and Kearney 1994). Nevertheless, migration rates throughout valley communities vary even as local economic opportunities worsened.

Given the pulls from north of the border and the continued attraction of internal migration, how can we explain the 40 percent to 70 percent of a community's households that have not yet migrated? In other words, how best can we explain community members' immobility? If we divide valley households into three groups—what I call marginal nonmigrant households, common nonmigrant households, and successful nonmigrant households—we can begin to define the variables that affect outcomes and limit or sometimes mitigate the need to migrate.

Marginal nonmigrant households are disadvantaged in terms of local resources and assets and thus cannot afford to migrate. Regardless of destination, something makes the decision too costly in economic and social terms. The common nonmigrant household can choose to send a member to a national or international destination; however, it does not for economic and or social reasons (owing to its insider advantage according to Fischer, Martin, and Staubhaar 1997). The difference between a marginal and a common nonmigrating household is that the common nonmigrating household is not limited by economic and social forces; rather, the common household, at least at the moment it was surveyed, had opted to manage while depending on local or regional opportunities. The successful nonmigrant household finds that its local achievements and resources outweigh the costs of migration so that crossing the border or moving to a national destination outside of the central valleys does not make sense.

Marginal nonmigrating households lack land, have no or few members involved in wage labor, and therefore have no (or extremely limited) regular sources of income. Marginal households also hold few kin or communal ties (the heads do not serve as godparents at the rate that is typical for their community). Their members hold low-status positions in the local *cargo* system (political hierarchy). Finally, male household heads use their labor to cover communal expenses that would typically be met through *cooperación* (cash payments to support local projects and festivals).[4] Marginal households cannot migrate, or they are in positions where the risks and costs of migration cannot be covered.

Common nonmigrating households usually hold some land (about a hectare on average) and include members who are able to combine farmwork with wage labor to cover expenses. These households are embedded in kin and community networks, and their members hold minor positions in various civil *cargos* and act as *compadrazgos* (godparents). Common nonmigrating households cover daily expenses and sometimes even save money for the occasional luxury purchase. Nevertheless, the typical household is never far from failure, and it is always possible that a crisis will sap resource and stress support networks. Typical households can migrate, and in the future, some may. However, the risks and costs of migration are carefully balanced against local opportunities and needs. Furthermore, the majority of nonmigrant households of all kinds lack linkages to friends and family with experience as migrants. In fact, less than 10 percent of nonmigrant households acknowledged a relationship with a migrant, whereas 43 percent of migrant households acknowledged the importance of kin ties and friendships in their decision making. In fact, 60 percent of all first-time migrants relied on ties to other migrants to facilitate their move.

Successful nonmigrant household are successful because they hold substantial high-quality land, include a number of different wage earners employed in various fields, and use their place in kin and communal social networks (particularly the *cargo* system and the sponsorship of godchildren) to increase or earn status within their community. Successful households make investments, manage small businesses, and have access to resources that make the risks of migration unnecessary.

NONMIGRANTS IN THREE COMMUNITIES

Each community surveyed for this project included nonmigrant households that fell into the three categories described. However, to illustrate my discussion, I have selected an ethnographic example of each type of household from three different communities. The example of a marginal nonmigrant household comes from San Juan del Estado. The common nonmigrant household is from the village of San Juan Guelavia. Finally, I use a household from Guadalupe Etla as an example of a successful nonmigrant household.

Marginal Nonmigrants

In June 2000, I went with my research team to the town of San Juan del Estado as part of the investigation of migration and remittance outcomes in the central valleys. San Juan is a community of 2,277 residents and is located twenty-seven kilometers northwest of Oaxaca City. The community includes land that supports a lumber industry and stone quarries in addition to agriculture. Historically, the town is known for producing wheat. San Juan also serves as a commercial center for the area, and its population continues to produces crops and dairy products (milk and cheese) for local and regional sales. The town looks prosperous: there are many small stores, some limited businesses, and many satellite dishes on rooftops. Primary roads in the village are paved, and many households have running water. The entire town is electrified.

In San Juan, I met the Martinezes (all names are pseudonyms), a couple with whom I conducted one of several surveys as part of a random sample of forty-three households. The Martinez family constitutes a household that cannot migrate and exists on the margins of the growing market system that characterizes rural life in Oaxaca. However, the family has been touched by migration: the oldest member of the household, Inez, spent nearly two decades independent of her daughter Flor and Flor's husband, Marco; she lived in Mexico City, where she worked as a domestic. Poor health forced Inez to settle with Flor and Marco and their two daughters. Inez's experience in Mexico City brought no resources to Marco and Flor's household. Rather, Inez is now a burden on her daughter and son-in-law due to her health.

The resources available to the household are limited, and the members of the household own no land. Marco farms a quarter of a hectare of wetlands (this is not irrigated land but land that has a high water table) *por la mitad* or *a medias* (for half of the harvested crops he produces). Flor takes in laundry and irons, earning about fifty pesos a week for her effort (approximately five U.S. dollars in 2000).[5] Inez never remitted to support her daughter, and she returned to San Juan with no savings. Her poor health means that she cannot work as fully as she would like and has come to rely on her daughter and son-in-law. Inez owns a sewing machine, and when she feels well, she takes in minor work repairing clothing. Marco and Flor's daughters are too young (four and six) to effectively add any labor to the household. Both are in school full-time.

I asked Marco, Flor, and Inez to describe their expenses for me. "Expenses? How can you have expenses if you don't have an income? We do not have any money. We have to ask for help and, God willing, we make it. But we really don't have anything." Marco adds, "My mother-in-law, she used to live away, but now we are taking care of her—she needs medicine, but we can't buy it, and here she is a widow, who will take care of her? Really, we just don't have anything."

I asked the couple how they cover the bimonthly charges for water and electricity. Marco answers, "I do extra *tequio*—I trade my service in the community to cover [water and electricity]. But sometimes the electricity is shut off because we can't pay for it. Other times we borrow money to pay—maybe fifty pesos, but I usually trade my time." The situation was the same in terms of water: "When we cannot pay for water, I go to the river [below the house] and carry buckets for cooking."

Trading labor to cover the costs of utilities is not a bad short-term solution. However, it does carry social consequences. Much of a household's social status and community standing is defined by its members' participation in local social institutions. These include participating in the system of *cargos*, paying *cooperación* (financial support of community events and projects), and regular service in *tequio* (voluntary work brigades; see description in Cohen 1999). Using *tequio* to cover weekly or monthly costs removes the reciprocal basis of the original social contract surrounding *tequio* and emphasizes the economic marginality of Marco's household. Thus, one outcome of Marco's actions is to increase the asymmetry that separates marginal and successful households in terms of wealth, status, and standing in the community.

A lack of resources also means that members of households in marginal positions hold only low-status offices in low-status *cargos* and *comités*. *Comités* (civil and political committees) are given responsibility for local institutions, such as schools and educational programs, streets, health clinics, and water systems. For Marco this has meant a series of positions as a *topil* (a person who provides informal security for the town) or a *vocal* (a voting member with no leadership) on a minor committee—in Marco's case, a vocal for the *casa de salud* (health clinic).

Later in the survey, I asked Marco, Flor, and Inez to talk a little about migration. Marco responded, "How can we afford to migrate? I have my children to feed; I have my wife and my mother-in-law. I can't leave them alone. Even if I did, where would I get the money to get across the border? Who would help me? Where would I live? I can't do it. I don't even think about it."

Inez talks about her time in Mexico City and having to separate from Flor beforehand. Following the death of her husband, she was forced to call on her mother to take Flor. Afterward, she left for Mexico City and worked as a servant for a family in the district, earning a very low wage, none of which she was able to save. "I went [to Mexico City] when my poor husband died. I had nothing to do, and I was very young, so I left my daughter with my mother, and I went to Mexico City. I spent twenty years there! Can you imagine, twenty years working my fingers to the bone, and now what have I to show for my time? A sewing machine and bad health!"

The lack of able-bodied workers in marginal nonmigrant households is an additional disadvantage that limits potential income, wealth, and status through periods in the developmental cycle of domestic groups. However, we should not assume that marginal households grow out of their predicament as their children mature and become effective workers. The challenges facing marginal households are not explained with Chayanov's crisis model (see Durrenburger and Tannenbaum 2002), where shortcomings in a household's output are solved over the long term as the worker-to-consumer ratio improves. Rather, the situation is one where marginal households lack fixed assets (social, cultural, economic, and political) and the human capital that might effectively help them to gain additional assets and respond to anything more than daily maintenance.

The situation that marginal nonmigrant households like Marco and Flor's face every day, a struggle to put food on the table and maintain a modest home, is not exceptional. Approximately 18 percent of the nonmigrating households surveyed are in a similar and sometimes worse situation. These are households with few resources. They lack land, own few consumer goods, and have few linkages to other households as defined by kin and *compadrazgo* ties. Such households often face crises at home (usually a medical crisis, as in Inez's case, or a death or an accident) that quickly consume any resources and stress network supports.

Common, Nonmigrant Households

Nearly 20 percent of nonmigrant households fall into the marginal category. However, the majority of nonmigrant households (about 75 percent of the nonmigrant households surveyed) hold some insider advantage. They typically own land and fill wage jobs that provide the money needed to purchase goods and services that members want, and they maintain social ties with other households that effectively establish them in local, and sometimes regional, national and transnational flows. For a few households, these connections become the basis for successful economic growth and for earning local status and prestige.

San Juan Guelavia has few of the outward signs of wealth noted in the San Juan del Estado case. Most of the streets are dirt; there are few satellite dishes and fewer cars in the town. This town of 2,919 residents sits at the bottom of the eastern (Tlacolula) valley, thirty-seven kilometers from Oaxaca City. It was once home to salt producers and basket makers who traded their goods throughout the valleys using the local rail line that passed through the community as it linked Oaxaca City and Tlacolula (Mendieta y Núñez 1960). Today, no salt is produced, and basket making is in steep decline. One artisan commented that basket making "just isn't worth it. You have to find *carrizo* [reed]. It doesn't grow here anymore. We don't have enough water. And *carrizo* costs a lot of money. No one buys our baskets either. Before, we would export even to Arizona, but not now. Today there are more basket makers in Papalutla. They have a market and carrizo."

Townspeople regularly told us that although there is arable, largely unirrigated, land in the community, Guelavia suffers from a lack of usable resources and, because of increased migration, a lack of skilled workers. It is interesting that Mendieta y Núñez found little migration as recently as 1957, when he conducted his study (1960, 321). At that time, he noted that young men and women travel occasionally to Oaxaca City to work as domestics or to seek additional education (a point I return to later).

By 1970, the situation had changed, and currently approximately 60 percent of the community's households are home to at least one migrant who has left for an internal or international destination. Nevertheless, not everyone elects to migrate in Guelavia. Some cannot for reasons similar to those noted in the example of Marco and Flor. For others, the decision to stay at home is made carefully and balanced against what are perceived as the costs and risks of migration.

Amador Mendez (fifty-eight years old) heads an extended household that includes eight additional individuals: his wife, Consuela; their daughters Lupe (twenty-two), Rosa (twenty), and Antonia (nineteen); their son Cornelio (twenty-seven) and Cornelio's wife, Maria (twenty-six), and their two young children. The family farms a hectare of temporal (unirrigated) land and grows enough maize and assorted vegetables to cover about a quarter of their yearly demand for tortillas. Money comes from raising animals and renting *yuntas* (teams of oxen). Amador describes the situation: "I can recover my costs for the house and expenses by raising and selling cows, pigs, *yuntas*, sheep, and goats. I use some of our corn to fatten my pigs, and then I take them to Tlacolula to sell. Every year I take [two] *yuntas* to sell in Tlacolula. I sell them and buy new *yuntas* to train. With my son, I rent out my team—I can earn maybe three hundred pesos a week, three hundred pesos!"[6] That price, however, is fetched only during the planting season.

Amador and Cornelio also work irregularly as day laborers in town building homes and additions. Occasionally, Cornelio will travel to Oaxaca if he hears about potential work on a building site. This work can earn up to about sixty pesos a day (nearly double the minimum wage for the state). Lupe and Rosa work in Oaxaca, where they have jobs as domestics. They are each paid two hundred pesos a week plus room and board (see the discussion in Howell 1999). They travel to Guelavia to spend their days off and to bring their salaries to their mother, who keeps track of the household's assets. Antonia travels to study accounting in Oaxaca City and helps Consuela and Maria with housework. When I asked Amador if he would think about migrating, he answered, "I cannot afford it. I don't know who to talk to and where would I go?" He described the border and migration to the United States in negative terms: he did not object to the process, but he was not sure of the outcome,

> My father was one of the first people to go to the States. He went in 1943 as a bracero. But to work now, you need a patron, you need papers. It is a way to earn a lot of money, but it is hard. I see what happens. People leave, and they don't want to come back, or they want to change everything. . . . I would rather see jobs come here and not suffer like those poor souls that cross only to be treated badly.

Amador, Consuela, and their household have the resources to carefully weigh the risks of migration and what they see as questionable success against the guarantee of low, but steady, wage labor. The issue is not one of whether there is money to cover migration (for, in fact, there is); rather, it is whether risking that money makes sense. While the household continues to pool its resources and manage its affairs with enough money to cover daily expenses, some entertainment, and the occasional luxury item, there is little reason to migrate.

If Cornelio and Maria are able to establish an independent home and if they leave Cornelio's natal home, with Amador and Consuela, the latter couple's status will likely shift. Particularly for Cornelio, migration to the United States may become an important alternative, as many typical first-time migrants are young male heads of newly formed households. A second factor that adds to Amador's status, and therefore increases the assets and resources the household can turn to in times of stress and crisis, is his continued service to the community through *tequio, cooperación,* and *cargos* and the family's one-time sponsorship of a *mayordomia* (Saint's Day fiesta), in 1991. In contrast to a marginal household member who must trade service to the community to cover costs, Amador is able to serve because that is what community members in good standing must do. He is able to build prestige and networks with others in the community through his participation in *cargos,* his service in *tequio,* and his support of community ritual life through the payment of *cooperación* and sponsorship of a *mayordomia.*

Successful Nonmigrant Households

The third example comes from Guadalupe Etla, a town of two thousand residents located nineteen kilometers to the west of Oaxaca City. Guadalupe Etla shares many qualities with San Juan del Estado: most of the streets are paved, and there is a booming local market system that includes a pizzeria and an Internet café. Guadalupe Etla is also home to a growing population of Oaxacans who are moving from the city to the town as they search for a suburban lifestyle.[7] This has started a small land boom in the area. We interviewed two families that were in the process of selling land that they had gained during agrarian reform in Guadalupe Etla (see DeWalt, Rees, and Murphy 1994). Farming and dairy production are important in Guadalupe Etla. The twenty households that reported keeping dairy cattle averaged four cows and earned up to five hundred pesos a week for their efforts.

In Guadalupe Etla, I encountered households that were able to use their locally defined strengths to climb the status ladder but also to effectively carve out a niche in the growing market system that links Guadalupe to Oaxaca City and beyond. Carlos Pérez (fifty-three years old) and Virginia Cano (fifty-one) live with two sons (Miguel, who is twenty-five, and Guadalupe, who is seventeen) and two daughters (Maria, who is fifteen, and Carolina, who is twenty). Virginia's mother, Soledad (sixty-seven), also lives in the household, since her husband died some years ago. The household members pool their resources to maintain the household itself but also to invest in higher education and business. Carlos divides his time between fieldwork (an irrigated plot that produces about a year's maize, in addition to some oats, beans, and squash) and renting his three-and-a-half-ton truck for deliveries. Carlos earns a minimum of 150 pesos per delivery and manages between six and ten deliveries a week. This is a far different situation for Carlos than the one he knew as a child:

> We used to be so poor in this town [Guadalupe Etla]. We didn't even have shoes, and we used our harvest to feed ourselves . . . but my poor, departed father, he suffered for me and my sisters—he was never satisfied with his life and he suffered. He would go to Etla to work or to buy and sell goods. He would make a few pesos, a few centavos, but he would take the extra harvest and sell it in Etla, or he would take firewood to sell. He saved for us, and when I was old enough, I was able to help him . . . the way my son [Miguel] helps me. It is correct, he helps his papa.

Miguel and his brother Guadalupe both work with Carlos in the field and as assistants with the truck. Virginia is occupied with the household, but she also earns a small income as a seamstress. In the house, her mother lends a helping hand, as do Maria and Carolina. Miguel's wife (Susanna) lives with him in the household and contributes by helping Virginia with housework and occasional sewing. Maria and Guadalupe attend the Instituto Tecnológico de Oaxaca, where each pursues a bachelor's degree in business. Guadalupe says, "It was my mom's idea for me to go . . . but I like it. I want to earn my degree and then find a job in Oaxaca [City] maybe working for a delivery service." Maria has no definite plans for her future but has hopes to be a store manager. When she is not in school, she works in a *papelería* (office supply store) and brings her salary back to the household.

No members of the household have ventured farther than Oaxaca City in search of work. When asked to talk about migration, Carlos stated, "Well, over the last years it has really grown, but it isn't something I would recommend. . . . What if you go away for five years? Your wife will suffer for you, and your children won't be satisfied with what they have. In my opinion, migration is not worth the time or suffering. . . . And the obligations you have to the community? You have to pay for that! And what about food? What about the *cargos*? It isn't worth it, not for me."

Carlos and Virginia have invested time and effort supporting the community. Carlos has served on a series of committees, and Virginia has worked in LICONSA (a state-supported food program that distributes commodities—including milk—to low-income communities), which is often described as the *leche* (milk) committee. The couple also contributes to community projects and programs regularly (contributions demanded by the town's leadership) and gives *tequio* yearly, and their sons have served as *topiles*.

In the last year, Carlos was asked to serve as the head of a minor committee. For the first time Carlos declined to serve on a committee and instead he paid five thousand pesos (about five hundred U.S. dollars at the time) for a substitute to take his place. He will still get credit for the position; however, he is free to pursue his growing delivery business.[8] Carlos's use of money to cover the social costs of *cargo* service contrast clearly with Marco's use of labor to meet household expenses. Marco is forced by his marginal status to use his labor to cover expenses that most households meet and budget for. In contrast, Carlos uses his savings to cover the time and energy that service demands, and in the process, he gains the opportunity to earn more money. This shift emphasizes the growing socioeconomic asymmetries that are present in rural Oaxaca and that threaten traditionally based and sanctioned reciprocity.

DISCUSSION: NONMIGRANTS AND MOBILITY

Given the aforementioned examples, immobility is not the best term to describe the ways in which nonmigrating households respond to their situations. Many of these households may elect to send members to internal or international destinations. Others households include relatives that have experienced migration in the past. Finally, while nonmigrant households have not yet seen members travel to other parts of Mexico or the United States, there is a constant movement of individuals between their hometowns and Oaxaca City (Howell 1999).[9] Many locals depend on these circuits to survive, and they will travel regularly to other communities and the city for education, work, health care, and on rare occasions entertainment (although this is of near-zero importance), even as they describe international migration in risky terms.

Circuit moves are not migrations—rather, they are the kinds of moves that take rural Oaxacans to nearby cities, much like commuters in the United States. Circuits fall into one of three classes: students who travel to Oaxaca

City for education; workers in the formal labor force who work in the city; and *campesinos* (farmers) and unskilled workers who travel to Oaxaca to sell produce and crafts or to find occasional work as day laborers. According to this survey, most of the people moving between rural towns and the city for work are men. Men form 75 percent of the professional workers who travel between rural towns and Oaxaca City holding jobs in politics, education, management, and health. Women who are professionals work in office jobs, teach, and hold careers in health and allied health fields. Students commuting to Oaxaca are more evenly divided. Men make up about 60 percent of the students and women about 40 percent.

Rural Oaxacans also travel regularly to Oaxaca City to find work in the informal labor market. Men like Amador and Cornelio seek out construction jobs, and women often find domestic positions. Women and men also travel to Oaxaca to sell goods. Typical are the experiences of women in San Pedro Ixtlahuaca who travel the short distance to Oaxaca City to sell tortillas. One such woman, Señora Mendoza, commented, "I can earn maybe sixty or seventy pesos in a day. . . . I used to walk to the city, but now I take the bus." Her three days of work are important to her household and, combined with the fieldwork of her husband and son, support the household and effectively limit the need to migrate. For other women, the earnings from the sale of tortillas supplement remittances form migrants in Mexico and the United States. By using locally earned monies for food, remittances are funneled into house building or expensive purchases or are saved for crises.

One key to the lower rates of U.S. and internal migration in the valleys may well be access to labor markets, whether formal or informal, locally and in Oaxaca City. Locals understand that wages are much higher in the United States; however, for those households that can earn enough locally, the option to migrate may not seem important. A man in Guadalupe suggested, "I know that you can earn six dollars an hour for minimum wage—that is like sixty pesos an hour! But if you spend a million pesos to get to the U.S. to buy something, what is the point? It isn't a good deal."

In 1993 and 1996, migrants and nonmigrants in Santa Ana del Valle described the process of border crossing in innocuous terms. They did not dwell on the risks or dangers of crossing into the United States. Sergio Bautista described his situation as follows: "I go to Tijuana by bus, and I'll call my brother Eloy. . . . He has a green card. He'll come get me in his car and take me up to

Santa Monica." Once in Santa Monica, Sergio slides into a job as a busboy in a Chinese restaurant that he has held off and on for several years.

By the year 2000, migration was a much more tense subject. The costs of crossing the border were high, as were the risks. Many households (migrant and nonmigrant) said that a crossing could easily cost thousands of dollars. For marginal nonmigrants the opportunity to find wage work in the United States had declined. Even some migrants argued that the situation had changed. Señor Mendez, a former migrant to the United States at home in San Martin Tilcajete, stated in January 2002, "Parents see the news, they know what is going on! They won't let their children migrate." A second informant, Señor Jimenez, also from San Martin, echoed this point and added, "You have to sell everything to get across the border! If I went, I would have to work just to pay for my trip!"

I regularly heard talk of border troubles, Mexicans dying as they struggled across the border and the threat of vigilantes in Arizona. While households with migrant experience were more likely to say that they would still seek work in the United States, nonmigrant households appear now to carefully weigh the risks involved in migration to the United States. Thus, a second factor that may lead to an increase in the numbers of nonmigrant Oaxacans in these central valley communities is the fears or risks that are perceived (whether real or not) around migration. These factors are difficult to quantify, however; we can note a tendency among nonmigrants in particular to describe migration in increasingly risky terms.

While access to Oaxaca City and its resources and fear of the border are important factors in defining migration outcomes, the most important influences on decision makers remain the insider advantages (sociodemographic, economic, cultural, environmental and geographic) that households can bring to bear in daily life. Central to the ability of a household to survive and prosper are the economic assets that are available to its members. These include fixed assets (land) and flexible assets (animals, skills), and they range from the economic to the social and from the geographic to those based in community practices (Conway 2000; Conway and Cohen 1998; Fischer, Martin, and Staubhaar 1997).

Fixed and flexible resources also include homes, stores, automobiles, and other big-ticket items that can be expensive to buy or build but that can sometimes be sold (land, animals) or used to enhance economic standing and status.[10] Households with large landholdings tend to dominate local affairs. Their reach extends first through contracts they maintain with land-poor households that farm *medias* (sharecrop) but also through their domination of local affairs through the service of their members on high-ranking *cargos* and committees.

Households also manipulate flexible costs and assets such as labor, education, health care, and leisure time. Health care is a flexible resource, and a household's members can choose either to cover those costs (as Marco and Flor do with Inez) or to minimize costs and hope that crises can be avoided. Leisure time can become an important resource for households as well. Participation in cultural programs in a community (such as the *casas de la cultura* that are found in San Martin, Santa Ana, and Diaz Ordaz) is one way to gain internal status and standing, but participation in these extracurricular activities can create opportunities for households to connect with regional and state leaders. In Santa Ana, for example, supporters of the town's museum have gained access to special funds through state programs and a nongovernmental organization affiliated with the museum. One leader received a truck to haul textiles from Santa Ana and Diaz Ordaz to Oaxaca City. In addition, he now has a vehicle, while the majority of his neighbors must still rely on bus service.

For marginal nonmigrant households, there may be few real assets available to members for investment or as hedges against potential risks. On the other hand, common and successful nonmigrant households are able to use their wealth to effectively enhance their standing and status. Certainly one of the challenges for anthropology is to follow how households continue to deploy their resources, how those resources change over time, and how the choice to migrate influences the strategic use of those resources.

While migration often fosters success, it is not a decision that is necessarily equated with success. Put more clearly, a household does not move into the category of a successful household simply by sending members to the United States or to an internal destination outside of the central valleys. Approximately 80 percent of all remittances received by migrant households in these villages are earmarked for household maintenance, home building, or renovations. Furthermore, the budgets of most migrant households are not substantially larger than the budgets of nonmigrants; rather, migrant households depend on remittances to cover shortfalls in local wages. Thus, migrant households in rural Oaxaca continue to invest their efforts into their homes. Whether the migrants themselves will return and join their neighbors who have not left is a question we cannot yet answer. Additionally, we cannot begin to know how marginal nonmigrants will respond to the changes that will occur as migrants return.

A second set of assets that are critical to understand are the social networks that migrants and nonmigrants rely on for support. Migrants depend on social networks (either familial or communal) as they travel across the border, look for work, and settle into communities throughout the United States. Migrants turn to other migrants already settled in U.S. communities, their families, godparents, and village leaders for monetary support to move across the border. Typically, migrants borrow money from these individuals and use their early months in their new homes to pay off their debts. Once in a new setting, nearly all of the migrants we interviewed stayed with relatives (brothers, cousins, fathers) or friends from their hometown, as Douglas S. Massey (1990) found for Mexican migrants in general.

Social networks are established within families and between households. They are amplified through kin and nonkin ties, communal labor, and service and support of village projects and programs (Cohen 1999; Mutersbaugh 2002). Thus, households that lack the network ties and the resources necessary to create more ties through participation are at a severe disadvantage. Shortcomings do not simply affect migration outcomes (or the decision not to migrate) but, as pointed out in the examples discussed here, set the stage for future development and growth that can make it quite hard for marginal households to effectively move themselves out of their position.

Finally, there are the intangible cultural beliefs that influence all outcomes. Oaxacan migrants, like their nonmigrating counterparts, participate in local systems of reciprocity and prestige. The members of households must make clear decisions when it comes to migration. Leaving for a construction job in central Mexico or the agricultural fields of Baja California has to be balanced against the requirements of service and support that community life demands. So, too, nonmigrants cannot turn their backs on community rules if they hope to maintain status and standing. Thus, rules of reciprocity and the burden of community participation confirm membership and status for migrants and nonmigrants alike.

CONCLUSION

Migration is evident throughout the central valleys, and the majority of communities in the state continue to lose their population at a high rate (Dirección General de Población 1999; Embriz 1993). Nevertheless, migration is not always the first choice, and it is not the only solution for local households. What I have shown here are the ways in which three rural Oaxacan households from three central valley communities use or rely on what Fischer and colleagues (1997) describe as insider advantage to mitigate the need to migrate. Nonmigrants rely on household resources (human and economic), local assets, circuit moves, agricultural labor, and local opportunities to meet the challenge of their changing economies. However, I have noted that not all nonmigrant households share insider advantages, and I argue that disadvantages also limit outcomes for nonmovers. Marginal nonmigrant households are at a disadvantage, and their marginality may increase as economic changes take place, even as common and successful nonmigrant households manage their situations quite effectively. The challenges for anthropologists working on this topic are threefold. First, they need to begin to outline how local examples such as those in the central valleys compare with other regions in Mexico and the world. Second, they must focus on the relationship of local practices to migration and, in particular, transnational migration in order to understand the foundation on which decisions to move are made. Third, they should recognize that although local systems are increasingly embedded in global systems and linked through powerful transnational ties, local inequalities can marginalize certain households of any community, even while a majority may succeed and flourish.

NOTES

Support for this project came from the National Science Foundation (grant 9875539); the Department of Anthropology, Pennsylvania State University; and the Instituto Tecnológico de Oaxaca. My thanks to Sylvia Gijon and Rafael Reyes for their assistance in the field and to Jayne Howell, Dennis Conway, Martha Rees, John Gledhill, and Jack Rollwagen for their helpful comments. Part of this chapter appears in "Migration and 'Stay at Homes' in Rural Oaxaca, Mexico: Local Expression of Global Outcomes," in *Urban Anthropology and Studies of Cultural Systems and World Economic Development* 31, no. 2 (summer 2002): 231–59. Any errors remain my responsibility.

1. In 1995, 13.63 percent of the state's population was moving; however, only a little more than 3 percent of that population was bound for destinations beyond national borders (Consejo Nacional de Población 2000). The 2000 census notes that only about 5 percent of Oaxaca's population is moving at any given time (Instituto Nacional de Estadistica Geografia e Informatica 2002).

2. I administered an ethnographic survey to a random sample of 15 percent of each community's households after selecting eleven communities (Cohen et al. 2003). The survey is combined with the collection of general information on each community, interviews with local leaders, the collection of oral histories, participant observation in the various communities, and work in state archives (including Instituto Nacional de Estadistica Geografia e Informatica, the national institute for statistics, geography, and information). An inventory documents local resources, infrastructure, transportation, and the structure of the local economy and political system.

By using a variety of methods, I am able to define patterns of work, migration, consumption, and community participation. I focus on the household rather than on individual actors (or a more macrofocus on communities) because households are the base from which the key social networks, relationships, and cultural beliefs develop that define and bound the resources available to individual actors (see, e.g., Cohen 2001; Netting, Wilk, and Arnould 1984; Wilk 1991). Additionally, the actions of any individual (whether he or she is rooted in the well-being of the household and community or in escaping a family's clutches) have ramifications for the maintenance and reproduction of the domestic group and community (Conway 2000; Mutersbaugh 2002).

3. While I classify households with no migrants as nonmovers for this chapter, such households may eventually choose to send members to national or U.S. destinations.

4. The *cargo* system is a local hierarchy of political and religious leadership found in most rural, peasant communities (for an introduction to the *cargo* system, see Cancian 1965). The *cargo* system is described by locals as being based in *usos y costumbres* (village customs) and continues to function in each of the communities discussed in this chapter.

5. The exchange rate hovered between nine and ten pesos to the dollar throughout this study.

6. A well-trained *yunta* can fetch as much as nine thousand pesos on the market.

7. This shift is so pronounced that Guadalupe Etla was listed as a net attractor of population and has one of the lowest degrees of marginality in the state (Consejo Nacional de Población 1987; Dirección General de Población 1999).

8. Tad Mutersbaugh (2002) finds a very different situation in the Sierra Norte of Oaxaca. In his example, villagers have developed serious sanctions in response to the nonparticipation of locals in *tequio* and the *cargo* system. Unlike the examples discussed here, migrants from Sierra communities must carefully balance migration against the demands that a community will place on their time and energy. Failure to participate fully in community politics can lead to heavy sanctions that range from fines to expulsion.

9. Instituto Nacional de Estadistica Geografia e Informatica (2002) notes that 10 percent of Oaxaca's daily workforce commutes from the surrounding villages.

10. This is clear in Guadalupe Etla and San Pedro Ixtlahuaca, where land speculation has begun as urban Oaxacans seek suburban settings to construct weekend homes.

REFERENCES

Basch, Linda G., N. Glick Schiller, and C. Szanton Blanc. 1994. *Nations unbound: Transnational projects, postcolonial predicaments, and deterritorialized nation-states.* Amsterdam: Gordon and Breach.

Cancian, Frank. 1965. *Economics and prestige in a Maya community: The religious cargo system in Zinacantan.* Stanford, Calif.: Stanford University Press.

Cockcroft, James D. 1983. *Mexico: Class formation, capital accumulation, and the state.* New York: Monthly Press.

Cohen, Jeffrey H. 1999. *Cooperation and community: Economy and society in Oaxaca.* Austin: University of Texas Press.

———. 2001. Transnational migration in rural Oaxaca, Mexico: Dependency, development and the household. *American Anthropologist* 103 (4): 954–67.

Cohen, Jeffrey H., Alicia Sylvia Gijón-Cruz, Rafael G. Reyes-Morales, and Garry Chick. 2003. Understanding transnational processes: Modeling migration outcomes in the central valleys of Oaxaca, Mexico. *Field Methods* 15:366–85.

Consejo Nacional de Población. 1987. Indicadores sobre Fecundidad, Marginación y Ruralidad a Nivel Municipal: Oaxaca. Mexico City, Mexico: Consejo Nacional de Población.

———. 2000. Carpetas informativas, retos demográficos 2000 la población, un desafío permanente. www.conapo.gob.mx/RELEVANTE/reto2000.htm (accessed November 8, 2001).

Conway, Dennis. 2000. Notions unbound: A critical (re)reading of transnationalism suggests that U.S.-Caribbean circuits tell the story better. In *Theoretical and methodological issues in migration research: Interdisciplinary, intergenerational, and international perspectives,* ed. B. Agozino, 203–26. Aldershot, Engl.: Ashgate.

Conway, Dennis, and Jeffrey H. Cohen. 1998. Consequences of return migration and remittances for Mexican transnational communities. *Economic Geography* 74 (1): 26–44.

Cornelius, Wayne A., and Jorge A. Bustamante, eds. 1989. Mexican migration to the United States: Origins, consequences, and policy options. San Diego: Center for U.S.-Mexican Studies, University of California.

DeWalt, Billie R., Martha W. Rees, and Arthur D. Murphy. 1994. The end of agrarian reform in Mexico: Past lessons, future prospects. San Diego: Center for U.S.-Mexican Studies University of California.

Dirección General de Población. 1999. *Oaxaca, indicadores socioeconómicos índice y grado en marginación por localidad (1995).* Oaxaca, Mexico: La Dirección General de Población de Oaxaca y el Consejo Nacional de Población.

Downing, Theodore E. 1979. Explaining migration in Mexico and elsewhere. In *Migration across frontiers: Mexico and the United States,* ed. F. Camara and R. Van Kemper, 159–67, vol. 3 of *Contributions of the Latin American Anthropology Group.* Albany: State University of New York.

Durand, Jorge, Douglas S. Massey, and Fernando Charvet. 2000. The changing geography of Mexican immigration to the United States: 1910–1996. *Social Science Quarterly* 81 (1): 1–15.

Durrenburger, E. Paul, and Nicola Tannenbaum. 2002. Chayanov and theory in economic anthropology. In *Theory in economic anthropology,* ed. J. Ensminger, 137–53. Society for Economic Anthropology, Monograph 18. Walnut Creek, Calif.: AltaMira.

Embriz, Arnulfo. 1993. *Indicadores Socioeconómicos de los Pueblos Indígenas de México, 1990.* Mexico City, Mexico: Dirección de Investigación y Promoción Cultural Subdirección de Investigación, Instituto Nacional Indigenista.

Fischer, Peter A., Reiner Martin, and Thomas Staubhaar. 1997. Should I stay or should I go? In *International migration, immobility and development: Multidisciplinary perspectives,* ed. T. Hammar, G. Brochmann, K. Tamas, and T. Faist, 49–90. New York: Berg.

Howell, Jayne. 1999. Expanding women's roles in southern Mexico: Educated, employed Oaxaquenas. *Journal of Anthropological Research* 55 (1): 99–127.

Instituto Nacional de Estadistica Geografia e Informatica. 2002. XII Censo General de Poblacion y vivienda 2000 Estados Unidos de México: Síntesis de Resultados. www.inegi.gob.mx/difusion/espanol/poblacion/definitivos/nal/sintesis/migracion.pdf (accessed February 18, 2003).

Kearney, Michael. 1996. *Reconceptualizing the peasantry: Anthropology in global perspective.* Boulder, Colo.: Westview Press.

Massey, Douglas S. 1990. Social structure, household strategies, and the cumulative causation of migration. *Population Index* 56 (1): 3–26.

Massey, Douglas S., Luin Goldring, and Jorge Durand. 1994. Continuities in transnational migration: An analysis of nineteen Mexican communities. *American Journal of Sociology* 99 (6): 1492–533.

Mendieta y Núñez, Lucio. 1960. *Efectos sociales de la reforma agraria en tres comuidades ejidales de la republica Mexicana.* Mexico City, Mexico: Universidad nacional autonoma de Mexico.

Mountz, Alison, and Richard Wright. 1996. Daily life in the transnational migrant community of San Agustín, Oaxaca and Poughkeepsie, New York. *Diaspora* 5 (3): 403–28.

Mutersbaugh, Tad. 2002. Migration, common property, and communal labor: Cultural politics and agency in a Mexican village. *Political Geography* 21 (4): 473–94.

Netting, Robert M., Richard Wilk, and Eric Arnould, eds. 1984. *Households: Comparative and historical studies of the domestic group.* Berkeley: University of California Press.

Runsten, David, and Michael Kearney. 1994. *A survey of Oaxacan village networks in California agriculture.* Davis: California Institute for Rural Studies.

Warman, Arturo. 1978. Politica Agraria o Politica Agricola. *Comercio Exterior* 28 (6): 681–87.

Wilk, Richard R. 1991. *Household ecology: Economic change and domestic life among the Kekchi Maya in Belize.* Tucson: University of Arizona Press.

4

Migration and Risk Taking

A Case Study from Kazakstan

Meltem Sancak and Peter Finke

One of the less-documented impacts of the collapse of the socialist regimes in Eastern Europe and the former Soviet Union is that it gave rise to population movements of considerable degree. This is hardly surprising given the hardships that people in the region face today. While many people from Eastern Europe and Russia moved to Western Europe and North America, the Russian metropolises became destinations for thousands of labor migrants and petty traders from Central Asia and the Caucasus.

A different strain of migration in the postsocialist period is the ongoing readjustment of ethnic and state boundaries. The arbitrariness of the Soviet boundaries and the sometimes voluntarily, sometimes forced resettlement of population groups resulted in significant numbers of individuals residing outside the boundaries of the republics bearing their names. Now that these have become independent states, large-scale migrations were expected and sometimes encouraged by the respective governments. Primarily affected by these were Russians, who had become the second-largest ethnic group in most of the Soviet republics as a consequence of the previous dominance of Russians in administration and industry (Laitin 1998; Zevelev 2001). Others who were affected include members of groups that had been deported by Stalin during World War II (Chinn and Kaiser 1996; Allworth 1988).

Overall, these migrations led to a net population decrease in Central Asia because of the large numbers of Europeans—primarily Russians, Ukrainians, and Germans—who left the region. In contrast, the motivation among the indigenous groups to change their residences in order to equalize citizenship with ethnicity was not particularly pronounced. Although most Central Asian republics contain minorities bearing the names of their neighboring states, large-scale mutual exchanges of populations did not occur. All governments hesitated to initiate a debate on border adjustments fearing that doing so might open a Pandora's box.

One exception to this fear is that of Kazakstan, due to its specific demographic situation where Kazaks form only a slight majority and have experienced heavy assimilation pressure in recent decades. To counter this, Kazaks living outside of the new state were officially invited to resettle in Kazakstan. Some two hundred thousand individuals followed the appeal by the president, most of them originating from other former Soviet republics. Others joined from outside the Commonwealth of Independent States—namely, Mongolia, the People's Republic of China, Iran, and Turkey. The fate of these migrants and their adaptive strategies in their new home in Kazakstan form the topic of this chapter.

Instead of looking at the motives for people to migrate and the changes in society these movements bring along, we look at a rather different aspect of migration: the connection between migration and economic behavior. In this case study, people with supposedly the same ethnic background have very different attitudes toward the opportunities and dangers of the new market economy. We argue that this is the result of their experiences. One issue in this respect is the longer experience with the working of markets and marketlike institutions that the migrants had while living in China and Turkey. Another aspect, however, that seems almost as important is the connection between migration and risk taking. We argue that the experience of migration not only points to a greater willingness to take risks but also—if it does not prove to be a total failure—reenforces people's self-confidence. The ability to cope with new situations and the experience that one has to start new things by oneself, rather than wait for outside help, may encourage people to invest into risky activities more so than others.

Anthropologists have approached migration primarily in the context of what drives people to leave their native places and how they accommodate themselves in different settings, either temporarily or permanent. The focus has been either on rural-urban migration within Third World countries or on migration to, and the problems of integration into, the societies of North America and Western Europe (Cohen 1995; Guilmoto 1998; Brettell 2000; Blaschke 2001; Heckmann and Schnapper 2003). Much of this literature is also concerned with the impacts of these movements on the societies from which the migrants originate in terms of gender relations or their growing dependency on external revenues (Yalcin-Heckmann 1997; Brettell 2000; Werbner 1990).

In explaining what drives people to leave their home, economists and demographers have relied primarily on the analysis of pull-and-push factors and on the assumption that people make cost-benefit calculations when they decide if and where to migrate (Sjaastad 1962; Jackson 1969; Mitchell 1969; Esser 1980; Borjas 1989). Migrants were therefore considered to be on average more ambitious and more entrepreneurial than others (Borjas 1987; Chiswick 2000). This was part of a grander modernization theory. International migration was considered one aspect of industrialization and urbanization trends that ultimately would equalize labor wages and demographic pressures in various parts of the world. It would also encourage migrants to slowly assimilate into the host society, a movement that obviously increases the benefit from migrating. The nonhappening of the "melting pot" was therefore a first major drawback to this strain of theories (Brettell 2000; Castles and Miller 1993).

Economic explanations of cost-benefit calculations came under attack by many social scientists who advocated viewing migration in its historical and structural context, as part of a global system of inequality and exploitation in which the industrialized First World seeks to recruit cheap laborers. Influenced by world systems and dependency theory, various authors tried to stress the embeddedness of migrations into a global order of privileged and disadvantaged (Sassen 1988; Portes and Rumbaut 1990; Brettell 2000; Cohen 1987; Castles and Miller 1993). Instead of promoting more equality in international relations and enabling investments in developing countries, the migrants often formed ethnic enclaves of unskilled workers (Portes 1998).

Struggling with the lack of agency that the latter approach is willing to concede to the individual migrant, some authors tried to combine elements of both, within the so-called migration systems theory. They stressed the importance of social ties and networks as the binding link between micro- and macroanalysis. Decisions to migrate are, according to this view, made in households or larger kin groups who may send individuals for testing the ground. Therefore, migrations usually take the form of "chain migrations." Following generations of migrants can benefit from the networks that already exist at their destinations (Massey et al. 1987; Werbner 1990; Brettell 2000; Faist 2000). Particular countries thus become the destinations for migrants from particular places in the Third World. Often two or more countries develop mutual dependencies this way (Castles and Miller 1993; Sassen 1988; Portes and Rumbaut 1990). Once started, migrations become self-perpetuating processes (Massey et al. 1987; Faist 2000).

Migration may thus become a "way of life" not only for the original migrants but also for future generations (Massey et al. 1993; Castles and Miller 1993). While many migrants had planned to return home after a couple of years, doing so proved difficult in most cases. Economic failure (e.g., not being able to save the money to invest back home) is only one aspect among many. Equally important is the reluctance of the second generation to move back to a place that is not its home anymore. Lack of economic success can, of course, be a reason to return, if doing so seems the more plausible solution. Again, other reasons—such as strong social ties, nostalgia for one's homeland, or discrimination in one's new home—may also contribute to this decision (Brettell 2000).

A more recent branch of migration literature deals with what came to be labeled *transnationalism* and the way that migrants maintain ties with both their previous and their current place of residence (Basch, Glick Schiller, and Szanton Blanc 1994; Levitt 1998; Portes and Guarnizo 1999). The idea behind this is that migrants do not decide on either integrating into their host society or keeping their place of origin as the focus of their identity but rather try to accommodate themselves in both worlds and create networks that encompass them (Massey et al. 1987; Margolis 1994).

In migration debates, the term *diaspora* is used to denote groups who are forced to take refuge outside their assumed home countries but who maintain strong emotional ties with their roots (Tölöyan 1996; Safran 1991). The archetypical cases were, of course, the Jewish and the Armenian diasporas. In recent years the term has come to stand more and more for any kind of minority that "should"—according to its name—live somewhere else. This terminological inflation was also taken up by many authors inside and outside the former

Soviet Union who were dealing with minority cases caused by the dismantling of the union. Many of these cases can hardly be called those of migrants at all, because the respective groups abroad owe their existence only to a more or less arbitrary definition of boundaries. They had resided in their contemporary regions well before these lines were drawn and are not the result of any type of migration (Tishkov 2002; Arutiunov 2002; Naumova 2003; Diener 2005). Many so-called diasporas actually do not intend to return to their presumed homelands but rather re-create their cultures in their places of residence (Tishkov 2002).[1]

Among the Kazaks, as in many cases, both types of diasporas exist: those that result from previous migrations as well as those that stem from a more or less arbitrary definition of a state border. The Kazaks described in this chapter refer to the first type. They are the descendants of groups who left the present territory of Kazakstan in the eighteenth and nineteenth centuries, fleeing the increasing pressure of Russian settlers (Olcott 1987; Benson and Svanberg 1988). In this sense they might be called diasporas who now return to their "ancestral homeland," although the meaning that this place had for them in the past decades is difficult to say.

The chapter describes the perceptions and strategies of these migrants and contrasts these with the attitude of the local population of the same ethnicity. Our approach is to analyze individual cases representing four different groups living together in one particular village in southern Kazakstan. The four groups in question are as follows: local Kazaks, that is, those born in Kazakstan and thus socialized within the Soviet system; two groups of migrants from distinct areas of the People's Republic of China, one from Xinjiang and the other Gansu; and migrants from Turkey. Members of each group bring along their own concepts of markets and different attitudes toward entrepreneurship that derive from their personal experiences.[2]

KAZAKSTAN AFTER INDEPENDENCE: ECONOMIC TRANSFORMATION AND THE SEARCH FOR NATIONAL IDENTITY

Kazakstan became an independent state, together with the other Central Asian republics, with the dissolution of the Soviet Union in 1991. The government publicly advocated a rapid transition to a market economy, although in reality the chosen path was one of a rather cautious policy of privatization. The consequences of the reforms were disastrous, especially in the rural areas, and ended in massive unemployment and a dramatic decline of living standards (Rumer 2003; Kerven 2003). Widespread corruption, a predatory fiscal policy, the lack of a functioning credit system, and the general neglect of development in the agricultural sector further exacerbated the economic situation. The delay in privatization also allowed former party functionaries and the heads of the socialist enterprises to appropriate major parts of the assets before they could be distributed (Robinson, Finke, and Hamann 2000; Werner 2002).

At the same time, the government saw itself confronted with the difficult task to define what the citizens of the new state had in common and what would distinguish them from others. This was a particular sensitive issue in Kazakstan because of its precarious demographic situation. Devastating famines and the flight of several hundred thousand Kazaks to China in the first half of the twentieth century, in combination with the massive influx of Russians and other European settlers, had made the titular group a minority in its own republic (Olcott 1987). Besides Russians, the Ukrainians, Germans, Uzbeks, Uygurs, and Koreans formed sizable minorities as well. Some of these came as deported people during World War II; others had been settling here for centuries. In 1989, when the last census before independence was taken, Kazaks had for the first time in decades surpassed Russians as the largest ethnic group but were still less than 50 percent of the total population. After the independence of Kazakstan, many Russians began to leave the country, but they still dominate many of the northern provinces, which border on the Russian Federation, as well as many of the industrial centers.

As in most of the new states, tensions along ethnic and tribal ties were soon to be expected, according to most Western observers (Bremmer 1994; Olcott 1995). Fortunately, these fears have proved to be largely unfounded, as has been the case in most of Central Asia. The few cases of ethnic clashes occurred mainly in the final days of the Soviet Union, not after the various republics had gained independence. Furthermore, the incidents took place between various indigenous groups and were not directed against Russians and other European immigrants. Ethnic relations in everyday life remained relatively peaceful (Eschment 1998). Frequent reports of Russians in leading positions being replaced by Kazaks contrast with the situation in rural districts, where both groups live in complementary rather than antagonistic relations (Wilms 2001).

As a result of the delicate demographic situation, the political discourse is carried out carefully between the idea of a Kazak nation-state and a multiethnic Kazakstanian identity. Undoubtedly, there are strong tendencies for the "Kazakisation" of the country at work, and the importance of traditional Kazak culture is invoked on countless occasions, such as the renaming of streets and villages or the public conduction of horse races. At the same time, the multicultural character of the state is equally celebrated as on the first of May ("The Day of the Unity of the Peoples of Kazakstan"). One reason for this is that the Russified contemporary Kazak elite are afraid they could be pushed back by a more nationalistic new generation of Kazak intellectuals (Eschment 1998).

The proposed multiethnic identity is not solely a political calculus by the elites but is shared by many urban as well as rural Kazaks. It is in fact stressed as a part of Kazakness to generously invite others to share one's space and resources. However, being a citizen of Kazakstan, a *Kazakstaniy* or *Kazakstandiq*, is sharply distinguished from being a Kazak. Ethnic affiliation is constructed quite primordially and can only be transmitted via a blood relationship, preferable in the male line. To be a Kazak, one has to be able to trace oneself to one of the Kazak lineages, a practice that ends in creating a society where everyone is akin to everyone else via a chain of patrilineal descent groups (Hudson 1938; Krader 1963; Svanberg 1988). This genetic link is ultimately more important for defining identity than for delineating territory, behavior, or even language (Finke and Sancak forthcoming).

For this reason, Kazaks residing outside the boundaries of the new state are perceived as being principally of the same kind. Within Kazakstan, these groups are officially called diaspora while achieving the status of repatriants (*oralman*) after their migration to Kazakstan (Mendikulova 1997; Naumova 2003). This terminology is at least a simplification of historical facts, since in their majority these groups, although ultimately originating in the area of present-day Kazakstan, have left long before there existed a state with this name. The advance of Russian colonization in the steppes since the eighteenth century caused hundreds of thousands of Kazaks to search for new pastoral lands in the adjacent regions of Xinjiang, today part of the People's Republic of China (Olcott 1987; Svanberg 1988). The movement of significant numbers of Kazaks into China continued well into the twentieth century, reaching another climax in the course of the forced collectivization during Stalinist rule.

Some of these returned to Kazakstan back in the 1960s while others remained to live in China.

Several other Kazak diasporas stem from these same groups who had moved to Xinjiang. Since the 1860s, in search of new pasture lands, Kazaks started to cross the border into western Mongolia (Finke 2004). In the 1930s and 1940s, bloody turmoil in many parts of Xinjiang, and the growing Chinese interference into local affairs, initiated further waves of migrations. On their way across the Tibetan plateau, the overwhelming majority of these migrants perished from frost, hunger, and hostile attacks by Chinese troops. Only a small group made its way into northern India and Pakistan, finally ending up as refugees in Turkey (Altay 1981; Svanberg 1989). During the flight, a part of the group was separated and stayed behind in the mountainous areas of Gansu. These people would form the origin of another diaspora group (discussed later; see also, Finke and Sancak forthcoming). All the eastern Kazaks settling in Mongolia, northern Xinjiang, Gansu, and Turkey belong to the same tribal groups and are often closely related. Some of them would later meet for the first time in the village in southern Kazakstan described later.

When Kazakstan achieved its independence in 1991, its president, Nursultan Nazarbayev, officially invited all diaspora groups to resettle in Kazakstan. The prime intention for this seems obvious: the migrants were to increase the proportion of the ethnic Kazak population. For this reason, those who came were settled primarily in the northern parts of the country, where Kazaks form a minority, sometimes less than 20 percent, and therefore seem endangered by claims of annexation by Russian nationalists. A second motive may also be the importance attributed to the diasporas for the revival of traditional Kazak culture, which is believed to be best preserved among these groups. The superior knowledge of Kazak language and culture as well as familiarity with Islam are mainly stated in this context (Finke and Sancak forthcoming).

The influence of the repatriants on changing the demographic balance of Kazakstan remained limited, however. There are no official numbers of repatriants available, but estimates hardly exceed two hundred thousand individuals (U.S. Committee for Refugees 2002). The majority of these people seem to be migrants from other former Soviet republics, primarily Uzbekistan.[3] The bulk of Kazaks who came from outside the Commonwealth of Independent States are the sixty thousand migrants from Mongolia. Their prime motivation seems to have been economic issues because Mongolia experienced a dramatic crisis in the early 1990s, one in which ethnic tensions are generally denied to have played a role. In the mid-1990s, the emigration from Mongolia came to a standstill, and since then a minor remigration to Mongolia has begun because of the difficulties the migrants faced at their new home in Kazakstan (Finke 1995, 2004).[4]

Smaller numbers of Kazaks came from China, Turkey, and Iran. Their motives differed to some degree from those of the migrants from Mongolia. Dissatisfaction with the economic situation was rarely mentioned. Many of those coming from Turkey hoped for a chance to function as "cultural brokers" between Kazakstan and the West. Some others had religious motives, intending to strengthen Islamic values in a seemingly secular or atheistic society. Migrants from China thought of the migration as an investment into their children's future. The children themselves might possibly suffer from this decision, but they would escape birth restriction and the limited access to land in China as restraints on the options of future generations. The fear of assimilation by the dominant Chinese culture was also mentioned as a reason to migrate. Oppression by Chinese authorities, on the other hand, seems not to have been a major issue (Sancak and Finke 2001).

All migrants from China, however, complained about the difficulty of leaving China. It took most of them several years to get final approval, and in many cases, part of the family had to stay behind. After the approval, however, the treatment by the Chinese authorities was relatively favorable. Not only were the migrants allowed to sell their nonmovable property such as livestock and houses, but they also received their already-paid contributions for pensions and were transported free of charge up to the Kazakstanian border. The reluctance of the authorities to allow people to leave while at the same time sponsoring the trip of those who succeeded in getting permission indicates that the migrants shall play a specific role in the future relations of both countries.

On arrival at the border, the concessions by the Chinese state were substituted by the crudeness and corruption for which Kazakstan has become infamous in recent years. The migrants complained bitterly that they not only had to pay for their further transport but were charged exorbitant amounts of money. Of the promised support, they have not seen anything so far. The reason for this denial, which is not disputed by the authorities in Kazakstan, is that the Kazaks from China came on their own will and organized their migration individually. They were not part of a bilateral agreement, as is the case for the Kazaks from Mongolia, for whom there exists a quota system regulating the migration flow (Sancak and Finke 2001).

THE VILLAGE OF AQ ZHOL

In the following, we introduce the village of Aq Zhol, in southeastern Kazakstan, which has become a major point of settlement for repatriants in recent years.[5] The village is a peculiar place for several reasons. It was founded in the mid-1980s at a spot where, up to then, only a few shepherds seasonally grazed their herds. The plan, which apparently was developed among the political elites in then-capital Almaty, was to create a village that looked like a small town. This should point to the idea that in a developed socialist system there is no difference between an urban and a rural lifestyle. Houses, streets, and public buildings were all designed to contribute to this image, and the planned character further adds to the image of a surreal place in the middle of a desert steppe (Sancak and Finke 2001).

The second purpose for the founding of Aq Zhol was to build a village to resemble the "Soviet House of Nations," a place where all ethnic groups would live together peacefully. Villagers were recruited from all over the Soviet Union, and streets and houses were designed according to different "ethnic styles." Kazaks from all over the republic were attracted to come to Aq Zhol, as were Russians, Ukrainians, Moldavians, Koreans, Azeri, and others. Most families arrived on an individual basis and had no previous ties to others who took up residence in Aq Zhol. This was true even for the Kazak part of the village population, although most of them originated from southeastern Kazakstan. In the following, they are called locals, irrespective of their original place of birth.

The village of Aq Zhol is located in one of the most fertile agricultural regions of Kazakstan. Precipitation is low, so the main water sources are the rivers originating in the surrounding mountains of the Ala Tau ranges, which are captured in an extensive network of irrigation channels. Prime importance for the extension of agriculture was due to the Great Almaty Canal, which was completed in the early 1980s and was a precondition for the establishment of Aq Zhol. Most villagers in the region live on the growing of grain and vegetables, with tobacco becoming an increasingly important cash crop in the last years. Pastoralism, traditionally the basis of livelihood for the Kazaks, has some relevance but is clearly secondary today. The steppes around Aq Zhol as well as the surrounding mountain ranges provide good grazing areas, but they are utilized only to a limited degree today. Most families keep only a few animals, primarily cows for their milk supply.

The dissolution of the Soviet Union and the steps toward privatization that followed caused a severe economic decline and increasing poverty in all of Kazakstan. A process of decay set in that would greatly alter the life of virtually everyone in the country. During the mid-1990s, the agricultural land of the Sovkhoz in Aq Zhol was distributed equally among the population, with every individual receiving 0.8 hectare, as well as some mechanical equipment and livestock. As in other villages, most of the livestock had already disappeared when privatization started, for a variety of reasons. During the early transformation, most of the heavily indebted collective and state enterprises were forced to trade their animals to acquire necessary inputs. Most villagers claim that the major portion was probably abstracted and sold off by the local elites, as seems to have happened in other parts of the country (Kerven 2003; Robinson, Finke, and Hamann 2000). Another factor was the unfavorable terms of trade that forced villagers to barter away the few animals they had been allocated for their plain survival.

As a substitute for the former Sovkhoz, neighborhood-based cooperatives were founded to use the technical equipment acquired during privatization in common. But these were also dissolved soon. The main reason was that tractors and other equipment were used until they broke down, and nobody felt responsible for their replacement or to get necessary spare parts. Members of one cooperative often had conflict with another over the use of machinery as well as over the distribution of labor for common projects. Until 1999, only one of these cooperatives had survived, and this one was the only one based on close kinship ties.

Upon their arrival, the migrants were allocated the same amount of land as the locals—that is, 0.8 hectare per person. Formal use rights, however, would have to wait until the migrants became Kazakstanian citizens. Locals did not own their land either, because the constitution so far did not allow private ownership of land, but they did have long-term contracts. In either case, by law, land may be taken away if it is not properly used for a number of years. We have not heard of any such instance to date.

The amount of land actually used for agriculture, however, has been halved during recent years because, one, people lack the necessary inputs and, two, prices for agricultural products have fallen constantly. The same may be said about livestock rearing. Meat prices decreased while the costs for veterinary services and fodder have risen (Kerven 2003). Vegetables grown in the garden area around every house are mainly consumed within the household, but a little may be sold as well. Some households own a few animals, mainly sheep and cattle. Tobacco is the most profitable cash crop, but it is a risky, labor-intensive undertaking. Many villagers complained about health problems occurring during the harvest and processing of the leaves. Economically, the crop is risky to market because of a monopoly situation on the demand side. In 1998, Philip Morris, the only buyer at that time, promised to buy a certain amount of to-bacco for an agreed price, but in the end it did not, and many households could not market their production.

The scenario described so far does not differ significantly from that in other villages. The situation in Aq Zhol was, however, especially precarious for several reasons. First, its artificial character made the village more vulnerable and dependent on electricity, heating, and other external inputs. In contrast to those of traditional villages, its buildings, streets, and courtyards are not furnished for the kind of self-sufficient lifestyle that the postsocialist period again promotes. Second, the fact that most of its inhabitants had arrived only recently did not encourage collective activities. Infrastructure, including electricity, heating, and public transport, almost collapsed because of the lack of money and lack of political interest.

As a consequence, people began to leave the village. Because they had only loose networks within the village, most of those who originated from other parts of Kazakhstan or were of non-Kazak ethnicity went back to their "home regions," some of which had become independent states. In 1996, of almost 400 families, only 150 had remained, mainly Kazaks who originated from the region around Aq Zhol.

The others, before leaving, tried to sell their houses. Because of the large numbers of people leaving, dwelling prices were so low that they were almost nonexistent. To make some money, the owners began to deconstruct their houses into pieces, sometimes even doing so to those of others who had left earlier. Wooden windows and doorframes as well as other construction materials were taken away and sold. By the mid-1990s, the former model village had turned into a ghost town. It looked like "the aftermath of a bomb attack," as the remaining villagers described it (Sancak and Finke 2001).

At that time, Aq Zhol became home to succeeding waves of Kazak *oralman*, as the repatriants are called in Kazak. Between 1991 and 1995 several dozens of families from Mongolia, Iran, and Karakalpakistan took up residence in Aq Zhol. All of them left the village again after a few years for various reasons. Then, in 1997, a new group of migrants arrived, this time from China. A part of these migrants originates from the autonomous region of Xinjiang, where the bulk of the 1.2 million Kazaks in China have settled. The majority, however, came from the neighboring province of Gansu, where a small community of three thousand to four thousand Kazaks makes a harsh living, mainly by raising livestock.

The character of Aq Zhol thus changed dramatically during the 1990s. The multiethnic character of the village has gone. Today, two-thirds of the population are local Kazaks; the remaining are migrants from China and Turkey. Together with the 150 families who had remained in Aq Zhol, the total population now approaches 250 families. Both local Kazaks and the village authorities welcomed the newcomers in the beginning, thinking that they could stop the decay of the village. Their integration, however, turned out to be difficult. Interaction between locals and migrants is characterized by mutual suspicion and distance. So far, there have been no cases of intermarriage, and the idea is strongly rejected by both sides. Private ceremonies, including funerals, are generally conducted separately. Up to now, there have been no cases of violence between the two groups, except for occasional fights between groups of young men. We are not aware, however, of any serious injuries or casualties.

Besides the low degree of interaction, there exist strong mutual prejudices from both sides. The migrants accuse the locals of being Russified, which is manifested primarily in the consumption of alcohol and the ignorance of traditional Kazak culture, as well as in the restricted knowledge of the Kazak language among the locals and their indifferent attitude toward Islam. The locals, on the other hand, are proud of their superior level of civilization—as they call it—which they attribute to the strong and prolonged Russian influence.

Locals and migrants, in fact, live in two separate worlds and feel uncomfortable with each other. They consider each other as being a member of the same ethnic group while at the same time exhibiting a completely different way of culture. What makes the interaction even more complicated is the fact that each group considers its respective pattern as being the proper and more "Kazak" one. Being traditional on the one hand and being open toward other cultures and a "modern" European lifestyle on the other become powerful positions in arguing over the true content of Kazakness (Finke and Sancak forthcoming).

ECONOMIC ATTITUDES: FOUR CASE STUDIES

In the following four case studies, with each being a household from one of the groups living in Aq Zhol, we want to show differences in economic behavior. The four groups in question are as follows: local Kazaks, who lived in Aq Zhol during Soviet times; two groups of migrants from provinces in the People's Republic of China, one from Gansu and one from Xinjiang; and, finally, Kazaks who came from Turkey.

The differences in the groups' economic attitudes derive, in part, from their respective experiences in their countries of origin—namely, their familiarity with market or marketlike systems. Besides arguing this point, we claim that the very fact of migration may contribute to a readiness to take risks. This is something that the migrants all have in common. Among the locals, on the contrary, feelings of helplessness and being betrayed are quite strong. The recent changes are commonly perceived as a kind of hostile attack by an unknown force on the locals' existence and by the former and present government, accused of deliberately destroying a state and system that secured a superior living standard than the present one. Both the policy of perestroika by Gorbatchov and the reform politics after independence are equally blamed for the current situation. People seem to be locked in a vicious cycle of hostility toward the new market economy and a refusal to engage in its opportunities, which at the same time reproduces the negative experience they make within that system.

A further element in this reluctance is a self-image of an educated and skilled worker that almost every local has of oneself. The percentage of people with higher education used to be relatively high in Kazakstan, and in the past, everyone had an official profession as a teacher, Sovkhoz director, driver, agricultural specialist, or Kolkhoz worker. There existed no category as a peasant (and no term either), since everyone was on the payroll of some state enterprise. Although the supplementary growing of potatoes and vegetables was common, as it was all over the Soviet Union, to be degraded to a peasant livelihood is unacceptable for many, even if it is the basis of one's livelihood today. The concept of work is strongly connected with receiving a regular monthly salary by the state. Growing vegetables to sell them on the market for one's livelihood is not part of that concept. When asked about their profession, people typically say, "I used to be a driver in the old days, but now I am without work."

The lack of paid jobs leads many into a state of apathy. Few try to find new revenues but rather expect the state to help them. Although the people lack any regular source of income, only half of the arable land is currently utilized. Part of this is attributable to the unfortunate terms of trades and obstacles for agriculture. However, many of the locals are also not willing to invest capital and labor in spite of their often-desperate situation. One informant gave an almost-caricaturist image of this attitude. After complaining extensively about his poor situation (and that of Kazakstan as a whole), we asked him if he had any agricultural land in current use. He answered, "No. We worked some land for two years in a row, so this year we decided to take a rest."

The experience that people had with the new market economy in Kazakstan contrasts sharply with the situation that the migrants from Gansu and Xinjiang encountered in China. Here economic reforms started in the late 1970s and by the early 1980s had reached the minority regions. Kazaks often benefited even more than other minority groups did, since their traditional product, meat, was in increasingly high demand in China, with the rise of urban incomes (Longworth and Williamson 1993; Robinson, Finke, and Hamann 2000). So, the personal experience that the migrants bring along is one of the possible benefits that a market economy may offer. What is maybe even more important is that it teaches them that once socialism is gone, there is no choice other than to try the market economy, even for those who do not like the idea. This is exactly the attitude that the migrants from China show in their new habitat in Kazakstan. While the locals tend to fall into a state of resignation, the migrants become characterized by a will to engage in whatever activity seems promising. It is not that all of them were able to establish flourishing businesses. But all of them tried, and some of them did fairly well.

One further aspect in the different attitudes of locals and migrants is the degree of cooperation within the respective groups. Social relations and mutual trust among the locals are rather weak because all of them came to the village only recently and on an individual basis. It seems also that they did not try to create relations among one another by marriage. Very few individuals have affinal relations within the village.[6] The socialist state—which existed far longer in Kazakstan than in China—equally did not encourage local cooperation, as there was little need for that. Economic relations were primarily vertical, toward a redistributive central authority. In contrast to many settings, in this case it is the newcomers who have denser networks and use them for activities where coordinated labor is necessary, such as harvesting and processing tobacco leaves.

The migrants, on the contrary, especially those from Gansu, came as a group made up of close relatives. They lived in China in a relatively compact area and knew each other. Besides their language and religion, they inhabited an economic niche, livestock rearing, which further distanced them from the Han Chinese. Presumably, the joint move to Kazakstan and the experienced hardships there further strengthened cooperation within the migrant groups. All feel to various degrees betrayed and mistreated not only by the government because of the lack of assistance but also by the population of Kazakstan.

Case 1: The household of Beysen, age fifty-three, born in southeastern Kazakstan.[7] Beysen and his family moved to Aq Zhol in 1989, five years after the founding of the village. He was born in the neighboring district of Kegen, where Kazaks form the overwhelming majority of the population. His wife was born in Esik, a district center near Almaty. Before their move to Aq Zhol, Beysen and his wife worked as teachers in Esik. They came to Aq Zhol because of the higher salaries and the excellent housing conditions in the village. Salaries were calculated according to the number of classes taught, and a new-founded village in the desert had more classes per teacher to allocate than a midsize town next to the capital city.

Neither Beysen nor his wife had any relatives in Aq Zhol when they came there, and they did not have any by 1999. They have five children, three daughters and two sons. All of them are university educated (some still attending, some completed), except for the youngest son, who is still at home. The eldest daughter has a degree from a Turkish university and works for a Turkish company. This enables her to support parents and siblings with some money, while the younger ones all are still dependent on their parents.

Beysen was among the first who tried to take advantage of the new economic situation. In contrast to most villagers, who hardly made use of their small allocated plots, Beysen started to become a midscale farmer. He quit his job at the school, rented twenty hectares of land, and hired several workers to help him grow wheat and tobacco. He received some of the equipment from the dissolved Sovkhoz, which he had to share with other farmers. This soon resulted in mutual accusations of neglect and destruction, and within a year most of the equipment had become completely unusable. Beysen still has a broken tractor in his courtyard originating from these days.

The land has remained in his possession up to the present day, but he has no capability to use it, except for a small strip where he grows some potatoes and vegetables. One year he had grown wheat in an agreement with the semi-formal mayor of Aq Zhol, who had promised to provide seeds, equipment, and laborers. None of this came to fruition, and after borrowing money from a couple of villagers for similar activities, the mayor disappeared and has never been seen again. Beysen had also been working on the land that the mayor had rented by himself, but he was never paid for his labor. He later joined with the owner of one of the two mills in the village and invested some of his money and even more of his time in building up a business with him. He not only never made any profit out of that but also suffered most of the losses.

Beysen's situation was different from that of most of the locals in that he tried to find new ways to make a living and use the new market opportunities. He lacked, however, experience and tended to ally himself with people who took advantage of him. He also had little support from his family, with only one son being able to help him, and he was weakly embedded into social networks within the village. In addition to this, he was not able to find any credit, which would have helped to realize his ideas into concrete action. The same is true for most of the local Kazaks. As mentioned, few of them even tried to make use of the small piece of land allocated during privatization, except for subsistence purposes.

What seems characteristic for the few locals like Beysen who are willing to become farmers is that, rather than merely grow some tobacco or wheat to make ends meet, they aim at creating an agricultural enterprise with hired workers and a relatively large-scale production. They also try to avoid activities that they consider arduous and of low prestige. As with most villagers, the idea of ending up as a simple peasant seems incompatible for a person with a university degree. However, like most other locals, Beysen had neither the experience nor the necessary resources to create such an enterprise successfully. He also lacked a sense of finding trustworthy partners, which is one of the fundamental concerns in any economic system based on privately organized exchange.

Case 2: The household of Muxammad, age fifty-four, born in Xinjiang. Muxammad was born in the Altay region of Xinjiang. He completed a secondary education but does not hold a college or university degree. In Xinjiang, Muxammad worked primarily in urban settings, factories, and small-scale businesses. He often changed jobs and never had an official position in government or any state enterprise. A steadier career was inhibited by his political activities. He spent several years in prison for disobedience toward the Chinese state, although he would not talk in detail about that.

Similar to most migrants from Xinjiang—and in contrast to those from Gansu—Muxammad came to Kazakstan only with his immediate family and had no relatives upon his arrival in Aq Zhol. His imprisonment in China delayed his marriage far beyond what is the norm in Kazak society. His eldest daughter married shortly after their arrival in Kazakstan, thus establishing affinal links with another influential family from Xinjiang in Aq Zhol. One elder son had stayed in China. The present household consists of him, his wife, and four young children, aged five to eleven.

Muxammad did not have much experience with agriculture when he came to Kazakstan. This did not hinder him from starting a small farming business within weeks after his arrival in Aq Zhol. He went to all possible agencies to obtain some credit in order to buy seeds, although he was not very successful in doing so. Finally, he managed to get seeds from more-affluent members of the migrant community in Aq Zhol. He devoted most of the land to the growing of tobacco, while approximately a quarter of it was used for subsistence. When we met Muxammad the first time, half a year after his arrival, he was busy looking for potential buyers of his tobacco harvest. Since he had come too late to arrange a precontract with Philip Morris, the sole buyer in the region, he could not be sure that he would actually be able to sell his produce. In addition, he started to collect milk from other migrants and sell it to an intermediary. So far, the milk production in Aq Zhol had been so low that it did not justify the transport to the next town. Now that the migrants have started to raise goats, the total yields make it worthwhile to collect and market them.

Muxammad's ideas about Kazakstan were negative. More than anybody else, he accused the local and national authorities of fraud and corruption. His primary concern was that he and all migrants from China had been abandoned by the government. Like others, he had interpreted the call by President Nazarbayev for the diasporas to come to Kazakstan as a promise for help. In contrast to many other migrants, however, he did not hesitate to challenge the authorities and try his way through the bureaucracy, even if he was not particularly successful in doing so. Even some of the locals admired him for this courage, although some felt insulted by his ongoing derogative statements about Kazakstan.

Muxammad was an energetic person. His experience in China helped him in a number of ways. He was not afraid of anyone, after all he had gone through in the past. Because of his age and his imprisonment, he also knew that he had no time to waste and that he would not achieve anything by waiting for help. The only way was to go ahead and try his best. It may be an exaggeration to call his start in Kazakstan a success story, but compared to the majority of the locals, he achieved more in a few weeks than others did in years. At least he was able to feed his family without relying on much help from outside. Even though Muxammad was not necessarily liked, many villagers did express their respect for his courage and uncompromising behavior.

Case 3: The household of Tölegen, age fifty-eight, from Gansu. As mentioned, migrants from Gansu settled in the Altay region of Xinjiang before joining the first wave of Kazaks who tried to flee China in the 1930s. During combats with Chinese troops, a part of this group was separated and stuck in the mountains of Gansu. They were not able to follow the rest and remained in Gansu for several years while the rest moved on to northern India and present-day Pakistan and finally to Turkey. In the late 1940s, the Chinese government decided to resettle a part of the group to Xinjiang but had them return to Gansu only a few years later. Since the 1950s the group has been living there permanently, primarily from the raising of livestock on high-altitude pastures.

Tölegen was the head of an extended family, which included besides his immediate household four married sons with their families. In Gansu, Tölegen was making a living in the pastoral sector. He had been working for the local socialist collective until the 1980s and since then has been a private herder, like the majority of the Kazaks. Before he left for Kazakstan, he sold a total of about five hundred livestock. This was the average stock number migrants from Gansu reported to have owned. Although the harsh natural environment was certainly taking a significant annual toll, this number was sufficient to make a decent living (Longworth and Williamson 1993).

Nevertheless, in the mid-1990s Tölegen decided to move to Kazakstan with his family. The main reasons for this, as stated earlier, seem to have been his concern with the future opportunities of his children, as China increasingly enforced its birth restriction policy on the minorities as well as the majority. In addition, the scarcity of arable and grazing land was perceived as a real threat for future generations. Like other migrants, Tölegen also mentioned health problems because of the altitude in Gansu.

Tölegen himself has eight children, three daughters and five sons, four of whom are married. Three sons have set up individual households while the fourth son still lives with Tölegen. One of the daughters was already married when the family left Gansu, and she stayed with her husband's family. A second daughter was married to another migrant from Gansu living in Aq Zhol. Like other migrants from Gansu, Tölegen has an extensive kin network within the village.

The fourth son married two years after they came to Aq Zhol. Since the migrant families are short of girls and the locals are not willing to marry their daughters to them, he abducted a woman out of the three Kyrgyz families who worked as hired laborers on the tobacco fields. She not only provided the extended family with a daughter-in-law but also some fluency in Russian and a familiarity with the previous Soviet system still currently important. On the other hand, her status as labor worker from a different ethnic group gave her fewer options at hand to resist the abduction. Doing the same with a local girl might have caused serious tensions within the village.[8]

After their arrival in Kazakstan, Tölegen and his family settled in the northeastern region of Zaysan for several years where they had some distant matrilateral kin. They moved there together with some thirty families from Gansu. Soon, however, the family joined the movement to Aq Zhol in 1997, where they would meet with former neighbors and kin who had first moved to Shüy, a district in southern Kazakstan. In Zaysan, which is a traditional pastoral area, the family invested in livestock but claimed to have suffered from widespread theft. Although they spent most of their savings from China in these first years, upon their arrival in Aq Zhol, they were able to buy at least a house and a few sheep and goats.

Today, the family subsists on a herd of approximately thirty small stock and a few cows. More than half of the small stock comprises goats, which is unusual for the region. Goats are well adapted to the local ecological conditions in the desert steppes around Aq Zhol but are considered less valuable than sheep because they do not provide wool and their meat is not much appreciated. Goats produce more milk than sheep do, but small stock is generally not milked in rural Kazakstan today. The migrants, on the contrary, do milk their goats and even sell a surplus within the village, among others to Muxammad. Some income is also derived from herding the animals of other villagers.

In addition, the family engages in some tobacco growing. Each of the four households was allocated some land according to family size, which they utilize in common. As with other migrants, they also assist other relatives during critical periods of the year. Tölegen was able to arrange a precontract with Philip Morris, which would then provide seeds and fertilizers. This increased greatly the chances of being able to sell one's produce, although some families reported that Philip Morris in the end did not fulfill its contractual commitments. Other families opened up small shops, as there is no grocery shop existing anymore in the village.

The situation of Tölegen was different from that of Muxammad. Tölegen had less experience with entrepreneurial activities because in Gansu everyone led a pastoral life with well-established channels of marketing. He shared, however, the basic understanding of a more or less private market economy, namely, to look out for market options and niches and then decide on a strategy according to one's resources and skills. With his experience as a herder, he realized that investing in goats would be a sensible strategy given the natural environment and market conditions. He was also grumbling about the attitude of local and national authorities, as did everyone else, but this did not hinder him (as it did not Muxammad) to try whatever was within his reach.

One major difference from Muxammad was that Tölegen came as part of a larger network of people. He was accompanied not only by his immediate family members but other kin as well, who could be called on in times of need. We estimate that approximately one-third of all migrants from Gansu were related to Tolegen in one way or another and that this number is fairly typical for other members of this group as well. Muxammad, coming alone, had to create these networks and, although he had some success in this, was clearly less advantaged. When it was time to clean and dry the tobacco leaves, which is labor intensive, he was left with his wife and small children, while Tölegen and other migrants from Gansu had a pool of relatives who would help each other in rotation. This embeddedness into a network of people provided some feeling of security in a situation that otherwise was experienced as being alien and often hostile.

Case 4: The household of Mustafa, age fifty-seven, born in Istanbul. There is a fourth group within the village, whose members have similar problems of redefining themselves as peasants as the locals Kazaks have. These are Kazaks who migrated to Aq Zhol from Turkey but ultimately originated from the Altay region in Xinjiang as well. As outlined, they were part of the same group that had fled Xinjiang during the 1930s and 1940s, but instead of being trapped in the mountains of Gansu, they were able to escape into northern India and today's Pakistan. From there, they later would end up in Turkey in the mid-1950s, where they were granted asylum (Svanberg 1989; Altay 1981). In fact, most Kazaks from Gansu have close kin who made it to Turkey, and some of these would later turn up in Aq Zhol. Some saw their half siblings or cousins for the first time in their lives in this small village in southeastern Kazakstan.

In Turkey, the Kazaks were assigned a village in central Anatolia (which they named Altay) and several other settlements in semiurban settings. The majority of them, however, moved to Istanbul within the next two decades, where the Kazaks had established an economic niche for themselves. It was the period when Istanbul became the gateway for the famous overland route from Europe to Afghanistan and India, and the Kazaks—being traditionally pastoralists—started to produce patchwork leather jackets for the tourists passing by. By the 1980s, the majority of Kazaks in Turkey were employed in this business (Svanberg 1989).

The idea of promoting a national or religious awakening among their former socialist brethren is certainly stronger among Kazaks in Turkey (and maybe Iran) than in other diaspora places. The majority of those who decided to move to Kazakstan after 1991, however, did so for economic reasons. Equipped with some capital (at least more than other people in Kazakstan) and some knowledge of the functioning of market systems and democratic societies, they were thought to be ideal mediators between Turkish businessmen (an exclusively male domain) and the local Kazak population. This proved unrealistic for a variety of reasons, and few Kazaks from Turkey actually decided to live in Kazakstan permanently.

Some, however, made it to Aq Zhol, where their relatives from Gansu often had acquired houses for them beforehand. They settled here primarily to be in their "home country," as they say. The savings brought along from Turkey enabled them a somewhat-superior living standard than that of the rest of the village, but the future seems less promising. Like the migrants from China, none of them speaks any Russian, which is still a necessity in Kazakstan for engaging in any kind of entrepreneurial activity outside the small boundaries of the village of Aq Zhol.

The family of Mustafa and his two married sons arrived in Aq Zhol in 2000 (including the two daughters-in-law, who were not very enthusiastic about this decision). They are one of three extended families from Turkey currently living in the village. While the reunion with their relatives from Gansu was certainly one of the prime reasons why they came to Aq Zhol, their contact with them is in fact rather limited. The differences in perceptions and life experiences proved to be stronger than the wish to live together after decades of separation. Similar to the local Kazaks, they consider the migrants from China as being culturally backward. However, they equally distance themselves from the local Kazaks, who are considered Russified and indifferent toward traditional and religious values.

Economically, the family of Mustafa was so far not able to make efficient usage of their capital and their supposedly superior knowledge of the working of market systems. They started growing some tobacco and vegetables, but they expressed a clear hesitance to turn themselves into peasants since they had been living in one of world's largest cities before. Although most of them have no higher education, they share this attitude with the locals. They nevertheless went on and introduced with some success agricultural products they were used to from Turkey but which are typically not grown in Kazakhstan, such as beans and lentils. Some of the locals expressed an interest in following their example to diversify the agriculture produces.

A sphere in which the migrants from Turkey did invest was communal affairs. Encouraging a religious revitalization had prime importance in this endeavor. Even more so than the migrants from China, the group from Turkey is acknowledged as being more devout Muslims, and they play an important role in the growing meaning that Islam has in the village. They were the prime financial as well as intellectual sponsors of the village mosque, which was founded in 2000. In addition, they invest time and money in maintaining and expanding the irrigation system of the village and aggressively try to fight the omnipresent corruption. Their willingness to engage in activities that benefit the community and not only themselves gives them some moral authority, which neither the locals nor the migrants from China have.

In social respects, the migrants from Turkey do not feel attached to any other group. They certainly feel closer to their kin from Gansu than to other villagers but do not cooperate much with them either. In particular, members of the younger generation frankly admitted that they miss their lives in Turkey and consider Aq Zhol not really as a place where they want to live. This greatly exaggerates their problem of accommodating themselves in the village. For this reason, the Turkish migrants also have little access to the labor force from outside their community in Aq Zhol, when they experience such a need for it.

CONCLUSION

The difference in economic attitudes between the various Kazak groups in this setting as exemplified by the described case studies is striking. The migrants from China are clearly more willing to invest in risky and unhealthy activities such as tobacco growing than others are. They have the experience of almost fifteen years of marketlike economy in China, which taught them not to wait for state help anymore. With some success they were able to adapt this to the current situation in Kazakstan, which is certainly far from promoting entrepreneurship. A somewhat-reductionistic summary for this scenario is the main problem as identified by members of both groups: while the locals' major complaint is *zhumis zhoq* ("There is no work," meaning they do not receive monthly wages from the government), for the migrants from China and Turkey it is *bazar zhoq* ("There is no market!"). For the majority of the locals, it is still the obligation of the state to create jobs and ensure one's livelihood.

But the argument of this chapter is that equally important for the difference in attitude is the very fact of migration. It encourages people to develop strategies that others shy away from. In addition, this strategy becomes self-enforcing if reasonably successful. That one migrated and was able to accommodate oneself, in turn, strengthens confidence for other engagements as well. Without losing time, the migrants from China started to engage in tobacco growing, which they had never done before. The migrants from Gansu are, in general, a little bit more conservative in their attitude. They nevertheless sharply contrast with the locals who seem to be captured in fatalism. The reluctance of the locals to become peasants may be partly explained by a feeling of inappropriateness, but it is equally fueled by the lack of experience and the fear of failure.[9]

Besides creating individual strategies, the migrants also developed and reinforced collective strategies to cope with the new situation. They could build on already-existing ties and a relatively high degree of social cohesion based primarily on kinship. This was further strengthened by the common experience of migration and the skepticism toward Kazakstan and its population. This is particularly the case among the migrants from Gansu but is valid to some degree for those from Xinjiang and Turkey. There is not only a mutual exchange of labor within critical times of the year but also a higher level of information exchange within the group. Some of them had their houses and livestock bought by relatives even before they arrived in Aq Zhol. This is partly to be explained by the density of networks within the group. In this respect, all the migrant groups have more in common than any of them with the local Kazaks.

The locals, on the other hand, not only came to Aq Zhol relatively recently but arrived from various regions. Even those who tried to develop new strategies, as was the case with Beysen, were rarely successful because they could not organize any kind of cooperation with others. Among the migrants, the higher degree of in-group solidarity lowered transaction costs and thus eased the development of collective action. Intergroup relations, however, were not based on long-term strategies, because of a lack of mutual trust.[10]

All groups agree, though, on the poor state of politics in Kazakstan concerning taxes, the lack of credit and marketing facilities, as well as corruption. In spite of their relative success, many migrants are deeply disappointed with the economic and political situation in Kazakstan, which is characterized by economic downturn, corruption, and mismanagement. In many cases, their living standards were far superior in their former locations, and they do not really feel welcomed in their new setting. Still, few express regret over their decision, because they believe it is for the better of the next generation.

The cases of the various Kazak groups described here does not neatly fit into any of the migration debates discussed. The groups' members are neither labor migrants—since there is hardly any wage labor demand existing in Kazakstan—nor are they political refugees in any sense. Like other migrants in the post-Soviet space, they "return" to a place where they had never been before. Thus, they do not fit into the category of return migrants, as it is usually defined (Gmelch 1980; King 1986).

Although the Kazaks from China and Turkey are each officially labeled a diaspora, this term bears difficulties in its application. As Valery A. Tishkov (2002) and S. A. Arutiunov (2002) stress, in the case of the new states in Central Asia, it is often not clear who is a diaspora and since when. Were the Russians a diaspora when they were in the Kazak Soviet Socialist Republic, then a part of the Soviet Union? Certainly not in the sense of feeling separated from their "native" country. Are they one today? This is a question of how they experience their new situation. Tishkov, for example, considers the Volga Germans a diaspora now that they are in Germany, not before. The case is similar with the Kazak migrants, many of whom feel more nostalgia now for China or Turkey than they did for Kazakstan.

The fact that the migrants generally came in groups—except for those from Xinjiang—gives credit to what system theorists have claimed about the way migration works. The decision to migrate was usually one made by families, sometimes also within larger kin networks. And once they arrived, the joint experience of migration and suffering reenforced a sense of solidarity, which they were able to use as social capital in organizing their livelihoods in Kazakstan (Schmitter Heisler 1984; Light 1979).

Social and political constraints obviously play an enormous role in shaping the decision to migrate. It was the government of Kazakstan that invited them in the first place, while China pursued a rather cautious and strategic policy. The reluctance by the Chinese state to allow a reasonable degree of free movement may also hamper the development of transnational ties.[11] Feelings for the homeland were less prominent in this context, as authors following the fate of other diasporas in the former Soviet Union have also stressed (Tishkov 2002).

Nevertheless, the cases point more to the importance of choice in migrations. This is not identical with a naïve maximization position. The existence of preferences other than economic ones, the influence of social ties, and differences in resource endowments between actors have long been acknowledged as important variables in rational choice theory. It may be a nice metaphor that it is "not people [who] migrate but networks" (Tilly 1990). But in fact, it is people who decide if, when, and where to move. Kin networks may be important in deciding, but it is still an individual or family decision regarding who is ready to join and who is not.

It remains important to look at the motives that make people leave the place they grew up in and are familiar with. T. Faist (2000) is amazed why so few people, out of the much more that live in miserable conditions, actually migrate. Besides concluding that those who have most reason to move have the fewest resources to do so, he also believes that people migrate only when a significant number of related individuals already live at the destination. He speaks out against attempts to attribute the global immobility to a fundamental sedentary trait in human organization. In our view, neither sedentarism nor mobility can be seen as the norm for human behavior, but decisions in favor or against migrating depend on a multitude of local and global variables (see also Trager, this volume, chapter 7). The reason for less mobility than implied by overall economic conditions is in fact quite a different one: people usually seek predictability. As long as potential migrants perceive current conditions as being tolerable, they will usually prefer them to a state of a possibly better, but unsafe, existence. Even when people experience a significant degree of stress and deprivation, this does not necessarily force them to move. Otherwise, the former Soviet Union would be empty today.[12]

The decision to migrate to a place where one has no previous ties therefore encompasses a willingness to take risks. It is important to learn more about how these decisions are felt and how they further influence the perception that people have about themselves and the world. In this chapter, we suggest that this decision necessarily forces people to reorganize their lives according to circumstances that are not totally predictable. It is difficult to say whether and to which degree migrants are entrepreneurial persons—for whatever reasons—or if the experience of having migrated encourages an entrepreneurial spirit. We try to make the point that it is likely a combination of both. Most of the groups in our case studies had experienced previous migrations, either personally or in their immediate ancestry. They thought of themselves as being capable of managing the consequences of this move, although the results undoubtedly fell short of their expectations. Nevertheless, once the migrants arrived, they showed a remarkably high degree of entrepreneurship, as predicted by economic approaches of migration (Chiswick 2000; Borjas 1987).

Whatever the individual preferences are, potential migrants respond to some kind of incentive before they decide to change their places of residence. More often than not, these incentives are economic, if defined in a broad sense. In the case of the migrants from China, it was anxiety about the options of the future generations. For this, they were willing to sacrifice a safer and superior living standard, which to them did not promise to be sustainable over the long run. They may well have experienced nostalgia for Kazakstan before, but—as Tishkov (2002) rightly remarks—a homeland attracts only when people anticipate an increase of well-being of some kind.

NOTES

1. Several Russian anthropologists remain skeptical about the usage of the term of *diaspora* (e.g. Tishkov 2002). Being or becoming a diaspora is not only a matter of boundaries but primarily a question of self-awareness, according to S. A. Arutiunov (2002).

2. Overall, we conducted forty-nine interviews in Aq Zhol in the form of life histories. Usually, these involved families, not individuals. Most interviews were conducted during a three-month stay in the summer and fall of 1999; the rest was during a visit in 2002. Of these, fifteen took place with local Kazaks, sixteen with Kazaks from Gansu (the majority of the migrants), thirteen with Kazaks from Xinjiang, and five with Kazaks from Turkey.

3. In Uzbekistan, the majority of Kazaks live in three different regions: the rural areas around the capital of Tashkent (close to the border with Kazakstan), in the Qyzyl-Qum desert (as pastoralists), and in the Autonomous Republic of Karakalpakstan. Especially the last, which is shaken by poverty and environmental disaster (the drying up of the Aral Sea), experienced a significant out-migration of Kazaks (Aman 2000).

4. The total number of Kazaks is estimated at some eleven million or twelve million. Out of these, approximately eight million live in Kazakstan and two million in other countries of the former Soviet Union, mainly Uzbekistan and the Russian Federation. Another two million Kazaks live outside of the Commonwealth of Independent States. The largest of these groups, one of approximately 1.2 million, resides in the People's Republic of China. Almost all of its members live in the Autonomous Region of Xinjiang. Scattered groups also settled in the neighboring province of Gansu as well as in Beijing and other industrial places (Benson and Svanberg 1988; Schwarz 1984). The second-largest Kazak diaspora settled in Mongolia, where they numbered 130,000 in 1989 (Finke 1999). Other countries with a sizable Kazak minority are Iran, Afghanistan, and Turkey. As part of the immigration of labor migrants from Turkey, some Kazaks moved to Germany, France, and other Western European countries in the 1960s and 1970s (Svanberg 1989).

5. The names of the village as well as those of informants cited have been changed for reasons of confidentiality.

6. Since most Kazaks still follow the rule of lineage exogamy, this is not due to the fact that one's relatives were living outside the village. The reason may rather be that young Kazaks have relative freedom on choosing their spouses by themselves. Because of the high percentage of children attending a university or college, most people met their future spouses during their stay in Almaty or another urban center, and these were not necessarily from the same region.

7. The case studies are all named after the household heads, although the interviews usually involved other members of the family as well. The aim here is not so much to present the ideas and perceptions of individuals as it is to describe differences in combined strategies of households. As Kazak society is very much male centered, economic decisions on the household level are usually made by the senior male, either the father or the eldest brother, particularly in regard to agriculture. Women may, however, often contribute substantially to household incomes, as they constitute a majority among teachers and medical personnel. This is less the case among the migrants, but here women are engaged in producing and selling traditional handicraft.

8. Bride kidnapping has become a fairly common practice in Kazakstan and Kyrgyzstan in recent years, although it is not a totally new phenomenon in both societies. It comes in various forms. Nonconsensual kidnapping—that is, that against the will of the girl—used to be a rare exception. Much more common was that the bride and possibly some of her relatives were involved in the planning. This may often have purely ritual character, as in when the bride's parents have knowledge about the imminent abduction (Finke 2004). In recent years, however, nonconsensual abduction is increasingly becoming a social problem in Kyrgyzstan and Kazakstan (Werner 2004).

9. The migrants, on the other hand, were careful enough not to give up their previous passport immediately but to wait until the situation in Kazakstan became settled. This enabled them to visit relatives in China, although doing so was much more complicated in their case than for migrants from Turkey or Mongolia.

10. A low degree of cooperation is, however, characteristic not only for the village described but for other regions in Kazakstan, as well as other postsocialist societies (Finke 2004).

11. In contrast, many Kazak migrants from Mongolia started to move back and forth between both countries in order to engage in petty trading (Finke 1999; Diener 2005).

12. This argument goes in line with theories of bounded rationality, according to which individuals are in principle risk aversive in their behavior and seek to secure a satisfactory level of utility rather than aim at maximization (Simon 1957).

REFERENCES

Allworth, E., ed. 1988. *Tatars of the Crimea: Their struggle for survival.* Durham, N.C.: Duke University Press.

Altay, H. 1981. *Anayurttan Anadolu'ya.* Ankara, Turkey: Ministry of Culture.

Aman, A. 2000. *Population migration in Uzbekistan.* Tashkent, Uzbekistan: United Nations High Commissioner for Refugees.

Arutiunov, S. A. 2002. The diaspora as process. *Anthropology & Archeology of Eurasia* 41 (1): 89–96.

Basch, L., N. Glick Schiller, and C. Szanton Blanc, eds. 1994. Nations unbound: Transnational projects, postcolonial predicaments, and deterritorialized nation-states. Langhorne, Pa.: Gordon and Breach.

Benson, L., and I. Svanberg, eds. 1988. *The Kazaks of China: Essays on an ethnic minority.* Uppsala, Sweden: Studia Multiethnica Upsaliensia.

Blaschke, J. 2001. Ost-West-Migration: Perspektiven der Migrationspolitik in Europa. Berlin: Ed. Parabolis.

Borjas, George. 1987. Self-selection and the earnings of immigrants. *American Economic Review* 77:531–53.

———. 1989. Economic theory and international migration. *International Migration Review* 23:457–87.

Bremmer, I. 1994. Nazarbaev and the North: State-building and ethnic relations in Kazakhstan. *Ethnic and Racial Studies* 17 (4): 619–35.

Brettell, Caroline B. 2000. Theorizing migration in anthropology: The social construction of networks, identities, communities, and globalscapes. In *Migration theory: Talking across disciplines,* ed. C. B. Brettell and J. F. Hollifield, 97–135. London: Routledge.

Castles, Stephen, and M. J. Miller. 1993. The age of migration: International population movements in the modern world. New York: Guilford Press.

Chinn, J., and R. Kaiser. 1996. Russians as the new minority: Ethnicity and nationalism in the Soviet successor states. Boulder, Colo.: Westview.

Chiswick, B. R. 2000. Are migrants favorably self-selected? An economic analysis. In *Migration theory: Talking across disciplines*, ed. C. B. Brettell and J. F. Hollifield, 61–76. London: Routledge.

Cohen, R. 1987. The new Helots: Migrants in the international division of labour. Aldershot, Eng.: Avebury.

———, ed. 1995. *The Cambridge survey of world migration*. Cambridge: Cambridge University Press.

Diener, A. C. 2005. Mongols, Kazakhs, and the Mongolian territorial identity: Competing trajectories of nationalization. *Central Eurasian Studies Review* 4 (1): 19–24.

Eschment, B. 1998. Hat Kasachstan ein "Russisches Problem"? Revision eines Katastrophenbildes. Köln, Germany: BIOst.

Esser, H. 1980. Aspekte der Wanderungssoziologie: Assimilation und Integration von Wanderern, ethnischen Gruppen und Minderheiten; eine handlungstheoretische Analyse. Darmstadt, Germany: Luchterhand.

Faist, T. 2000. The volume and dynamics of international migration and transnational social spaces. Oxford: Clarendon Press.

Finke, P. 1995. Kazak pastoralists in western Mongolia. Economic and social change in the course of privatization. *Nomadic Peoples* 36/37:195–216.

———. 1999. The Kazaks of western Mongolia. In *Contemporary Kazaks: Cultural and social perspectives*, ed. I. Svanberg, 103–39. London: Curzon.

———. 2004. Nomaden im Transformationsprozess: Kasachen in der post-sozialistischen Mongolei. Münster, Germany: LIT-Verlag.

Finke, P., and M. Sancak. Forthcoming. *Contested identity: Inter- and intra-ethnic relations in southeastern Kazakstan*. Halle, Germany: Max Planck Institute for Social Anthropology.

Gmelch, G. 1980. Return migration. *Annual Review of Anthropology* 9:135–59.

Guilmoto, Ch. 1998. Institutions and migrations: Short-term versus long-term moves in rural West Africa. Population Studies 52:85–103.

Heckmann, F., and D. Schnapper. 2003. *The integration of immigrants in European societies: National differences and trends of convergence.* Stuttgart, Germany: Lucius & Lucius.

Hudson, A. E. 1938. *Kazak social structure.* New Haven, Conn.: Human Relations Area Files.

Jackson, J. A., ed. 1969. *Migration.* Cambridge: Cambridge University Press.

Kerven, C., ed. 2003. Prospects for pastoralism in Kazakstan and Turkmenistan: From state farms to private flocks. London: Taylor & Francis.

King, R., ed. 1986. Return migration and regional economic development. Dover, N.H.: Croom Helm.

Krader, L. 1963. Social organization of the Mongol-Turkic pastoral nomads. The Hague: Mouton.

Laitin, David D. 1998. *Identity in formation: The Russian-speaking populations in the near abroad.* Ithaca, London: Cornell University Press.

Levitt, P. 1998. Social remittances: Migration driven local-level forms of cultural diffusion. *International Migration Review* 32:926–48.

Light, I. 1979. Disadvantaged minorities in self-employment. *International Journal of Comparative Sociology* 20:31–45.

Lindstrom, David P., and N. Lauster. 2001. Local economic opportunity and the competing risks of internal and U.S. migration in Zacatecas, Mexico. *International Migration Review* 35 (4): 1232–56.

Longworth, J. W., and G. J. Williamson. 1993. China's pastoral region: Sheep and wool, minority nationalities, rangeland degradation, and sustainable development. New York: Oxford University Press.

Margolis, M. 1994. Little Brazil: An ethnography of Brazilian immigrants in New York City. Princeton, N.J.: Princeton University Press.

Massey, D. S., R. Alarcon, J. Durand, and H. Gonzalez. 1987. *Return to Aztlan: The social process of international migration from western Mexico.* Berkeley: University of California Press.

Massey, D. S., J. Arango, G. Hugo, A. Kouaouci, A. Pellegrino, and J. E. Taylor. 1993. An evaluation of international migration theory: A review and appraisal. *Population and Development Review* 19:431–66.

Mendikulova, G. 1997. Istoricheskie sud'by kazakhskoi diaspory: Proiskhozkdenie i razvitie. Almaty, Kazakhstan: Gylym.

Mitchell, J. C. 1969. Structural plurality, urbanization, and labour circulation in southern Rhodesia. In *Migration*, ed. J. A. Jackson, 156–80. Cambridge: Cambridge University Press.

Naumova, O. B. 2003. The Kazakh diaspora in Russia (Rossia). *Anthropology & Archeology of Eurasia* 41 (2): 23–42.

Olcott, M. B. 1987. *The Kazakhs.* Stanford, Calif.: Hoover Institute, Stanford University.

———. 1995. Central Asia's new states: Independence, foreign policy, and regional security. Washington, D.C.: United States Institute of Peace Press.

Portes, A. 1998. Divergent destinies: Immigration, the second generation, and the rise of transnational communities. In *Paths to inclusion: The integration of migrants in the United States and Germany*, ed. P. Schuck and R. Münz, 33–57. New York: Berghahn Books.

Portes, A., and L. Guarnizo, eds. 1999. Transnational communities. Special issue, *Ethnic and Racial Studies* 22 (2).

Portes, A., and R. Rumbaut. 1990. *Immigrant America: A portrait.* Berkeley: University of California Press.

Robinson, S., P. Finke, and B. Hamann. 2000. The impacts of de-collectivisation on Kazak pastoralists. Case studies from Kazakstan, Mongolia, and the People's Republic of China. *Journal of Central Asian Studies* 4 (2): 2–33.

Rumer, B., ed. 2003. Central Asia in transition: Dilemmas of political and economic development. Delhi, India: Aakar Books.

Safran, W. 1991. Diasporas in modern societies: Myths of homeland and return. *Diaspora* 1 (1): 83–84.

Sancak, M., and P. Finke. 2001. Nurli: Glanz und Verfall eines sowjetischen Musterbetriebes. In Zwischen Markt- und Mangelwirtschaft: Berichte eines Feldforschungsaufenthaltes im ländlichen Kasachstan und Kirgizstan im Jahre 1999, ed. P. Finke and Meltem Sancak, 96–103. Almaty, Kazakhstan: Friedrich-Ebert-Stiftung.

Sassen, S. 1988. *The mobility of capital and labor.* Cambridge: Cambridge University Press.

Schmitter Heisler, B. 1984. Sending countries and the politics of emigration and destination. *International Migration Review* 19 (3): 469–84.

Schwarz, H. G. 1984. *Minorities of northern China: A survey*. Bellingham: Western Washington University Press.

Simon, H. 1957. *Models of man: Social and rational*. New York: Wiley.

Sjaastad, L. A. 1962. The costs and returns of human migration. *Journal of Political Economy* 70 (Suppl.): 80–93.

Spencer, S., ed. 1994. *Immigration as economic asset: The German experience*. Staffordshire, Eng.: Trentham Books.

Stark, O. 1991. *The migration of labour*. Oxford: Basil Blackwell.

Svanberg, I. 1988. The nomadism of Orta Zhüz Kazaks in Xinjiang, 1911–1949. In *The Kazaks of China: Essays on an ethnic minority*, ed. L. Benson and I. Svanberg, 107–40. Uppsala, Sweden: Studia Multiethnica Upsaliensia.

———. 1989. Kazak refugees in Turkey. A study of cultural persistence and social change. Uppsala, Sweden: Studia Multiethnica Upsaliensia.

Tilly, C. 1990. Transplanted networks. In *Immigration reconsidered: History, sociology, and politics*, ed. V. Yans-McLaughlin, 79–95. New York: Oxford University Press.

Tishkov, Valery A. 2002. The diaspora as a historical phenomenon. *Anthropology & Archeology of Eurasia* 41 (1): 54–88.

Tölöyan, K. 1996. Rethinking diaspora(s): Stateless power in the transnational moment. *Diaspora* 5:3–36.

U.S. Committee for Refugees. 2002. *Country report: Kazakhstan*. N.p.: U.S. Committee for Refugees.

Werbner, P. 1990. The migration process: Capital, gifts, and offerings among British Pakistanis. New York: Berg.

Werner, C. 2002. Economic change in a Kazakh village. In *Shared diversity: Peoples and cultures in the global village*, ed. N. Dannhaeuser and D. Carlson, 288–95. Dubuque, Iowa: Eddie Bowers.

———. 2004. Women, marriage, and the nation-state: The Rise of non-consensual bride kidnapping in post-Soviet Kazakhstan. In *Reconceptualizing central Asia: States and societies in formation*, ed. P. J. Luong, 59–89. Ithaca, N.Y.: Cornell University Press.

Wilms, Bernd. 2001. Kasachstan—ein ethnisches Pulverfass? Ein Blick auf das interethnische Verhältnis zwischen Russen und Kasachen vor und nach der Unabhängigkeit 1991. In *Zwischen Markt- und Mangelwirtschaft: Berichte eines Feldforschungsaufenthaltes im ländlichen Kasachstan und Kirgizstan im Jahre 1999*, ed. Peter Finke and Meltem Sancak, 89–95. Almaty, Kazakhstan: Friedrich-Ebert-Stiftung.

Yalcin-Heckmann, L. 1997. The perils of ethnic associational life in Europe: Turkish migrants in Germany and France. In *The politics of multiculturalism in the new Europe: Racism, identity, and community*, ed. Tariq Modood and Pnina Werbner. London: Zed Books.

Zevelev, Igor. 2001. *Russia and its new diasporas*. Washington, D.C.: United States Institute of Peace Press.

5

Migratory Modernity and the Cosmology of Consumption in Côte d'Ivoire

Sasha Newell

Paris has already captured me, just like our own genies do when they cast a spell over someone and remove their power of speech. Isn't that what's happening to me? I seem to be floating; I barely acknowledge anything or anyone. I tell you Paris must be a wicked city indeed; to be able to work that kind of magic from that great a distance means only one thing: the evil spirits there must definitely be stronger than ours, whom we abandon, and who in turn abandon us.

—*Bernard Dadié, An African in Paris*

C'est pas en France tu vas partir, c'est France qui va venir te trouver [You aren't going to France, France is going to come find you].

—*Magic System, Secret d'Africain*

The Ivoirian novelist Bernard Dadié wrote *An African in Paris* on the eve of independence from French colonialism, describing the reverie that Paris produced on West Africans as that of a magical force. Forty-one years later, the premier Ivoirian pop band Magic System continues to sing about France's mystical hold on Ivoirian minds. To travel to Europe and return was the foremost desire of almost every Ivoirian I met. This desire crossed over the deepest social oppositions: those of gender, class, religion, and the pervasive north–south dichotomy that is currently tearing apart the country. At the same time, most Ivoirians were extremely proud of their national identity. The desire to emigrate was not one of permanent escape but of personal transformation. The target of this migration was *Beng*, an Ivoirian slang term best translated as "the land of the whites."[1] Migrants who succeed in reaching this near-mythical destination and return to Côte d'Ivoire undergo a radical transformation in identity. Thereafter, they are known by friends and family as a *Bengiste*, or sometimes more specifically as a *Parisien* or *Statois*. The *Bengiste* of popular myth travels to the "land of the whites" for several years, becomes very rich, and returns with enough money to build a large house for one's family and to sustain oneself and family in a life of luxury happily ever after. But the transformation is not purely economic, for the returned traveler is no longer merely Ivoirian, but a *Bengiste*, a European by proxy. The *Bengiste* is considered to exist on a somewhat different social plane than one's peers. As Karim Bamba writes in his master's thesis at the University of Abidjan,

> [Ivoirians] manifest a particular attachment to all that comes from the Occident, especially Europe and North America. In this sense one often sees that an Ivoirian who has returned from France or the United States is the object of particular attention from his friends and family, who confer a great deal prestige on him. (1982, 2)[2]

In practice, however, the dream of the *Bengiste* very rarely comes to fruition in an economic sense. Those few Ivoirians who successfully manage to cross the many obstacles between them and Europe or America do return bearing the appearance of wealth. They distribute gifts to family and friends and spend extravagantly at the best nightclubs and *maquis* (semilegal outdoor bars, the most popular of social spaces in Abidjan). In reality however, they are producing a temporary display of wealth that cannot be sustained for long, and typically after a month of such conspicuous consumption, they disappear again, returning to *Beng* for another few years. Rather than upsetting the myth of copious wealth available to the migrant, most Ivoirians remaining in their home country see this as proof positive that life in Europe is really as glorious as *Bengistes* tend to boast. Once someone has tasted the bounty of *Beng*, Ivoirians claim, they forget all about their origins.

This chapter is an exploration of the symbolic process of migration, the ways in which people reconstruct their identities through the transformative (even magical) journey to *Beng*. Within Côte d'Ivoire at least, such migrants have become Europeans. In opposition to many contemporary theorists of migration who focus on hybrid identities, the destructuring of nations, and remittances from migrants to their home countries (Rouse 1991; Appadurai 1991; Basch, Glick Schiller, and Szanton Blanc 1994; Clifford 1994; Kearney 1995; Hannerz 1996), I examine migration patterns from the perspective of the home country. My focus highlights the overlapping relationship between consumption and migration, each symbolic process paralleling and feeding into the other. At the same time, I examine the Ivoirian cosmological map of global relations and the way in which Ivoirians construct their identities in relation to a local conception of modernity. I argue that Ivoirian "modernity" is a kind of magical force through which social hierarchy is legitimated according to a theory of social evolution. This angle on the cosmology of migration complements the work of Katy Gardner (1993), on the villages from which Bangladeshi migrant populations stem, and Luin Goldring (1999), who argues that transmigrants maintain connections with their native community because in only the native community do they find a shared set of values. Likewise, it parallels the work of James Ferguson (1999) on Zambian understandings of modernity, and Liisa Malkki's exploration (1995) of the Hutu "cosmological order of nations." In contrast, a near universal of "transnational" theory is the focus on the perspective of migrants outside their home country. Perhaps this seems intuitively correct—after all, it is migration we are talking about. But if we are to understand why migration happens in the first place and how it perpetuates itself, then it is important to examine the home communities from which migrants emerge ethnographically. It is precisely because of such a lacuna in anthropological theorizing of diaspora that migration theorists overwhelmingly assume that the motivation for the process is economic or political (ultimately relying on the modernization/dependency theories of earlier migration models). My research on Ivoirian migration indicates that motivation is much better understood in terms of consumption theory and cosmology than in terms of world system theory or, at least, that the latter perspective is incomplete without the former. As Dolores Koenig indicates in this volume (chapter 2), for West Africans, migration itself is a "positive social value," one apart from the political and economic factors outside observers insist on. As stated in the Akan song she cites, "you don't get civilized if you do not travel."

I begin by exploring the construction of social hierarchy in lower-class urban Ivoirian communities, which is a hierarchy legitimated according to who is more "civilized." I relate this to the Ivoirian cosmology of global national hierarchy through which the migration process is evaluated. I then examine the myth of *Beng* and the dreams of personal transformation that youths hold, followed by a description of the difficult preparations necessary to make the trip possible. Finally, I discuss the return of the migrants and their focus on ostentatious display, contrasting it with realities of their true economic position. To maintain the prestige they have garnered, they are forced into a cycle of migration and display, from which it is difficult to extricate themselves without sacrificing their reputation. However, so long as they maintain the *bluff* (a local term indicating an image of success), they live as mythical figures of power and wealth in Côte d'Ivoire, and in this sense migration has a kind of magical transformative efficacy.

CONTEXTUALIZING TREICHVILLE YOUTH

I conducted field research in Abidjan, the capital city of Côte d'Ivoire, between 2000 and 2001. Abidjan has a population of over three million people, almost half of whom are immigrants from other West African nations, such as Burkina Faso, Mali, Nigeria, and Ghana (Institut National de la Statistique 1994, 2000). These immigrants come to Abidjan in search of work and wealth; Côte d'Ivoire was one of the wealthiest African countries and is still the economic center of the region (David 2000). My research was focused on lower-class urban youth in Treichville, one of several poor residential communities that dominate the city's population and the first black quartier established in the city during the French colonial period (Diabate and Kodjo 1991). Although I focus primarily in this chapter on Treichville youth who have not yet succeeded in leaving the country, many lower-class youth actually do succeed. Getting an accurate representation of how many succeed is difficult, given that they tend to cross borders undocumented—*sans papiers*, as the French put it. The fact that the phenomenon was widespread, however, was clear not only from the numerous *Bengistes* I ran across but from the continual laments of older Ivoirians that youth were abandoning their country.[3] Furthermore, the values surrounding migration I describe here are not limited to lower classes; university students and the children of the elite were equally absorbed in the dream of traveling abroad (and the latter were far more likely to succeed). Although my research took place primarily in Treichville, I encountered a number of university students there as well as in other regions of the city I visited. The cosmology of modernity I elaborate on here is shared to some extent by Ivoirians from all classes, although the discourse in which it is presented varies. What makes the Treichville youth particularly interesting is that, for them, migration is seen as a means of profound social advancement and transformation. Since they are often jobless and survive primarily off exchanges within their social networks, that they make the expensive journey at all is somewhat miraculous. That they return bearing material abundance and rolls of French francs is nothing short of magical.

Economically, the Treichville community is supported largely by criminal activity. A loosely hierarchical criminal network holds the center of the local economy, supplying the principal commodities of informal exchange through theft (muggings, carjackings, pickpocketing, purse snatching, burglary, armed robbery). The network's activities complement a second group, the larger majority of people involved to varying degrees with the informal economy, which Ivoirians call *bizness* (illicit dealings). *Bizness* encompasses activities such as selling stolen goods (as intermediaries for the criminal network), making counterfeit money, forging documents, stealing phone lines, and so forth, and almost all young men have a hand in it, as well as significant numbers of women and older men. Although many of the activities categorized under the rubric of *bizness* are relatively innocuous (such as selling minutes on a cell phone under a false account), they ultimately depend on the criminal network for the supply of stolen cell phones, clothing, and jewelry (as well as protection from police and other thieves). Finally, there is a third category of people, those in the legitimate workforce, which is dominated by the immigrant community. Urban Ivoirian youth feel that most physical work is demeaning and that the only jobs fitting for Ivoirians are "desk jobs." Thus Luc and Jacques, two young men in their early twenties, explained that

> Ivoirians are too proud, too self-inflated. Here one can not sweep the streets, drive taxis, sell food. All that is shameful for an Ivoirian. No, there is no way I could go clean things off the street. . . . I prefer to stay at home. All those jobs

like that, they're for foreigners, people from Mali, Burkina, places like that. . . . We Ivoirians like to work in an office, seated properly. It's like the Garagistes sing *"Ivoiriens comptent en bureau"* [Ivoirians count on an office]. They like to be seated somewhere, writing, and the money comes to them. They just sit there and count their money.

Thus, Abidjanese view labor not only as an index of class hierarchy but, more important, as an index of cultural hierarchy and their own national identity within this evaluative schema. They perceive physical labor as an indication of a lack of development, a missing modernity.[4]

CONSUMING "MODERNITY"

This opposition between Ivoirians and foreigners on the one hand, and crime and work on the other, is expressed through the slang terms *yere* and *gaou*. *Yere* comes from the Dioula for "seeing"; it is someone *qui voit claire* (who sees clearly). Someone who is *yere* cannot be scammed: they see through attempts at fakes and forgery; correspondingly, they are capable of tricking others. To *yere* someone is to steal from them. A *gaou*, however, is an idiot, someone incapable of discerning his or her surroundings and therefore someone easily duped. This relationship of seeing to ignorance is transposed onto the social relationships between those who are integrated and socialized into the urban setting and those who are new arrivals from the villages or immigrants from other West African countries. The distinction corresponds to an idea of cultural evolution. Even Ivoirian presidents are evaluated in these terms, judged according to their Western education, mannerisms, and their ability to dress well. People disparage presidents as *gaou* by referring to them as ignorant villagers who do not know how to act in formal or "modern" situations.

In this way, urban Ivoirians understand migration as a kind of geographic ladder of modernity, such that "peasant" West Africans travel to Abidjan to become more "civilized" while Abidjan residents make the voyage to Europe seeking further cultural transformation. As a young Cameroonian university student explained to me, "many Ivoirians think they are already European. They think that they are already civilized, *évolué* [evolved]. They think they are a superior race." And as described earlier, Ivoirians who succeed in the dream of going to Europe come back transformed as *Bengistes*, occupying a new social category considered inherently superior to that of those who have not yet left the country. This hierarchical conception of geography is further expressed in the francophone African expressions for the journey to Europe. Someone who has made the trip is said to have *monté* (climbed up) while the return voyage is called *le descent* (the descent). Europeans and Americans themselves are looked on with a great deal of ambivalence, but the "land of the whites" is revered as the source of power and prestige. In this way, Ivoirians seem to distinguish between the power of a geographic location and the people who live there. It is the place itself that imbues people with prestige and success.

These cultural transformations taking place within the person are indexed in his or her appearance. Worn properly, clothing is thought more or less directly to reflect the cultural level that a person occupies. According to urban Ivoirians I spoke with, they could spot "uncivilized" qualities merely by the garb someone with a "peasant" mentality would wear. One day I was walking down a familiar street wearing admittedly somewhat ugly bright green pants and flip-flops, when an acquaintance named Charles called me over and began to ask me about America, talking about how cool it must be over there and how well he would dress if only he could get there. He said, "But when we see you, we don't understand how you can dress all *gaou* like that, you who are American." Intrigued, I asked him to explain what it means to dress *gaou*, and he pointed out several people on the street, including a man pushing a cart.

> People who push carts are always *gaous*. They come from Nigeria, Burkina Faso. *Gaous* are always people who come from outside the country. But not Americans. That is what we don't understand. You are who we imitate here, those of us who are *yere*. Jeans, baggy pants, things like that, that is what Americans wear. But you, you can't really wear that over there, can you?

For Charles, clothing should be a transparent indicator of "modernity." It was impossible that someone as "civilized" as myself (being from America) could dress like someone who did not understand urban sartorial norms.

Thus, a central figure in Ivoirian social life is the *bluffeur*—that is, a master of the art of bluff. *Bluffeurs* garner prestige not through migration but by producing an image of success beyond their real economic means. Ivoirian bluff is constructed primarily around the consumption of Western clothing and other prestige commodities. Unlike people in our own society, Ivoirians do not see such bluffing negatively. Members of Western societies fear clothing's potential to confuse social categories; such acts are seen as dangerous artifice. When Westerners dressing "above their station" are unmasked, not only does their prestige typically dissolve, but they often face negative social repercussions (this is the tension underlying the plot of *My Fair Lady*, for example). Although Ivoirians recognize quite explicitly that many people who appear wealthy are merely presenting a false front, they do not typically consider such acts as being inauthentic, superficial, or dishonest. Bamba writes that "to possess these imported goods seems to confer admiration on the individual, and even a certain power over others who find themselves in a position of inferiority" (1982, 3). In Côte d'Ivoire, the possession of Western commodities confers immediate prestige on the person in contact with them. To quote a dated maxim, clothing really does make the man.

I argue that Ivoirian consumption works through a kind of physical absorption of the value of objects such that qualities of an object from the external "otherworld" become qualities of the person. In this way, Western objects have a kind of magical efficacy to produce success, drawn from semiotic associations of contiguity with *Beng* (for a full explication, see Newell 2003). By *magical efficacy*, I refer to the collective belief in the power of signs to produce causal effect. Like John Langshaw Austin's linguistic performatives (e.g., "I promise"), magical acts have the ability not only to signify but to produce the very effect they signal (see Tambiah 1990, 359). As in all systems of signification, magical signs derive meaning through principles of metaphor and metonymy, or what Sir James George Frazer calls the "laws of similarity and contiguity" (1950).[5] A figurine of someone can have real-world effects on them by virtue of its similarity. Fingernails and hair clippings have power over their former owners because the part retains its connection to the whole, and a footprint, once in contact with the foot, retains influence over the person who imprinted it. Frazer considers these "laws" to be a primitive and misconstrued "science"; however, Marcel Mauss argues that these were not laws at all but rather culturally specific categories of objects with certain properties (1972). Sorcerers apply a "science of the concrete," in which signs are rearranged to produce new meanings, rather than apply laws to produce effects (Lévi-Strauss 1961).

In the Ivoirian case then, I am arguing that the magical efficacy of consumption stems from a belief in the power of objects to bring the consumer into metonymic contact with "modernizing" power of the symbolic West.

Ivoirians evaluate objects hierarchically according to their authenticity as imported goods originating in *Beng*. Objects, like people, can be *gaou* and *yere* because they embody the transformative force of "modernity" on which that distinction is based. Modernity is transferred from the object to the person according to the principle of contiguity so that by wearing American clothing, Ivoirians transform themselves into more-potent social beings. In this contemporary Ivoirian cosmology, "modernity" acts as a kind of force or quality that inheres in places, objects, and people, rather than as a state of development, as it is typically used in Western academic discussion.

I suggest here that to consume imported goods is to become that much closer to the Occident itself; it is a kind of partial migration. More important for this chapter, one can also argue that for Ivoirians, migration itself is the ultimate act of consumption. If the bluff of modernity transforms the person, then Ivoirians consider the voyage to the source of value as an irreversible and total metamorphosis, for the *Bengiste* has traveled beyond the bounds of the mundane and everyday to the source of power itself; they have become beings from another world.

MIGRATING DREAMS

The dream of travel is an obsession for many. As in Didier Gondola's descriptions (1999) of Congolese youth spending the majority of their days discussing stories of elysian bounty and strategies for Paris, Ivoirians are devoted to the imagination of *Beng*. It was my friend Christophe's favorite subject of discussion. The following statements were collected from a series of conversations with him over several months:

> For the last two days I have felt like I am in France. I think about nothing else. It is like I am not really here. Even in my sleep, I dream I am there. [When an airplane passes overhead, he points it out to me, looking at it lovingly and with an air of significance. I say, "You're thinking of France." He nods in pleasure.] . . .
>
> I'm sick of Côte d'Ivoire. All my friends have gone to *Beng*. I am a guy who likes cash, who lives with *pierres* [money]. I am not meant for this lifestyle. Right now everything annoys me here. I need to go join my mother in *Beng*, where I belong. . . .
>
> I am wasting my time here, achieving nothing. If I could only get to *Beng*, I could do some great things.

Others focused their dreams more specifically on what they would do once they arrived in *Beng*. I met two young thieves with the street names Biggie and Scarface—dressed to the T in Façonnables, Timberlands, Docksiders, and jeans—who told me excitedly of their plans:

> America is so great, life is sweet over there! All those cute little "chicks," they all drive cars over there. You cruise, listen to rap, you are satisfied. Yes, it is good over there. When I go to America, I'm going to sell cocaine. That sells well there, no? Yeahhh. But in order to last over there [not get caught], I will have a clothing store. Beautiful shirts that will sell for at least fifty dollars, and then I will put a little bag of coke in pocket, like a present. I could do the same thing with shoes, hide a little baggie in them, you know.

Scarface explained that he was supposed to be in Paris by now, but he had been scammed. The guy who was supposed to sell him a visa gave him a fake, and he was turned back at the border. He showed me where the police had unstuck the forgery from his passport, complaining that it had cost him CFA francs 500,000 (approximately US$715). In comparison, a middle-class salary is about CFAF 50,000 a month, still much more than what most Treichville youth bring in through their day-to-day *bizness*.

Charles, another young thief, had similar plans:

> No, I need to get myself to the States. I've got to do it. . . . I won't work there, though, I am going to "get by" there just like I do here. I want to sell drugs, I think, because in a single day you can make sooo much. Drug gangs? No, I'll be able to handle it. I won't be a *gaou* there because I know from my experience here how to get along. When I arrive in the airport, I will kick off my sandals while crossing the street and head straight for a nice clothing store . . . then go into changing room like they have there and put on some brand new sneakers, a new hat, a nice jacket, and I'm out of there, man.

Notice that the most important element of this story for Charles is the transformation in his appearance. He has to rid himself of his demeaning flip-flops as soon as he is out of the airport (apparently, he sees bare feet as being less conspicuous). And he seems to be offering this suggestion about his new clothing as an explanation of how he will avoid trouble with American gangs.

The pressures to make such a voyage were not merely internal. People experienced social pressure from both family and friends to succeed in such an endeavor. Noël had gotten close to entering Germany, but at customs his papers were identified as forgeries and he was repatriated immediately. Since he had already told everyone he knew that he was going to Europe, he dropped his old social circles. This had taken place in 1994, but even as late as 2001, when we ran into his old acquaintances, they often said, "Tiens, I thought you had *monté* [gone to Europe]." Noël told me he wanted to "hide himself in shame" at such encounters because all his old friends had already made the journey to Europe, some multiple times. Often, he carefully let people believe he had actually been inside Germany (after all, he had been on German soil), saying, "but I didn't last long over there." Noël felt not only that his own reputation depended on his eventually succeeding in reaching Europe but that his whole family's reputation rested on this achievement.

Although Treichville men tend to rely principally on their informal social network for day-to-day support (loans, food, gifts, and knowledge of where to find the next "deal"), most maintain strong ties with whatever kin they have in Abidjan. Older Treichville residents placed their hopes on their children. For an older couple, the myth of *Beng* consisted of a dream of owning their own house in their natal village. They expected their children to return from Europe wealthy enough to support them through the rest of their lives. But even beyond this dream, becoming a *Bengiste* was among the highest aspirations available to unemployed, undereducated youth. The returning *Bengiste* was a source of pride to all who knew him or her and produced prestige for the entire family. Thus, Noël's father, who had helped Noël raise funds for his first attempt to reach Europe, was sometimes almost desperate for him find the means to try again.

Michèle was a university graduate working as a telephone repairman, who considered himself to be more enlightened than his peers. His difference in opinion is not really an expression of class difference so much as a critical political stance, as many of his peers in the university system were equally obsessed with Europe as were the Treichville youth I focused on. He explained,

> It makes me sad. People just want to leave the country, they don't care. They have no respect for intelligence, it's travel only. For example, in a family where one son has a degree in engineering and another dropped out but went to *Beng*,

it is the second son the family is more proud of. They don't care what he is doing there, don't even want to know, it is the fact of arrival that counts. Ivoirians
are proud of this country in relation to other neighboring countries, but when
it comes to Europe or America, they forget their origins gladly.[6]

MIGRATORY PRACTICALITIES

For many years, university students from wealthy families dominated travel to
Europe, being sent there to further their education. But in the early nineties, a
widespread popular change in taste commenced such that France became the
central goal of most Treichville youth, especially those connected to the criminal networks. Some of the first street kids to achieve this dream were the musicians leading a new form of Ivoirian pop music, *zouglou,* who used their
success at home to travel to Paris and record their music. Their representations of Paris (both mystifying and demystifying) did much to spread lore of
the bounty available in Europe. In the late 1980s, Houphouët-Boigny began to
sponsor the criminal organization in exchange for political support, and the
influx of money sent many of the gang leaders to Europe to such an extent
that formal hierarchical gang structure largely disintegrated. However, at the
same time that migratory demand was increasing, it was becoming more and
more difficult to penetrate European borders. France in particular severely restricted entrance by African immigrants during this period. An Internet café
owner named Keita described the difficulties involved today in gaining access
to the appropriate paperwork.

> But visas, that is a difficult thing. It is not even possible to enter normally, one
> doesn't get in through legitimate means. . . . That's how it is now. I know a
> woman who took out loans, her parents borrowed on their retirement pension,
> plus she had worked and saved money and went [to the embassy] and applied
> and was refused. She shook the white guy in there and cried, saying kill me now,
> I can't go on. . . . Now she has given up, she put herself and family in debt in or-
> der to go to France and make money, and now there is no source of money.

According to Keita, the going rate for a French visa was over two thousand
U.S. dollars, double that for America. While corruption existed within the em-
bassies themselves (according to the stories of bribe takers told to me by
friends at the American Embassy), there was even more going on in the space
surrounding them. The guards at the gate also required bribes to allow access,

and others who knew the guards could get you past the line for another fee. An entire branch of the criminal economy is devoted to document forgeries, with its own slang term for the profession: *camoracien*. The *camoraciens* tended to focus their activity around the peripheral documents required to get a visa: proof of work, a letter from the boss granting a vacation, proof of sufficient funds in a bank account, and so forth. Leguen and Billy (in their late twenties) had stolen stamps from local businesses and worked long hours in Internet cafés trying to imitate their letters. Stolen passports were one of the most valuable items on the underground exchange networks. *Camoraciens* sometimes worked elaborate scams to con their clients, giving them all the peripheral documents and asking for a large advance to procure the passport and visa, then running off with the money. Because of these difficulties, many people choose more direct and dangerous methods, the principal one being to bribe someone working on a ship bound for Europe and to hide oneself somewhere on board. But these journeys require a great deal of money as well, and it is difficult to understand how any of these poor unemployed youth with little or no resources manage at all.

Much of the money needed for such a voyage had to be procured through success in the world of *bizness* or some kind of large theft, but unless an actor was fairly elevated in the hierarchy of thieves, this was not enough. Indeed, as hinted at in Keita's description, the journey was usually the result of collective effort, pooled resources from close family and extended kin as well as smaller contributions from friends. Many of those who help see such contributions as investments, as the *Bengiste* will be forced to distribute their newfound wealth generously when they return in order to prove their success. Family members hoped that their children would find success in Europe and provide for them, and they looked forward to the prestige of having a *Bengiste* in their midst; likewise, friends expected that their peers would "remember" them upon their return with some kind of valuable gift. In this volume (chapter 2), Dolores Koenig describes the intricate negotiations between families and their children over "going on adventure" in Mali. In Abidjan as well, social networks were crucial to departure—the voyage was difficult to make without their support. However, unlike the agricultural communities she describes in Mali, the labor of Abidjanese men was not highly valued by the family. In many cases, young men continued to depend on older relatives for food, shelter, or occasionally even money.

THE DESCENT AND THE BLUFF

The *Bengiste* who makes his or her descent must continually present superiority through personal display; glorious stories; and massive distributions of wealth, goods, food, and drink. Michèle describes the *Bengistes'* arrival:

> Soon we are going to enter the season when the *Bengistes* arrive. They come with their cars and their clothes, showing off what they have achieved, seducing girls by saying that they will find them a visa to bring them to France. There are people even who have only been hiding out in Burkina that show up and say there were in *Beng*. Those who come back always talk about how wonderful it is. They never talk about what they did there. There is one who I know who has gone back and forth several times, he always comes back with lots of money. When you ask what he does there, he always says he is a businessman. But you have to understand the relationship of the CFA to other currencies. If you make one thousand francs in France, it is one hundred thousand in [Côte d'Ivoire]. So who is going to challenge him? Even if someone comes and says that they saw him there as a crook or a prostitute, people are more likely to believe the adventurer. Because he is rich. How could he make that money otherwise? They come back and tell of the marvels of Europe, how they worked behind a desk in a big office building, how everyone is rich, and how easy it is to get money.

There was always an air of excitement and anticipation around the recently arrived *Bengistes*. One day, while approaching the street corner on which my friends and I spent most evenings, Solo pointed out a *Bengiste* standing by his somewhat-battered Opel convertible, wearing pristinely clean sportswear of the highest-ranking American and French labels. He was surrounded by a crowd of people, several of whom turned out to be other *Bengistes*, the rest eager onlookers and old friends. Although to untrained eyes there was nothing unusual happening, the gathering had a keyed-up energy that indexed the extraordinary. Everyone was trying to talk to the man at once. Solo remarked, "His hand goes into his pocket, and it just keeps coming back out." Practically everyone who approached the man (named Ibrahim) asked for money in one way or another. After awhile, Noël also approached Ibrahim. Despite the fact that Ibrahim chastised Noël for avoiding him, Noël explained to us afterward that he does not like to be seen around the man, because Ibrahim used to be one of his *petits* (his underlings in the criminal hierarchy). He did not want anyone to think that he is mooching money off of a *petit*, nor would he want Ibrahim to have that impression. The power of the *Bengiste* identity is revealed here, for Ibrahim clearly transcended his former subordination to Noël such that even to be seen in the presence of Ibrahim causes Noël humiliation. The importance of distribution of wealth in establishing these hierarchical relations also emerges. So long as Noël avoids receiving from Ibrahim, he avoids confronting the transformation in the relationship. Ibrahim's former equals, however, eagerly accept his offerings, recognizing his now-superior social status (and the possibility of benefiting from it).

Other people described their anger at having been forgotten by their former friends. Mathilde, a university student working in a printing and photocopy booth, was excited to hear that I was an American and began to tell me how much she would like to get there herself:

> It seems that over there life is sweet. There are good jobs. OK, maybe I couldn't get an important job, but one can find a little job, and when you return here, the money becomes big like that. But our brothers over there forget us quickly! When they return, we always ask them to bring us American clothes. We want jeans, Sebagos, Façonnables . . . but then often they bring us nothing. They lie to us, tell us the bag got lost at the airport, or that they haven't unpacked yet, and then a couple days later they are off to another part of town, and you never see them again. Often they are even ashamed to sleep in their own house where they grew up. They prefer to go sleep at the Ivoire [one of the most expensive hotels in town], at Ibis, like that. But what is certain is that when people come back they have money, and then they have gotten so fat, you can't imagine what they've been eating over there, really now. In any case, they get here and they forget about us immediately. They forget about their own family.

I would like to point out here that while most of my sources here are male, and indeed the majority of migrants are male, the dream of migration is just as prevalent among women, and there are many women who do succeed. Since they have limited access to the informal economy through which many men pull together their income, women rely more heavily on family support. An alternative (if less respectable) strategy is to try to sleep with foreign (mostly French) travelers, in hopes of getting these men to bring them back to their countries of origin. In any case, though migrants often attempt to cut off their former connections (and corresponding obligations) when they realize the very real difficulties of life in *Beng*, Mathilde's statements clearly reveal the norm they are breaking.

Evidence of the social dangers of transgressing such obligations can be found in the Ivoirian pop music called *zouglou*. *Zouglou* lyrics heavily emphasize humor, wordplay, and sharp social commentary. Ivoirians of all ages learned these words by heart and sang along with the music. The stars of *zouglou* music, who usually rose to success from the streets of poor quartiers such as Treichville, were the idols of Abidjan youth. Unlike most *Bengistes*, *zouglou* musicians were secure enough in their status to criticize their experience of Paris, and their lyrics often attempt to disrupt the myths of *Beng*. Nevertheless, observers pointed out that these musicians kept going back to Paris, despite all their complaints, and so were disinclined to put too much faith in such negative portraits. The following song, "Parigo," describing an ill-fated migrant to Paris named Gloglou was written by Fitini (Fitini 2000, translated by the author). This particular song is important for its description of a family's reactions to the failure to live up to social obligation.

Your parents build houses,
while for the sake of a few coins you follow people all over,
but you should stay home a bit, stay home.
A youth from our quartier, who dreamed of going to Paris
Since his birth, he dreamed of going to Paris.
In the quartier, he gave us a lot of shit.
"I want to go *derrière l'eau* [behind the water, Europe], to seek my future."

"My brother Gloglou, France is not like Cote d'Ivoire.
Over there it is cold, problems with papers.
Individualist, every man for himself
You have all the time you need to ask questions."
Example: If you are Dioula, "Ani sogo ma" [salutations]
Television *bei waa*? Are there *bei* radios? [Are their lots of televisions, radios?] Money
bei waa? Everybody has *bei* ? [Is there lots of money? Does everybody have a lot?]"
Nevertheless, Gloglou wanted to know nothing.

"I want to go *derrière l'eau*, to seek my future."
It is at the base of a wall that you see the true house.
So we began to save money.

"Here is your money, go now *derrière l'eau*, but there is one condition.
As soon as things are going ok, you must bring Zouzoi over.
Zouzoi in his turn will bring over Nyaware."

Certainly, right away, Gloglou accepted, he went off to Paris.
Three months later, a letter arrived.
Gloglou has written, Mama, Gloglou has written.
All the youth of the quartier gathered around to read the letter.
Gloglou has written, Mama, Gloglou has written!
My brother read us the letter.

"Truly things are not going well.
The cold will kill me, the white people ignore me.
Petit Yode was right, Paris is hard like a rock.
Come and bring me back, I sense that I will die."
He was really full of *donyere* [shit].

For the response, we didn't have to think long.
We also wrote a response: "go ahead and die."
He screamed mama. He sobbed papa, *djebelekou* [cry of sadness].

In the song, a youth dreams of going *derrière l'eau* to seek his fortune. *Derrière l'eau*, meaning literally "behind the water," is another slang term for *Beng* (as I argue later, this conception of *Beng* parallels representations of the "otherworld" in Ivoirian thought). Gloglou's family reluctantly agrees to provide the money to send him to *Beng*, so long as he will reciprocate by bringing over his brothers once he succeeds. When Gloglou fails to meet the expectations of the family's investment, they sever their connection with him and tell him he might as well be dead.

It is important here to consider the role of reciprocity (and lack thereof) in the migratory process. Mauss describes material exchanges as both expressing and defining social relationships (1923–1924). As Marshall Sahlins writes, "A material transaction is usually a momentary episode in a continuous social relation. The social relation exerts governance" (1972, 186). At the same time, however, "the connection between material flow and social relations is reciprocal. A specific social relation may constrain a given movement of goods, but a specific transaction—'by the same token'—suggests a particular social relation.

If friends make gifts, gifts make friends" (186). Gifts and their reciprocation, in other words, are obligatory acts for the maintenance of social relationships, but they also have the power to transform the nature of such relations. Both of these processes are at work in Ivoirian migration. Migrants are obligated to legitimate their newfound "success" through extensive gift-giving practices. At one level, as I have suggested, such gift giving can be understood as a reciprocal return for the economic support that family and friends have given in helping initiate migration in the first place—it is a necessary expression of the bonds between migrants and their kin and friends. But such gifts are often in the form of objects unavailable to the recipients or of sums of money beyond the means of those who receive it. In this sense, the returning migrants' gifts are marked by an unreciprocable surplus. Such asymmetrical exchange inevitably involves relations of social hierarchy and is often, as in this case, constitutive of them (or to put it another way, the equation is balanced by the prestige that the donor acquires as a result of the gift; Leach 1951). The massive distributions accompanying the return of the migrant can thus be understood both as a performative legitimation of one's newfound identity and as an act of self-production through unreciprocated giving. As such, these return gift-giving performances conform to relationships between authority and distribution in other spheres of urban social life. For example, within the social networks of the informal economy, the older, more-established criminals give to their younger acolytes in order to maintain loyalty. Christine Denot claims, "He who is affluent is called *grandfrère* or *tonton* [big brother or uncle], even by people who are older. The latter pay allegiance to the individual with the most material wealth, delegating their power in exchange for his protection which manifests itself concretely in gifts" (1990, 42).

BENGISTE NETWORKS, MIGRANT ECONOMIES

The economics of the *Bengiste* lifestyle are somewhat mysterious. From my own research among the African immigrant community in Paris, as well as from reports from older Ivoirians no longer concerned with their reputation, the reality of migration is somewhat different from the stories of success that *Bengistes* proliferate. Without proper papers (visa, passport, work permit, etc.), most immigrants cannot get legitimate work. Their income tends to come from within the African immigrant community itself. Working in underground African bars and restaurants, selling black-market goods smuggled in from other European Union countries with lax borders, hawking drugs, prostitution: these were the sorts of occupations on which most of my acquaintances in Paris survived, a far cry from the office job of which Ivoirians dream. Their living conditions are often extremely difficult, four or five people sharing low-income one-room apartments with no hot water, no bathroom, and sometimes even no electricity. In their work on the Congolese informal economy in Paris, Janet MacGaffey and Rémy Bazenguissa-Ganga (2000) have described an entire market based on renting or selling squats to other immigrants, housing that gains value the longer it remains undiscovered by the authorities. However, because the French franc is worth many times its value in Côte d'Ivoire, the meager savings that immigrants accrue over several years of living in these conditions are enough for them to spend one or two months' worth of luxurious wealth back in their home country. Such displays are enough for one to maintain an identity as a person of success, a *Bengiste*, and to bolster the prestige of one's entire family in the eyes of the local community.

While migration literature has tended to focus on remittances to the home country (see the introduction to this volume), Ivoirians are far more concerned with questions of accumulating social status through consumption and asymmetrical gift exchange. Of course, these two practices are closely related, but they have different social and analytic ramifications. Remittances are largely understood as a means for accumulating capital in the homeland (people migrate for the purpose of bringing otherwise inaccessible income to their families), while an emphasis on gift exchange brings attention to the expression and transformation of social relationships. Thus, Lisa Cliggett (2003) argues that Zambian urban migrants do not engage in remittances but rather bring gifts to maintain social relationships with their rural villages. I choose to call Ivoirian economic distributions "gifts" rather than "remittances" because I believe this better reflects the intentions and interpretations of the actors. A possible explanation for this difference in emphasis may have to do with the way relationships are maintained. Remittances would seem to be a means of maintaining relationships over distances of space and time. As in Nancy Munn's (1986) description of the *kula* in Melanesia, actors enhance their names across "spacetime" by sending material wealth. In contrast, Ivoirians seem to be more concerned with the maintenance of face-to-face relations and the production of hierarchical relations through giving. Migrants often maintain only sporadic contact with family while away and rarely send money. Families of Ivoirian migrants do expect remittances, but they are often disappointed and complain that their kin have forgotten them. Rather than through an extension of one's name through "spacetime" with remittances, it is in the concrete act of performative distribution of gifts that power is created, by giving profusely in front of the audience one wishes to impress. Ivoirians gain prestige through the action of potlatch-style competitive exchanges: it is by doing, not having, that they produce a name for themselves. Exchange here is about public performance rather than extending fame or increasing family capital. Ultimately, such youth do aspire to build in their communities and contribute to their family's welfare (most elite migrants and many unusually successful lower-class migrants actually fulfill this goal), but the social obligations for display are typically of greater importance.

In reality, the *Bengistes* economize in similar ways to those of the youth in Abidjan. Just as many Ivoirians rely on informal and criminal networks for their survival and income, the *Bengistes* develop similar networks in their destination countries and even back in Côte d'Ivoire. In the same way that youth at home in Abidjan invest such income primarily into clothing and other forms of conspicuous consumption in order to maintain and advance their reputation, *Bengistes*, whose resources are usually limited in the countries to which they migrate, use their savings in a grand display of wealth and success back in the home country and leave empty-handed to begin the process again. They also reenter the informal economy immediately, selling the prestige goods they have brought with them to support their luxurious lifestyle (often including used cars, which Ivoirians call *France Au Revoirs*).

In a rare moment of reflection on the inner workings of *Bengiste* networks, Christophe explained,

> In principal, guys who talk about going to France are full of shit. To go over there, if you have nobody there, you get repatriated fast. You have to have somebody to help you, to give you somewhere to stay for a while, all that. First someone from our *ghetto* has to get there and establish himself, then, others can come, little by little. *Bengistes* are like that, that is their system, their *manyerage* [way of manipulating the system]; they are together. Here, when they come, they have their kiosk, their bar. You wouldn't even believe that it is for them, because it is always in some forgotten corner, *coin façon* [messed up place], without a sign. You see them there figuring out their network. They are on the phone

to France: "ok, he's coming in on the plane at such and such a time, then he will be in this place, and you will find him over here." They are all connected, the *Bengiste* group.

According to Christophe, many *Bengistes* have to commit crimes in order to get the money to leave; they are even more caught up in the criminal hierarchy than before (one wonders, given that he knows this, why he continues to imagine France as such a utopia). The point is that *Bengistes* continue to operate within the same informal economy as the one they left when they emigrated—or, rather, it should be said that they never properly left it.

Instead, what has happened is that they have jumped up the hierarchy within this system. In this way, Noël was no longer superior to his former *petit* Ibrahim, who now had whole circles of acolytes supporting him. Thus, the magical transformation of migration actually has real social effects; even if in economic terms they are not that much better off than when they left, they have far greater social influence. In an informal economy in which "who one knows" is the difference between starvation and success, such influence and fame actually have real economic effects. However, to preserve this superior status—which is, after all, based on a kind of bluff—they spend much of their time within the delimited network they established in *Beng*. Among their own peers, they can drop pretense, while the exclusivity they cultivate reinforces their perceived importance from the outside.

THE MEDIATION OF THE OTHERWORLD: MIGRATION AS A FORM OF CONSUMPTION

I want to argue that migration can be considered a form of consumption. Rather than migrate for the purpose of increasing capital (in other words, as an act of economic production), migrants seek the symbolic and social capital of personal transformation. In fact, according to my friend Michèle, the popularity of migration was a recent phenomenon, one that emerged directly out of the collective importance placed on fashion. While youth used to put all of their income and energy into achieving the proper style, the importance of clothing has greatly diminished in relation to the dream of travel. In a sense then, migration is itself a fashion, a form of consumption that has replaced earlier modes of self-production. In the eighties, Michèle explained, everyone was trying to imitate the Congolese *sapeurs*, who dressed in European *haute couture* clothing.

Everyone was trying to get suits and ties and labels. People would cut tags off shirts and stick them on the back of their pants. They would say, "Look, what are you wearing, that is nothing, not even labeled. My pants are such and such," and then they would point out the label. This was all over Abidjan in those days. . . . But in 1990 . . . after the economic crisis began, everyone who had money left for France, and then there was no money at all. Meanwhile, some of the people going to France were coming back filled with stories of how great life was there, of how the money was more powerful, and even if you were a prostitute there, you could come back rich. By 1995, everyone wanted to go to France. If you put ten people in a row and asked them, nine out of ten would have said they wanted to go to France. *La voyage est devenu a la mode* [the voyage became the fashion]. This is how immigration became so important. Even the pop music stars, some of the most famous and successful people in Côte d'Ivoire at the time, have left for France and never came back.

In this sense, migration is merely a continuation of an ongoing relationship to consuming otherness, to a fascination with the external. While consumption was itself the incorporation or metonymic absorption of otherness, the migration process became a total self-transformation, one that ended up dramatically increasing one's social status while producing a "set apart" or, in Durkheimian terms (1912), a "sacred quality" to the *Bengistes*, who ended up congregating mainly among themselves.

As in the pop song "Parigo" cited earlier, Ivoirians commonly referred to "the land of the whites" as *derrière l'eau* (behind the water), revealing a sense of geography more influenced by hierarchical conceptions of power than cartography. Not that Ivoirians were ignorant of maps; indeed, maps were cherished and gazed at reverentially as sources of information about the land of dreams. Rather, by using the phrase *derrière l'eau*, I suggest that Ivoirians place "the land of the whites" in a conceptual category of otherworldliness, for the world of the dead is thought by many Ivoirian cosmologies to exist on the other side of a body of water (Wiredu 1996). While I do not think that Ivoirians consider white people to be supernatural beings, I am arguing that an abstractly conceived *Beng* has come to stand in a structurally homologous position to the otherworld, as the external source of the force of value itself, which Ivoirians discuss in terms of what they call "modernity." In this sense, the Ivoirian discourse on modernity and social evolution is an idiom for the explanation of social hierarchy, an idiom structured according to a local cosmology of the power from the otherworld. Migration and consumption both provide mediating access to this source of value, allowing social actors symbolic contact with modernity itself and the transformative potential it embodies.

In conclusion, I believe that Ivoirian consumption of Western goods and the migration to *Beng* are parallel symbolic operations. Migration is a more powerful and total version of the temporary transformation that the *bluffeur* achieves through clothing; the *Bengiste* not only absorbs the "modernity" of the West but becomes a purveyor of that modernity. This transformation takes place at two levels: cosmologically, through migration the "adventurer" becomes someone from "the land of the whites," the ultimate source of value, while socially, this symbolic operation expands the hierarchical position and social network of the actor. The prestige of the *Bengiste* gives them new social influence within the informal networks that dominate the Treichville economy, allowing them opportunities and resources they would have had great difficulty achieving without leaving Côte d'Ivoire.

This parallel between consumption and migration as magical transformations has important ramifications for our understanding of both spheres of social action. I follow the likes of Daniel Miller (1987, 1995), Jonathan Friedman (1991, 1994), Arjun Appadurai (1986), and Igor Kopytoff (1986) in theorizing consumption as personal symbolic action through which the categories of person and thing intermesh. However, I insist with Mary Douglas and Baron Isherwood (1979) that consumption is ultimately a social process, both constrained by cultural categories and ultimately producing not only individual identities but social ones. It is the principal means through which cultures attach meaning and value to persons and things alike. Unlike former theorists of consumption, I consider consumption as a form of partial migration and thus emphasize the importance of contact in the Ivoirian cosmology of persons, things, and places. Scholarship on consumption has tended to focus on questions of appearance and imitation to the neglect of indexical relations of contiguity as sources of value and symbolic transformation. But by examining migration as a form of consumption, we can examine local constructions of the relationship between place and value, allowing us far greater insight into the motivations through which migration comes about.

I suggest here that in neglecting the cosmological underpinnings of migration, anthropological accounts of transnationalism or diaspora often miss the crucial local effects of the process, effects that determine the motivations for migration in the first place. It is important for anthropologists to be sensitive to the ways in which the "Western" discourse of modernity can be appropriated and used within local cosmological systems. Thus, explanations of the postcolonial cultural hegemony of the metropole often rely on a working misunderstanding between cultures, one in which concepts such as modernity and civilization produce quite different resonances and associations in their culture of origin than in the culture that adopted them. Indeed, by disrupting these coordinated misconceptions of global hierarchy, the space is opened up to interrogate Euro-American cosmologies of modernity, value, and place. I suspect that modernity is imbued with just as much transformative power by the social actors directing the politics of global economies as it is by urban Ivoirian youth.

NOTES

1. Urban Ivoirians almost all speak some version of French, the official language of Côte d'Ivoire. However, those who make their living from *bizness* tend to speak among themselves a slang language called Nouchi. Nouchi maintains an essentially French grammatical structure but involves a great deal of lexical incorporation from a variety of local ethnic languages and immigrant languages. There is also a great deal of *détournement* (altering the meaning) of French words. Words found in italics throughout this text are of Nouchi origin, even though in a number of cases they may appear to be French.

2. At the time Bamba was writing, almost all migration was conducted by elites. It had not yet become the trend for lower-class youth to emigrate. Indeed, Bamba's study on the consumption of Western products focused entirely on the attitudes and practices of college students, drawn mostly from the wealthier echelons. Migration has been an important practice among the elite since the colonial period, in which *évolués* (the French term for educated elite) were sent to the metropole for further education. Although the elites are more likely to gain economic benefit from their voyage (they have student or work visas and so can do something productive and legitimate during their stay), their attitudes about cultural transformation are surprisingly similar to those of the lower-class youth I focus on here.

3. This chapter focuses on urban youth, but of course the question emerges, what happens to these values when the youth get older? Because this lower-class, clandestine migration is relatively new, only becoming a widespread phenomenon

in the 1990s, it is impossible to know for sure. Certainly, at present the older generations were divided over the significance of migration. Many hoped that their children would bring back the resources to build them a house and allow for their retirement. They were proud of the status such a voyage brought, regardless of economic benefits. On the other hand, many recognized that these voyages were dangerous, that too many people were leaving and not coming back, and that *Bengistes* did not always "remember" their kin materially. Others even scorned migration as a tragic waste of human and financial resources.

4. However, I was also told by friends from the same group that Ivoirians expect to have to work these same demeaning jobs when they get to Europe, just as the Burkinabe and Malians do in Côte d'Ivoire. Thus, this group saw a perfect hierarchical parallel, one in which it is permissible to demean oneself in the process of migration knowing that upon return one will be transformed. Of course, this also corresponds to the liminal phase of a rite of passage. On the other hand, many youth seemed to imagine that they would succeed in America without doing work, like Biggie and Scarface.

5. I draw on semiotic theory here without having the space to give it full consideration. The laws of magic can be compared to metaphor and metonymy in Roman Jakobson (1990), paradigmatic and syntagmatic in Ferdinand de Saussure (1983), and indexical versus iconic in Charles Peirce (1931–1935). All of these are different formulations of the two axes of language and the interrelations between signs. I am attempting here to bring theories of magic, language, and consumption together.

6. While Michèle may be exaggerating here, his point rings true to the general attitude. Although education was highly valued, most people thought of it as being fairly impractical, since the economy was such that few could make use of their degrees. One popular song tells of how university students go crazy when they graduate because their heads are so full of ideas and they have nothing to do. So it was not so unreasonable for a family to prize a son or daughter who raised the esteem of the entire family over one with a degree in engineering who brought in no income. Of course there were those who disparaged such travel altogether, but these critics were extremely rare.

REFERENCES

Appadurai, Arjun, ed. 1986. *The social life of things: Commodities in cultural perspective.* Cambridge: Cambridge University Press.

————. 1991. Global ethnoscapes: Notes and queries for a transnational anthropology. In *Recapturing anthropology: Working in the present*, ed. R. Fox. Santa Fe, N.M.: School of American Research Press.

Bamba, Karim. 1982. L'importe des produits d'importation occidentale sur la vie socio-economique des Ivoiriens à Abidjan. Memoire de Maitrise, Department de Sociologie, Université Nationale de Côte d'Ivoire, Abidjan.

Basch, Linda, Nina Glick Schiller, and Cristina Szanton Blanc, eds. 1994. *Nations unbound: Transnational projects, postcolonial predicaments, and deterritorialized nation-states*. New York: Gordon and Breach.

Clifford, James. 1994. Diasporas. *Cultural Anthropology* 9 (3): 302–38.

Cliggett, Lisa. 2003. Remitting the gift: Zambian mobility and anthropological insights for migration studies. Paper read at Society for Economic Anthropology meetings, at Monterrey, Mexico.

Dadié, Bernard. 1959. *An African in Paris*. Trans. K. C. Hatch. Chicago: University of Illinois Press.

David, Phillipe. 2000. *La Côte d'Ivoire*. Paris: Éditions Karthala.

Denot, Christine. 1990. *Petits Metiers et Jeunes Descolarisés à Abidjan*. Socliology, University de Paris 1, Panthéon-Sorbonne IEDES.

Diabate, Henriette, and Léonard Kodjo. 1991. *Notre Abidjan*. Abidjan, Ivory Coast: Ivoire Media.

Douglas, Mary, and Baron Isherwood. 1979. *The world of goods*. New York: Basic Books.

Durkheim, Emile. 1912. *The elementary forms of religious life*. Trans. K. E. Fields. New York: Free Press.

Ferguson, James. 1999. *Expectations of modernity: Myths and meanings of the copperbelt*. Berkeley: University of California Press.

Fitini, le createur. 2000. *Tout Mignon*. Showbiz, 144/2000. Audiocassette.

Frazer, Sir James George. 1950. *The golden bough: A study of magic and religion*. Abridged ed. New York: MacMillan.

Friedman, Jonathan. 1991. Consuming desires: Strategies of selfhood and appropriation. *Cultural Anthropology* 6 (2): 154–63.

————, ed. 1994. *Consumption and identity.* Chur, Switz.: Harwood.

Gardner, Katy. 1993. Desh-bidesh: Sylheti images of home and away. *Man* 28 (1): 1–15.

Goldring, Luin. 1999. Power and status in transnational social spaces. In *Migration and transnational social spaces,* ed. L. Pries. Aldershot, Eng.: Ashgate.

Gondola, Didier. 1999. Dream and drama: The search for elegance among Congolese youth. *African Studies Review* 42 (1): 23–48.

Hannerz, Ulf. 1996. *Transnational connections: Culture, people, places.* London: Routledge.

Institut National de la Statistique. 1994. *Abidjan la Cosmopolite: Une Etude Demographique de la Ville d'Abidjan.* Abidjan: Institut National de la Statistique, Republique de la Côte d'Ivoire.

————. 2000. *Recencesement Generale de la Population et de l'Habitation 1998: Premiers Resultats Definitif.* Abidjan: Institut Nationale de la Statistique, Republique de la Côte d'Ivoire.

Jakobson, Roman. 1990. *On language.* Ed. Linda R. Waugh and Monique Monville-Burston. Cambridge, Mass.: Harvard University Press.

Kearney, Michael. 1995. The local and the global: The anthropology of globalization and transnationalism. *Annual Review of Anthropology* 24:547–65.

Kopytoff, Igor. 1986. The cultural biography of things: Commodification as process. In *The social life of things: Commodities in cultural perspective,* ed. A. Appadurai. Cambridge: Cambridge University Press.

Leach, Edmund. 1951. The structural implications of matrilateral cross-cousin marriage. *Royal Anthropological Institute Journal* 81:23–55.

Lévi-Strauss, Claude. 1961. *The savage mind.* Chicago: University of Chicago Press.

MacGaffey, Janet, and Rémy Bazenguissa-Ganga. 2000. *Congo-Paris.* Indianapolis: Indiana University Press.

Malkki, Liisa. 1995. *Purity and exile: Violence, memory, and national cosmology among Hutu refugees in Tanzania.* Chicago: University of Chicago Press.

Mauss, Marcel. 1923–1924. *The gift.* Trans. W. D. Halls. New York: Norton.

————. 1972. *A general theory of magic.* Trans. R. Brain. New York: Norton.

Miller, Daniel. 1987. *Materialism and mass consumption.* Cambridge: Blackwell.

———, ed. 1995. *Acknowledging consumption: A review of new studies.* London: Routledge.

Munn, Nancy. 1986. *The fame of Gawa.* Durham, N.C.: Duke University Press.

Newell, Alexander F. 2003. Fashioning modernity: Consumption, migration and the production of Ivoirian identities. Ph.D. diss., Cornell University, Ithaca, N.Y.

Peirce, Charles. 1931–1935. *Collected papers of C. S. Peirce.* Vol. 1–4. Cambridge, Mass.: Harvard University Press.

Rouse, Roger. 1991. Mexican migration and the social space of postmodernism. *Diaspora* 1 (1): 8–23.

Sahlins, Marshall. 1972. On the sociology of primitive exchange. In *Stone Age Economics.* Chicago: Aldine-Atherton.

Saussure, Ferdinand de. 1983. *A course in general linguistics.* Trans. R. Harris. Chicago: Open Court.

Tambiah, Stanley Jeyaraja. 1990. *Magic, science, religion, and the scope of rationality.* Cambridge: Cambridge University Press.

Wiredu, Kwasi. 1996. African philosophical tradition: A case study of the Akan. In *African philosophy,* ed. P. English and K. Kalumba. Englewood, N.J.: Prentice Hall.

II

REMITTANCES
AND BEYOND

6

When Houses Provide More Than Shelter

Analyzing the Uses of Remittances within Their Sociocultural Context

Silvia Grigolini

A large debate exists in the social sciences over the role of migration (both national and international) and remittances in the development of the migrants' home communities (see Eversole in this volume, chapter 9, for a comprehensive review of both sides of the debate, as well as that of the literature on remittances in general). Although the literature clearly shows that migrants send home large amounts of remittances every year, the majority of studies have concluded that these are most frequently used in what scholars consider unproductive ways. In other words, remittances are said to be employed for the fulfillment of the immediate needs and wants of the migrants' family members rather than to be invested in activities that might increase the household's regular income (Burki 1984, 680; Reichart 1981, 57; Rubenstein 1982, 241; and Whittaker 1988, 21; see Rempel and Lobdell 1978 for a review of the literature that reaches the same conclusions). This behavioral pattern is considered not only worrisome but also puzzling. The migrants and their families are believed to be acting against their own best economic interest and contributing to the perpetuation of poverty in their own communities.

However, a few other scholars disagree with this pessimistic view of remittances and migration. They do not deny that a large percentage of remittances are indeed consumed, but they argue that productive uses of remittances also occur. For example, Norman Long (1968) describes the building of large-scale agricultural enterprises with remittance money in the Serenje District in Zambia. Lillian Trager (1984, 335–36; 1991, 189) shows instances in the Philippines in which remittances are used directly for investments in agriculture and education and might also help in freeing other resources for productive activities. Dennis Conway and Jeffrey H. Cohen (1998, 39) discuss cases of remittances being used for the establishment of small informal businesses in the valley of Oaxaca, even if they consider these ventures more important as forerunners of future expansions of the village economy than as proof of current success, due to the limited returns that they presently provide. Furthermore, some scholars have reported that remittances are used to sponsor public development projects in the communities of origin, such as repairs to public buildings and the pavement of roads; the establishment of public transportation systems, schools, and banks; and even the support of small local industries (Conway and Cohen 1998, 39–40; Massey et al. 1987, 230; Montes Mozo and García Vásquez 1988; Smith 1992; Trager 2001, 188–98).

In addition, some scholars have argued that the productive uses of remittances have been underestimated and misrepresented due to flaws in methodology. They argue that researchers tend to focus mainly on what is purchased directly with remittances. However, we should also take into consideration what purchases and investments are indirectly allowed by remittances by freeing other resources for this purpose (Adams 1991, 702; Stark 1980, 373; Trager 1984, 336; 1991, 189). Another possible problem with past methodology is the often-excessive reliance on informants' statements and, thus, on reported, rather than actual, uses of remittances (Trager 1984, 319). On top of this, in most cases only certain members of the household (either in the host or home community) are interviewed about remittance uses, without much evidence that they would be particularly knowledgeable on this topic. The tendency has been to interview only male household heads, under the assumption that they would be in charge of all decisions and that all other household members would simply follow their directions. However, there is no real empirical evidence to support this assumption. Indeed, the ethnographic literature shows that many conflicts occur within the household, as individual household members have different personal needs and wants that do not coincide with those of the unit as a whole. Thus, a variety of opinions and types of behavior often exist within a household (Abu 1983; Ayers and Lambertz 1986; Bentley 1989; Bruce 1989; Cheal 1989; Grimes 1998; Pahl 1980; Poats, Feldstein, and Rocheleau 1989; Rapp, Ross, and Bridenthal 1979; Saul 1989; Tapia 1995; Wilk 1989). Furthermore, even if households were found to behave as unitary actors, there would be no real reason to assume that in each household one adult male would be in charge of making all decisions all the time.

In addition to all of this, Conway and Cohen (1998) argue that we should move away from the simple dichotomization of remittance uses into "consumptive" and "productive" alternates and that we should instead focus on a wider range of positive (both monetary and nonmonetary) effects of migration and remittances than previously considered.

I would also add that remittance uses should be analyzed within the broader cultural and economic contexts in which they take place so that we can fully understand their significance at the local level. This would also help us better comprehend the reasoning behind actors' selection of certain uses of remittances rather than others that might appear more productive to an outsider. This type of analysis might reveal that some of the uses of remittances that scholars have generally viewed as being unproductive actually contain income-generating potential within certain communities and that under certain circumstances the simple consumption of resources might be more economically advantageous than their productive investment.

To illustrate my point, I present data on international migration to the United States from the village of San Pedro Mártir, Oaxaca, Mexico.[1] First, a few clarifications are in order. In this chapter, I focus on all economic resources originally obtained by migrants outside of the village but later spent or otherwise utilized within it either by the migrants themselves or by other people to whom the resources have been transferred. I analyze both the resources used by the migrants themselves and those utilized by others who receive them from the migrants, and I label them both "remittances," as it is commonly done in the literature. Both types of resources originate in the migrants' host communities and are eventually utilized in their home communities, and they both need to be analyzed within their sociocultural context in order for us to fully understand their significance at the local level. However, I distinguish between these two types of remittances throughout this chapter, as I consider them to be different in substantial ways. In the first case, there is no real transfer of resources from one individual to another, while such transfer does occur in the second case, playing an important role in the maintenance of ties between senders and recipients. Furthermore, these two types of resources are often utilized differently within the home communities. One might even argue that different labels need to be used for each type of phenomenon, but I do not wish to attempt this here. Instead, I limit myself to noting the nature of each type of remittance discussed.

It should also be noted that resources move in both directions—from the United States to the village and from the village to the United States (although they take different forms)—but here I am only analyzing the former type.

Finally, the migration dynamics that I discuss in this chapter are directly tied to the nature of intergenerational relations within village households. While I analyze this tie in detail and describe the strain that exists between generations in the village, here I cannot fully explore the overall issue of intergenerational relations.

San Pedro Mártir is a Zapotec community located in the central valley of Oaxaca, about forty-three kilometers from the capital and thirteen kilometers from Ocotlán (to whose district it belongs). It is only a few kilometers away from the village of San Martín Tilcajete (discussed by Cohen, in this volume, chapter 3). Indeed, these villages belong to the same district of Ocotlán (see figure 6.1). In 2000, San Pedro Mártir had a population of 1,902, distributed across 413 households (Instituto Nacional de Estadística 1995). A large percentage of the villagers (especially men) travel periodically to the United States to work but come back home regularly. A much smaller percentage of them have permanently moved abroad and rarely, if ever, visit the village.

Most of the migrants send remittances to their relatives in the village or bring substantial sums of money with them each time they return to their home community, although the amounts remitted vary greatly, from fifty to almost ten thousand U.S. dollars per year. The migrants and their relatives use this capital in a variety of ways, some of which are clearly productive. I have observed remittances being invested in the purchase of land, fruit trees, fertilizers, and a variety of agricultural tools; and in the establishment of little businesses, such as bakeries or grocery stores. In addition, remittance money is often spent on extravagant celebrations, which although unproductive in themselves often provide jobs for many other villagers (through the production and sale of flowers, bread, and chocolate; the resale of mescal and soft drinks; and the performance in brass bands and musical groups, among other

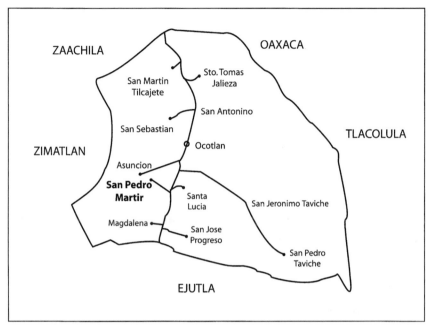

FIGURE 6.1.
The district of Ocotlán and the village of San Pedro Martir

activities). Still, the most frequent uses of remittances in the village are ones that typically occur before any other type of investment is even attempted: the purchase of consumer goods and the construction of fancy houses. These uses are also among the most commonly reported cross-culturally. To an outside observer, these do not appear to be economically productive or even truly advantageous ways of spending money, and the villagers' behavior appears even more absurd when we observe that a small but substantial percentage of the houses they build are left empty for many years.

However, this use of resources is perfectly understandable if analyzed in light of the cultural, social, and economic circumstances of their community and, in particular, the nature of intergenerational relations within village households. Many of the consumer goods bought with remittance money actually have productive uses in the village, and the construction of houses, while not economically productive in itself, plays an essential role in the acquisition of control over one's economic resources. Furthermore, the construction of a specific type of house can provide the owners with upgraded social status and popularity in the village and can improve the productivity of their future businesses.

In the rest of the chapter, I show the importance of these uses of remittances through an analysis of their local sociocultural and economic contexts. In particular, I show the close tie that exists between migration dynamics and intergenerational relations. I first present the village family context, with an emphasis on children's lack of freedom and the strains that exist between different generations within village households. Then I show how migration can represent a route to independence for children, especially if aimed at accumulating enough funds to build their own house. Next, I discuss remittance uses in the village, showing the hidden economic advantages of certain forms of apparent consumption. Finally, I focus on the importance of housing as a form of investment of remittances.

FAMILY/HOUSEHOLD CONTEXT OF MIGRATION

Children's Dependence on Parents before Marriage

In San Pedro Mártir, one is not considered an adult until he or she gets married and has at least one child. Until that day, youths typically remain under the authority of their parents (in particular, their father). They are not fully free to choose the economic activities in which they want to engage, although they might express their general preferences hoping that these will be taken into consideration. Parents have the right to decide whether their children should pursue higher education or enter the workforce, and it is a decision based on what the household as a whole needs the most (whether they need more labor to work the fields or can invest in education). Furthermore, parents tend to monitor their children's daily activities closely. In one household I observed, each morning at breakfast, the father would explicitly tell each household member what tasks they should perform that day and in what order. At night, he would check to see if they had conducted their duties adequately. Although fathers in other households did not seem to exercise the same extreme degree of control, they nevertheless were generally found to have at least the power of authorizing or prohibiting their children's own choices of activities. In addition, children are expected to turn in their entire incomes to their parents. Most children need to ask their parents for money each time they require it, specifying the use they will make of it. A few are luckier and receive a regular pay to cover minor personal expenses, but even in this case, their daily subsistence and any major expenses are the responsibility of the parents, who consequently possess the right to monitor all wants and needs of their children. Such economic dependence, of course, ties children to their parents in other ways. Parents maintain the right to supervise all of their single children's activities, regardless of the age of the child. Children have to ask their parents' permission to interact with any friend, to engage in recreational activities, to attend school, and even to leave the house at any hour and for any reason.

Of course, this is only the ideal situation, and there exist numerous exceptions. Children employ a variety of strategies to get past their parents' disapproval of their decisions and accumulate income of their own. However, all these strategies can usually only provide minimum relief from the parents' control, and they all need to be practiced in secret (thus again emphasizing the limitations to children's freedom of action). When children's disobedience is discovered, it can be sanctioned harshly, and it usually results in the exertion of even stronger control. The only children who gain total freedom from their parents before marriage are those who decide to sever more or less all ties with their families and move out of their parents' home, becoming fully economically independent. They can only maintain limited contact with their parents, and they typically lose their right to inherit from them.[2]

The extreme control exercised by parents is hard for children to endure. When this is accompanied by alcoholism and physical abuse, as it is often the case in the village, the children's situation becomes almost unbearable. Alcohol abuse among male villagers is typical.[3] Furthermore, within the village, excessive drinking is commonly associated with the physical abuse of wives and children.[4] Although this type of violence is, for the most part, socially accepted in San Pedro, it still understandably creates great hatred on the part of the victims, especially when it is done frequently or when it is caused by simple drunkenness. I have heard many complaints from both wives and children (but more frequently from the latter) on this matter. Many children have even told me of having completely lost respect for their fathers and to wish that their mothers would seek a divorce. This type of abuse, coupled with the lack of freedom that most children suffer, causes most young people to strongly desire leaving their parents' households. However, many fear social disapproval within their community or the loss of their parents' inheritance. Thus, they are left with only one socially acceptable alternative: marriage.

Indeed, in the village, marriage confers adult status on the bride and groom and allows them to achieve financial independence and greater freedom to make their own choices in all aspects of life. Although many young couples remain to live with the husband's parents for at least a few years (usually until the birth of their first child), they are now expected to be able to completely take care of themselves, whether they wish to be independent or not. One of the main requisites for marriage, in the eyes of most villagers, is to be able to work on one's own and support oneself. Both men and women need to demonstrate this ability during the early stages of marriage. During the engagement party, the prospective husband is required to provide and slaughter the turkeys that will be eaten during the celebration at the bride's house. Later, he will work for his future father-in-law every Sunday until the day of the wedding. The bride will then prove herself when, on the Tuesday following the wedding ceremony, she will be responsible for preparing all the meals of the day for all the guests completely on her own. Once the young couple has demonstrated that they can work on their own, they are expected to do so for the rest of their lives together, thus gaining much greater independence.

In spite of the hardships that it might represent, this acquisition of independence is strongly desired by youths, who wait anxiously to get married and often do so at very young ages. Just in my last five months of fieldwork, I witnessed the elopement of six teenage couples. In fact, most people get married before they turn twenty-five. The common desire to get married can be easily heard during conversations with young people, and it is expressed even more strongly during arguments between children and parents. Children often threaten to elope, or they otherwise daydream about it when they find their current living conditions disagreeable.

The Need for Separate Housing after Marriage

Even though marriage does confer greater independence onto young people, some tension between the newlyweds and the husband's parents often remains as long as the two couples are living within the same lot, which is the traditional arrangement until the younger couple can afford to build their own house. In this case, parents still feel as though they are partially supporting their son since they are allowing him to live on their property for free, and they believe that this privilege, coupled with their generally greater experience, still confers onto them some rights over him. However, the son, who has now been given social recognition as an adult, is typically less willing to stand his parents' control.

Furthermore, problems often arise between his mother and his wife. Stories of conflicts between these two are famous in the village and are the source of innumerable jokes. Indeed, a person who is fastidious and bossy is commonly called a *suegra* (mother-in-law). In addition, mothers often reprehend their unmarried daughters for failing to complete their tasks by telling them that once they marry, their mothers-in-law will not be as understanding of their mistakes as they are being now. Indeed, I have observed older women treat their daughters-in-law rudely, and just about every woman I interviewed on the matter has told me of problems with her mother-in-law (either presently or in the past). Young brides gain freedom from their parents only to end up under the control of their parents-in-laws. At the end of the wedding ceremony, the wedding godparents *entregan* (ritually "give away") the bride to the groom's parents. From that day on, she is considered their daughter, and as such, she is under their authority. Through marriage, she has earned adult status, at least in theory, but she will not be able to fully exercise her rights as an adult while she is still living under her in-laws' roof. Mothers-in-law typically try to substitute the labor of their real daughters, who by this time have often already married and left the household, with the labor of their daughters-in-law. They can become controlling and demanding, forcing their daughters-in-law to take time off from their own housework to help them out and insisting that they adopt their mothers-in-law's habits and preferences, abandoning those of their parents' household. Daughters-in-law often patiently accept a certain degree of abuse but nonetheless nurture some resentment toward their mothers-in-law. They have experienced a similar situation in their parents' household, but this is now harder to accept given their social recognition as adults. Thus, conflicts between the two generations are inevitable.

These problems are usually attenuated by the construction of a separate kitchen for the younger couple so that they can exercise more freedom in their domestic life. Daughters-in-law begin doing their own grocery shopping and their own cooking, thus avoiding interference from their mothers-in-law. Still, this is only a partial solution and usually a temporary one.[5] Parents themselves often prefer to see their married children leave the household, especially once they have given birth to grandchildren. With the birth of grandchildren, the household lot can become crowded and uncomfortable, and domestic work can increase dramatically.

Thus, it is in everybody's best interest to have the young spouses build their own separate house and move out of the lot of the husband's parents (although they typically move close by). Indeed, in many cases, young women will not even consider marrying somebody who does not already have his own house or is not at least in the process of building it. Many potential husbands are judged based on their houses or their available resources that allow the construction of a good house. Even if the couple is to remain with the husband's parents for a while (usually while the construction of the house is completed or while the husband is spending long periods abroad), the existence of a house where the younger couple can go guarantees them a certain degree of security. Furthermore, that they were able to build such a house symbolizes to others that they are fully capable of taking care of themselves and thus even more deserving of independence and respect. Consequently, the ownership of one's house becomes almost a requisite for marriage (or at least for a conflict-free marriage) and thus for the acquisition of total independence.

MIGRATION AS A ROUTE TO INDEPENDENCE

The unavailability of land, as well as lack of cash, can make the acquisition of one's own house difficult for young couples, except for those who inherit a piece of land or a house from their parents (and since most couples have numerous children, only a few of them are usually lucky enough to receive such inheritance). To make matters worse, the economic dependence of unmarried children on parents can make their accumulation of funds for housing purposes even slower. Parents are often sympathetic to their children's wish to build their own houses, but at the same time, they might also need them to spend their energies on other household projects (and some parents might even want to purposely delay their children's marriage to retain their labor within the household longer). Furthermore, few jobs in the village allow the quick accumulation of cash.

The best way to save enough money to build a house (and then get married and finally obtain economic independence) is to work outside one's community where jobs are more plentiful and the pay is higher. This place is usually the United States. However, this strategy is usually reserved for men.[6] When asked why they decided to migrate to the United States, most young men mentioned one or both of two reasons (aside from the general desire to earn more money). One is the need to earn enough money to get married (in other words, to sponsor the wedding and build a house for their bride), and the other is the desire to distance themselves from their parents in order to gain greater independence. Indeed, migration is considered a great way to both save money relatively quickly and gain greater freedom.

Most young men from the village travel (illegally) to the Fresno area in California, but an increasing number are now migrating to other areas of California as well as to Washington State, Colorado, Wyoming, and Utah. Most of them work in the fields harvesting fruit or in fast-food restaurants. A few find jobs in slaughterhouses or as gardeners or house painters. In any case, in the United States, they are able to earn in an hour what it would take them an entire day to earn in their home community. Living frugally during their residence abroad, they are able to save relatively large sums of money that they will then send home to their parents.[7] Furthermore, these sums will seem even greater in Mexico due to the difference in exchange rate.[8] Some of the money will be spent by the parents as they see fit, but migrants have the right to require that at least part of it is kept for their return home so that they can build their own house and sponsor a wedding. Parents cannot refuse to comply with the migrants' wishes in this case, as the desire to prepare for marriage is considered a noble and natural one in the village, and it is the parents' duty to support it or even encourage it (and parents should even help their children economically in this endeavor if their finances allow it). Parents who fail to do this are harshly criticized both directly and through gossip, but so are children who demand that all their remittances be saved for their return without providing their parents' household with some economic help. The accumulation of enough funds to sponsor a wedding and build a nice house, while still sending money to one's parents for their own use, tends to require several years of work abroad, as one usually needs at least three thousand to four thousand U.S. dollars to sponsor a wedding and at least eight thousand to nine thousand U.S. dollars to build a two-room brick house. Migrants often begin migrating around age fifteen (when they are first expected to become economically active) and are finally economically ready for marriage when they turn twenty-three or twenty-four. Some do not come back home at all until that day, and when they do, they expect to find a bride quickly and start putting their savings to work.

The case of Juan exemplifies the migration and remittance patterns just described.[9] Juan left the village for the first time when he was fifteen to harvest fruit in California. He had no pressing financial need to do so, as his family was relatively well off by village standards. However, he told me that he wished to be more independent both financially and in other aspects of his life, and he disliked his father's insistence to have him work in the household's bakery. He remained abroad for five years straight and eventually was able to legalize himself during the 1989 amnesty. His father was initially upset about his son's migration. Juan was the youngest of several siblings, many of whom had also migrated, and his father was hoping to have him stay home to cultivate the household's fields and help prepare bread for sale. However, Juan's regular remittances (which started about six months after he left) pleased him, and he eventually came to accept and even welcome his son's decision. Juan would send cash home through the telegraph each month, although sums varied according to his earnings (he would normally send between fifty and two hundred U.S. dollars). Juan's father used the money at his will, usually on medical bills and food but also to cover some expenses related to his bakery business. Juan soon started to also accumulate cash for his own purposes. He sent this to his mother, whom he trusted more to save money for him without spending it. He did not begin the construction of his house while he was abroad, since as the youngest son, he was expected to remain to live in his parents' house until their death and then inherit it. However, he did use the money he earned in the United States to sponsor his wedding, which occurred almost immediately upon his return to the village. He continued to migrate even as a married man, but he would return home every October to visit his family and cultivate the land that his father loaned him. He would leave again in April or May to work as a house painter in Colorado. During his absences, his wife would remain with his parents, although she had her separate kitchen, which helped alleviate conflicts. After his father's death, a couple of years later, Juan decided to build his own house, in spite of tradition and his automatic loss of his parents' house as inheritance. Again, he used money earned in the United States for this purpose. He told me that owning his own house, where he, his wife, and children could act freely, was well worth giving up part of his inheritance and risking to upset his mother. His mother was indeed displeased but soon found consolation in the presence of an unmarried son and daughter who lived with her at home. Juan's construction of a separate house, of course, did not only represent a loss of rights but also freed him from most of his obligations toward his mother, leaving the responsibility for her well-being to his two unmarried siblings.

In addition to providing economic advantages, migration allows young men to achieve greater freedom even before marriage. It represents sort of a relief from the strains of intergenerational relations that are so common in the village. Far from the supervision of their parents, young migrants begin to take more decisions on their own. They can choose a line of work they find more pleasing, select their own social activities and friends, administer their own earnings to some degree, and make at least some purchases on their own. Although most keep in contact with their parents, they can much more easily hide their true activities and earnings from them. Some even take this freedom to an extreme and virtually disappear for years, not even letting their parents know if they are alive. Indeed, many young men choose to migrate exclusively as a way of obtaining more freedom, with little real intention to save up money for their return home. This has been revealed to me many times during interviews with young migrants, and I have even heard it from youths currently planning their first migration.

However, migration is not a definitive way of gaining complete independence, unless one is willing to sever all ties with his home community and lose all social and economic rights there as well as the respect of his fellow villagers. Even when living in a different country, unmarried children continue to be considered part of their parents' household and maintain both duties and rights within it. As mentioned, they are obligated to continue contributing to the household economy. In addition, even the funds that the children are allowed to save in order to build their houses and sponsor their weddings should be sent home to their parents for safekeeping. In theory, the parents will not spend any of this money on themselves (other than in case of extreme emergency), and in addition, they will monitor the construction of the house, making sure that their sons' instructions are followed closely. However, the physical distance between them and their children makes it easier for them to abuse their role as safekeepers of the children's savings. As their sons can gain a little more freedom over their own resources because their parents are not present to monitor their earnings, the parents can more easily make up false emergencies that need the support of their children or they can exaggerate the prices of the house construction. Indeed, I was told about, and personally witnessed, many arguments and even physical fights between parents and children surrounding the alleged misuse of money sent from abroad.

The case of Eduardo is probably the most extreme but not a particularly unusual one. He migrated to California at an early age and worked in the fields there during almost his entire stay abroad. He did not return home for almost ten years, but during his absence, he communicated often with his family and sent regular cash remittances to his father. According to what he told me, he allowed his father to administer all the money, but he clearly stated that he expected his father to save some of it for the construction of his house. Indeed, he encouraged his parents to begin the construction as soon as possible, although he understood when his father claimed to prefer to wait to have his son oversee the work himself. Eduardo never told his father how much money should be saved for the construction of the house and how much could be used for other household expenses. He figured that strict rules could not be set, as emergencies and special circumstances could occur at any moment, but he trusted his father's judgment. However, upon his return home, he found that *all* the money he had sent had already been spent. He became extremely upset with his parents and his brother (who lived in their household the entire time). His parents argued that they had gone through very difficult times financially and simply could not save any of the money, but Eduardo was not at all satisfied by their explanations. He felt bitter, and popular opinion was on his side. Villagers gossiped that his parents and brother had used all the money supporting themselves instead of working for ten years. Their behavior ruined Eduardo's life. He was in his late twenties and had come home with the intention of finding a bride, but given his financial situation, he had to give up on that goal. Furthermore, he lost all interest in working and started to drink excessively. Every time he became intoxicated, he remembered his misfortune even more strongly and became enraged. In more than one occasion, he even physically attacked his father and brother.

Not only do children maintain economic responsibilities for their parents' household, but they are also obligated to regularly report their activities to their parents and ask permission before taking major decisions. Their behavior is monitored through other migrants residing in their host community, both in the form of gossip and direct conversations with the migrants' parents.[10]

Of course, as mentioned, there are cases of migrants who fail to meet these standards. At times, they are simply unsuccessful as migrants. They might be unable to find good jobs abroad; they might end up in jail, making their future trips to the United States even riskier; or they might even end up killed. A few fail to choose their "coyotes" (persons hired to smuggle migrants abroad) carefully and are robbed of all their possessions before they even cross the border. In addition, some migrants simply choose not to respect the village rules. Several migrants have admitted to me (usually expressing a high degree of regret and guilt) of having spent all their funds on alcohol, drugs, and other expensive forms of entertainment while abroad rather than sending the money home or saving it for their own use. At other times, they make much more responsible use of their resources, but they simply do not share them with people in the home community.

In any case, these migrants automatically lose most of their rights in their home community, including any inheritance they might otherwise have received from their parents. They might gain total independence, but they will have to exercise it mainly abroad. This is the case of Francisco. He left the village in his late teens and went to work in a restaurant with two of his brothers in Utah. During the first few years abroad, he sent remittances home more or less regularly. Then he visited the village with the desire to find a bride. He had not saved enough money for a wedding, and his house was not under construction yet, but he planned to finish accumulating enough funds for these two purposes during his next trip. In the meantime, he intended to ask for the hand of a woman in marriage and set the date of the actual wedding. After courting a few young women without success, he decided to give up on his search and leave again for the United States. Later, he married a Mexican American woman against his parents' wish and stopped sending all forms of remittances (with the exception of a few inexpensive birthday gifts) to his parents and other relatives in the village. Although he is legally married and even went through a Catholic ceremony, his mother still considers him single, as he did not choose a village wife. In addition, his parents are not including him in their plans to divide their possessions between their children. Since he has not visited the village in several years, nor has he built a house there, he is also not considered a true member of his home community at this point.

Thus, those who wish to remain full members of their home community and obtain independence and recognition as adults there need to keep respecting their parents' authority and keep contributing to their household economy at least until they get married (preferably to a village woman) and acquire their own house in the village.

REMITTANCES IN SAN PEDRO MÁRTIR

The Main Uses of Remittances in the Village

As discussed, young unmarried migrants from the village typically send some remittances home to be used by their parents as they wish and some to be saved for their own use. Once the migrants marry and become independent from their parents, they start sending remittances home to their wives, usually for her support and that of their children or to be saved for later use by the husband (but in theory for the benefit of the entire household). The resources sent home for the use of parents or wives and children (which might also be sent in kind) are commonly utilized for the purchase of consumer goods (although this is not the only use I have encountered). On the other hand, the remittances saved for the migrants' later use are most commonly (but not exclusively) reserved for the construction of fancy houses (even after marriage, if the young couple is still living in the lot of the husband's parents).

In the literature, both types of uses are often classified as simple forms of consumption with no income-generating potentials (although one should not forget that the construction of houses provides work for a vast number of people in the community and the surrounding areas, and thus it is a productive use of remittances in that sense). However, a more careful analysis of the San Pedro situation reveals that at least in the village these uses of remittances provide hidden economic advantages. The consumer goods are rarely purchased exclusively for personal use. On the contrary, the buyers typically aim at putting them to work to generate at least small earnings that complement their regular income or even establish small businesses as their primary form of livelihood. For example, I have observed cars, trucks, and vans being utilized as taxis to transport people, animals, and crops between the village and the nearby town of Ocotlán (a very profitable business in the village, if one is able to obtain a public transportation permit). In fact, of the eight village taxis, three have been directly purchased with remittance money, and in two other instances, vehicles were purchased within households that received remittances from members temporarily residing abroad. Tractors can also be rented out (besides being used to increase one's own agricultural productivity), and the same is often done with a variety of other consumer goods, such as televisions, videocassette recorders, washing machines, and the like. In addition, the villagers who purchase a phone tend to set up public phone booths in their houses, while those who buy a refrigerator can then start selling cold drinks, ice, ice cones, and a variety of perishable snacks. Those who can afford both a refrigerator and the construction of a small extra room in their house often open *tiendas de abarrotes* (small groceries stores; in the village, they also commonly serve as bars). Those who own a still or video camera are frequently hired to record important celebrations, such as weddings and baptisms. Often, even the simple purchase of an electric shaver can be enough for one to start working as a barber.

These uses of remittances are frequent in the village. One example is that of Valentín, who purchased a refrigerator and paid for adjustments to be made to one room of his mother's house (such as the opening of a door onto the street) so that she could open a little store right in her home. He saw these expenses as a partial substitution for the remittances he had been regularly sending his mother before, as she could now earn a small income of her own without much extra work (she could continue her regular activities within the home, interrupted only briefly by the arrival of clients at the store). Similarly, Artemia received a phone as a gift from her son, who also paid the initial installation fee. He meant the gift as a way for the two of them to remain more easily in contact, but Artemia found an even better use for it. She had a little wooden "phone booth" built and furnished it with her new phone, a wooden shelf, and a chair and started encouraging neighbors and family to come make phone calls at her house for a fee. She charges one peso per minute in addition to the cost of the call. She also gives out her phone number so that villagers can receive phone calls at her house, and she walks to people's homes to let them know when someone is calling them (she charges ten pesos for this service). Since the majority of villagers do not own a phone and the privacy of Artemia's phone booth is greatly appreciated, she now has many clients. Furthermore, this activity takes little time off Artemia's regular schedule and does not require much physical effort. Finally, Crispín brought a video camera with him to the village the last time he came for a visit. He mainly planned to record a large fiesta that was to take place at his sister's house so that he could take the video back with him to California and show it to his siblings who lived there. He also decided to tape a few weddings that occurred during his stay in the village. He then offered the videos to the parents of the bride and groom, who always happily accepted to purchase them. Soon more people started to actively seek his services, and they started providing him with food and drinks during the wedding, in addition to cash, in exchange for his work. He did not make a living this way, but he did accumulate some useful extra funds. Other people learned from his experience and started to provide the same type of service after Crispín went back to the United States. Some even began to specifically ask for video cameras as "gifts" from their migrant relatives abroad. Since celebrations are frequent in the village, there are many opportunities to make money in this way.

Similarly, the use of remittances for housing purposes brings about economic advantages greater than the simple fulfillment of a need for shelter—in other words, people might benefit from spending large sums in building such a house even if they do not intent to reside in it. As discussed, the acquisition of one's own house is necessary to establish oneself as being economically independent, and thus it is best completed before attempting any other economic endeavor (this is true for migrants and nonmigrants alike). In addition, for migrants, a particularly luxurious house works as a symbol of success that can bring them a variety of other benefits.

Remittances and Housing

The Economic Advantages of Owning One's Own House

In the village, the main advantage of owning one's own house is that it enables children to marry and become independent (financially and otherwise) from their parents, relieving some of the strain that exists between the two generations. While under the authority of their parents, children cannot ensure that their economic needs and wants will be fulfilled nor that there will be a direct correspondence between the effort they put into their work and the economic rewards they attain. In the village, at least ideally, household members are not supposed to accumulate resources for their individual purposes (with the exception of funds intended to build a house, as discussed) but should instead pool all their earnings to have them redistributed by the household heads as they see fit. Although the household heads are supposed to take into consideration the needs and wants of all household members, they are typically more likely to prefer to fulfill their own or those of a preferred child first. Thus, children might be working hard and still not be able to meet their own personal goals, while seeing the resources they have accumulated be utilized to satisfy somebody else's wishes. Only once they start a household on their own can they start making sure their needs and wants are fulfilled to their satisfaction (and even utilize the labor of other household members to that end as their parents have done with their labor before). Furthermore, they will be no longer responsible for the well-being of their parents and siblings (other than under special emergency situations).

Thus, young villagers see the construction of one's own house as an important investment. It allows them to marry and gain economic independence and then start investing their own resources in other ventures of their choice. If they were to make these other investments *before* the construction of one's house, they could not dispose of their earnings as it suited them, nor would such earnings be necessarily utilized to their best interest. Such investments, from their point of view, would be wasted. The construction of one's house is the investment that allows them to later benefit from other ventures. This is one reason behind the existence of a relatively large number of empty houses in the village (currently, about 11 percent of all houses in the village remain empty for most of the year, while the owners reside outside the community). Many migrants build houses in the village even when they do not intend to inhabit them, because they are simply trying to establish their economic independence and their status as adult members of the village.

This is stated frequently and explicitly by young men. For example, Carlos told me, "Cuando aceptas vivir en casa de tus padres, también debes de atenerte a las consecuencias. Él [tu padre] puede mandarte y no puedes decir nada. Si él dice, 'vete al campo,' debes obedecer. Si él dice, 'préstame ese dinero,' debes dárselo. También tu mamá puede mandar a tu vieja; puede ponerla a ser tortillas cuando quiere. Pero si tu ya tienes tu casa y tu cocina, ya puedes ver por ti mismo" [When you accept to live in your parents' house, you have to abide by the consequences. He (your father) can order you around and you cannot say anything. If he says, "Go to the fields," you have to comply with it. If he says, "Loan me that money," you have to do it. Also, your mom can order your wife around. She can have her make tortillas whenever she wishes. However, if you already have your own house and your own kitchen, you can decide for yourself]. Another young man, Luis, told me that he decided to migrate with his wife (his is actually a case of internal migration to the Oaxacan coast) because he was tired of earning money that would go to pay his parents' expenses. Away from home he is able to administer his own money. He told me that he would come back home only once he could afford to build or buy his own house. His parents wanted to leave their house to him in exchange for his assistance during their old age, but he refused. He told me in confidence that he could not handle remaining under the control of his parents any longer and that the type of sacrifice requested was not worth receiving a better inheritance.

One would expect, then, that migrants prefer to utilize their savings (part of their remittances) to build houses before attempting any other type of investment. Indeed, this tendency does not apply exclusively to migrants. All young couples in the village aspire to building their own houses to enjoy the benefits described here, but migrants typically have an easier time accomplishing this (and doing so relatively quickly). Furthermore, migrants usually distinguish themselves by building houses stylistically different from those of other villagers (and usually of better quality), and this often brings them further economic and social advantage.

Traditional versus Migrants' Houses in the Village

Most traditional houses in the village are made of either adobe or reed grass (or a combination of the two), often with metal or thatched roofs and unpaved floors, although wealthier houses often have cement floors. They all contain a central yard, where most of the daily activities are conducted and around which are built a few (usually one to three) bedrooms and an open-fire kitchen (always made of reed grass). Another common feature of traditional village houses is the *corredor* (literally, corridor), a roofed area with only one wall (or at times none) where crops are typically stored and prepared for market sale. Farm animals are usually allowed to graze freely around the yard and even to enter the bedrooms. The bathroom, when present, is built far from the main house construction, and it never includes a plumbing system. An example of this traditional type of house, belonging to a family of low economic means, is presented in figure 6.2.

However, in the last few years, the many migrants who have resided or are currently residing abroad began to build a new style of house in the village. These migrants typically prefer to construct houses that (in their eyes) resemble more closely those they have observed while in the United States and that

FIGURE 6.2.
External view of a traditional house built with reed grass

are generally of better quality. All migrants' houses are made of bricks with cement roofs and tiled (or cement) floors. Most have at least two stories. The internal yard is often absent, although a back or front yard is always maintained.
The number of bedrooms is usually higher (three to five), and the bathroom
is often built inside the main structure.[11] The open-fire kitchen made of reed
grass is still present (usually built on the side of the main house), but it is
complemented by a modern-style one furnished with at least a gas stove and
a refrigerator. Animals and crops are kept outside the house, in special enclo-
sures built specifically for them. Although not all migrants' houses are built
exactly in this fashion (only about 10 percent of all village houses present all
the features listed here), these characteristics are nonetheless common among
migrants' houses (about 30 percent of village houses present several of these
features, and virtually all of them were built by migrants).[12] Thus, we could
talk of a "migrant's style," although the owners themselves consider this to be
an "American style."[13]

The preference for such style is certainly due in part to the migrants having
acquired new tastes abroad, which they now try to reproduce in the home
community. However, I believe they are also purposely trying to distinguish
their houses from those of other villagers. Indeed the difference is immediately

obvious to any observer, and to the villagers it represents a difference not only in wealth but also in level of success, personality, and style of life.

The Symbolic Nature of Migrants' Houses

On my first visit to the village, the taxi driver who was taking me to my new, temporary residence insisted on first showing me what he considered a great tourist attraction, comparable to the ruins of Monte Albán and the church of Santo Domingo. He drove me by a large two-floor brick house (shown in figure 6.3), which was surrounded by thick brick walls. The building was painted with bright colors that could be detected from far away. It stood out among the modest reed grass or adobe constructions that were visible all around it. I later learned that this was the most luxurious of several migrants' houses built in the American style in the village and that it represented an ideal to be emulated by all migrants seeking social recognition. My self-appointed tourist guide told me that the owner of the house hardly ever visited the village but that he was remembered with pride by fellow villagers as somebody able to rise from the poverty of the village and reach wealth and success in a foreign land. The taxi driver, who was himself a circular migrant, dreamed of someday obtaining the same level of success.

FIGURE 6.3.
The most luxurious of all village houses built in the "American style." It represents an ideal to be emulated by all migrants seeking social recognition.

As illustrated by this anecdote, owning a house built in the American style has become a status symbol in the village. It equates to announcing to all observers that the owner is a successful migrant who has obtained great wealth abroad and, thus, in the eyes of the villagers, is likely to be highly intelligent, industrious, and trustworthy.[14] For this reason, one can typically gain the respect of other villagers through the simple construction of this type of house. However, it should also be noted that some villagers do feel more envy than respect for these successful migrants (as most feel toward successful nonmigrants), and indeed there has been at least one case of murder committed due to such envy.

Nonetheless, migrants can lose the respect of fellow villagers if they fail to acquire an American style house. It is common to hear people criticize a male migrant and doubt his abilities or general success by stating that he did not even build a small house in the village yet or that he only built one in the traditional style.

Furthermore, the status of "successful migrant" can help considerably in the establishment of little local businesses. Villagers tend to be more willing to work for or collaborate with such a person, as they expect him (or occasionally her) to succeed in the future as he or she has done in the past and to be able to help others to reach a similar type of success. This is important, as the availability of wage laborers is often low in the village. Also, a "successful migrant" finds it much easier to obtain loans from other villagers in order to start a venture, as he or she is expected to be able to repay the debt easily earning money abroad, even if his or her local business fails. Most important, "successful migrants" tend to attract greater numbers of clients. Villagers are eager to purchase the products or hire the help of these migrants, as the former expect the latter to provide high-level products and services (and villagers are often also curious to meet these almost-heroic figures and have the opportunity to hear their stories). Thus, the migrants' grocery stores, bakeries, *molinos* (corn mills), barbershops, and so forth, are typically filled with clients.

The importance of achieving the status of successful migrant, especially for men, can be better appreciated by looking at what happens to a migrant's social status when he is not able to obtain such success. Failure as a migrant can bring great social derision on a person. For example, one villager I met early in my fieldwork failed twice in his attempt to earn a fortune through migration: the first time he had to return home quickly because he simply could not get used to the new environment, and the second time, he was robbed of all his money before he even crossed the border. His misfortune was cause of much hilarity in the village and a reason of shame for his entire family. His wife and children would make fun of him constantly in my presence, and he lost all rights to control the activities of other household members. Indeed, when his daughter decided to migrate herself, he could do nothing to stop her. His wife soon left him, and he eventually committed suicide.

Of course, as mentioned, many migrants do not actually inhabit the fancy houses they build, nor do they establish businesses in the village, because they prefer to continue spending most of the year working abroad. While these migrants still gain social recognition, they cannot enjoy the economic advantages that this involves. In this case, they simply earn the potential of these benefits, and they might be able to put these to use later on in their lives, if they decide to settle more permanently in the village. Some migrants, however, do return to the village to inhabit their new homes and start new ventures. They might continue circular migration, but they return to their home community each year for several months, and their spouses and children remain there year round, almost as the migrants' symbolic presence in the village. They are the ones who truly benefit from the construction of the fancy houses just described.

A good example of how a house built in the migrant's style can bring economic benefits is the case of Juan, already partially described earlier. As I mentioned, he used part of his U.S. earnings to build his own house. According to what he told me, he purposely built it in a style that reminded him of houses he had painted in Colorado, but on seeing it, I recognized a strong similarity with the big house that the taxi driver had shown me on my first visit to the village. It is made of bricks, with cement roofs and floors (although Juan plans to refinish it with tiles). It lacks the traditional central yard, but it does have large front and back yards, all enclosed by a brick wall. It is also furnished with a modern kitchen, and Juan was in the process of building a second-floor bathroom with a water tank. When the house was in only the early stages of construction, Juan's social prestige was already increasing considerably. People were often commenting on his industriousness, and he started to receive more requests for being a godfather during various religious occasions in the village (something that can bring both social prestige and economic advantages while significantly draining a person of resources if done too frequently). When he purchased a tractor and began to rent out his services, he immediately acquired a large number of clients, in spite of the fact that several other people were already providing this type of service in the village. His sale of gasoline has also proved profitable. In addition, when he needs day laborers to work in his fields, he never seems to have any problems finding them, whereas numerous other people have complained to me about the difficulties of finding available workers. Of course, it is hard to know with certainty if the success of Juan's businesses and the ease he has in finding workers can be attributed exclusively to the prestige he gained through the construction of his house. However, he seems to think that this is at least a contributing factor, although he does not state it directly. He told me that people like to work with him because they know that he is skilled and hardworking. They can easily judge his qualities by simply observing his accomplishments. "Mira [look]," he told me while pointing at his house and the truck parked in the front yard, as if saying that those things exemplified his success. Some of his clients have also told me that they admire him for his economic abilities and success as a migrant and have presented his house, car, and tractor as evidence of such success.

Thus, in San Pedro Mártir, the construction of houses is a way of increasing one's chances of success in later economic ventures, as well as a way of guaranteeing that the profits of such ventures will be cashed in by the migrants themselves rather than by their parents. It could even be described as a form of "investment" in advertisement and in the establishment of economic independence.

CONCLUSION

A debate over the role of migration and remittances in the development of the migrants' home communities exists in the literature. This debate has been framed in terms of the productivity of the uses of remittances sent by migrants to their home communities. The tendency on the part of researchers has been to simply gather data on amounts remitted and direct uses of remittances, through interviews with the migrants in the host communities or the male household heads in the home communities. The uses listed by interviewees are then typically (and uncritically) divided into "productive" and "consumptive" categories based on an outsider's perspective. The sociocultural context in which these remittances are sent, received, and utilized is rarely analyzed, and no attention has been given to other economic advantages that can derive from remittance uses beside the increase in productivity. Presumably, the consumption of resources does not possess any productive potential. Most research conducted in this manner has as its conclusion that migration cannot lead to the development of the migrants' home communities.

Some scholars (Adams 1991; Conway and Cohen 1998; Stark 1978, 1980; Trager 1984, 1991) have criticized the methodology utilized in these studies and have started to show that more careful analysis can reveal a more positive situation and that remittances are indeed often utilized in productive or at least economically advantageous ways. This chapter is meant as a contribution to this more-optimistic side of the debate.

I have provided examples of productive and otherwise economically advantageous uses of remittances. Most important, I have demonstrated the importance of analyzing remittances within their sociocultural context, focusing on their actual and reported uses and on the statements of all members of migrant-sending households. Through an in-depth analysis of this type, I am able to show the following points:

1. What might appear to be conspicuous consumption of remittances to an outsider can actually have income-generating potential, as in the case of the purchase of certain consumer goods (such as refrigerators or phones) that are then used to start small businesses in San Pedro Mártir.
2. The simple dichotomization of remittance uses into "consumptive" and "productive" categories prevents us from appreciating the value of remittance uses that do not directly generate income but do have economically advantageous effects (ones that might even be more useful than the immediate increase in productivity). This is the case of the use of remittances for housing purposes in San Pedro as a way of achieving financial independence from one's parents. According to custom, constructing one's own house should be accomplished before attempting new productive activities so that later income will be disposed at one's wishes. Similarly, the construction of particularly luxurious houses does not in itself guarantee economic returns, but it can function as a form of advertisement of one's accomplishments that might later be useful in the establishment of small businesses or in conducting other economic activities (by attracting more clients, providing greater availability of labor, etc.).

3. The true understanding of the significance of remittances involves the analysis of both economic and sociocultural effects on home communities. Both senders and recipients of remittances give importance to the acquisition of social prestige and power in their communities as well as to the production of greater incomes. If we fail to understand this, we will not be able to fully comprehend the actors' behavior, and we will risk misinterpreting it.

Only once these three points have been fully considered can we begin to formulate opinions on the economic effects of remittances on migrants' home communities.

NOTES

1. I am currently conducting dissertation research on the uses of remittances sent to San Pedro Mártir by migrants residing in the United States. To date, I have spent a total of twenty-two months in the village, spread out over a period of almost three years. I have selected six village households for intensive study, but I have also conducted in-depth interviews with members of thirty-two other households and collected extensive data about the village as a whole. Data have been gathered through participant-observation, direct observation, both informal and unstructured interviews, the drawing of house maps, and archival research.

2. I have also observed a couple of instances in which unmarried children live in the same lot as their parents, while maintaining themselves economically independent and allowing little interference from their parents. However, this seems to occur infrequently and usually only when the children have already reached an advanced age and their parents are too old and weak to really exercise much control.

3. I have observed innumerable instances of excessive drinking while conducting participant observation in the village, and many interviewees have admitted to me that they drink excessively on a regular basis.

4. I have been told many stories of wife and child battery by the victims themselves (besides hearing an even greater number of rumors on this matter). Furthermore, a number of jokes and sayings surrounding this topic exist in the village, and it is common for mothers to warn their young daughters about marrying men who show any violent tendency. During the wedding ceremony, when it is time for relatives to

give their blessing to the young couple, it is common for people to advise the groom not to beat his wife and children "unnecessarily" and the bride not to run away to her parents' house each time she is beaten by her husband.

5. An exception to this rule is the case of the youngest son, who should inherit his parents' house and remain to live in their same lot (even if with a separate kitchen) until the parents' death so that he can take care of his elders. However, due to the problems described here, many of these children prefer to build their own houses and move out at marriage, even if this means giving up part (or all) of their inheritances and in spite of parents' opposition and general social disapproval.

6. Until recently, village women would rarely migrate abroad and only when accompanied by their husbands or fathers. In the last few years, an increasing number of women have started migrating on their own (although usually when they already have family awaiting for them in the host community), but this is still not done frequently and never with the intention of saving money for a wedding. Men, and not women, are responsible for sponsoring weddings and building houses for their brides. Women's favorite strategy to obtain economic independence from their parents is simply to find a husband who already owns his own house. Furthermore, women's migration is still seen with a certain suspicion, and women who do migrate often have a hard time later finding a spouse in the village, as life in the United States is thought to corrupt one's morals.

7. Most young migrants are able to limit their expenses in the United States by sharing small apartments with as many as ten other people, purchasing very little furniture and often eating free at work.

8. During my last fieldwork trip, from December 2002 to March 2004, the value of the peso fluctuated between ten and eleven pesos to the dollar.

9. All informants' names have been changed to protect their privacy.

10. The desire to avoid this type of control is the reason reported by several migrants for leaving the security of their first host community, where they already have a close network of friends and relatives, to venture into new unknown areas where no people from their home village reside and where their behavior will not be monitored so closely.

11. Plumbing systems are still absent, as they are too expensive in a village that lacks a sewage system. Water tanks, which need to be refilled periodically, are usually installed instead.

12. There are only three houses in the village that were built in a similar style by wealthy nonmigrants. Of course, there are also migrants who do not build houses in the American style, because either they cannot afford to or they are not interested in the advantages doing so can entail. However, this chapter is mainly focused on those who do and the reasons behind their decision to do so.

13. Many migrants refer to these houses as being *tipo departamento* (apartment style). When using this term, they are usually referring to houses that lack a central yard and in which one can move from one room to another without ever stepping outside, as in the apartments where they lived in the United States, which often represent their only experience with this style of housing.

14. Of course, a nonmigrant can also build a house in the same style (and three nonmigrants have done so, as mentioned), but the construction of such a house does not bring one the same level of recognition and respect, as it does not represent a symbol of one's success in a foreign land (which is considered a rare accomplishment worth of admiration). Furthermore, most wealthy nonmigrants are often thought to owe their money to inheritances and other circumstances that required little skill on their part or to have even acquired it illicitly. Nonmigrants are usually better off not advertising their wealth so that they do not bring upon themselves the envy of others. Indeed, George Foster's concept (1965) of the "image of limited good" seems to apply mostly to the villagers' attitude toward nonmigrants but not so much toward migrants.

REFERENCES

Abu, Katharine. 1983. The separateness of spouses: Conjugal resources in an Ashanti town. In *Female and male in West Africa*, ed. Christine Oppong, 156–68. London: Allen & Unwin.

Adams, Richard. 1991. *The effects of international remittances on poverty, inequality, and development in rural Egypt.* Washington, D.C.: International Food Policy Research Institute.

Ayers, Pat, and Jan Lambertz. 1986. Marriage relations, money, and domestic violence in working-class Liverpool, 1919–39. In *Labour and love*, ed. Jane Lewis, 195–219. Oxford: Blackwell.

Bentley, Jeffery W. 1989. Eating the dead chicken: Intra-household decision making and emigration in rural Portugal. In *The household economy: Reconsidering the domestic mode of production*, ed. Richard Wilk, 73–90. Boulder, Colo.: Westview.

Bruce, Judith. 1989. Homes divided. *World Development* 17 (7): 979–91.

Burki, Shahid Javed. 1984. International migration: Implications for labor exporting countries. *Middle East Journal* 38 (4): 668–84.

Cheal, David. 1989. Strategies of resource management in household economies: Moral economy or political economy? In *The household economy: Reconsidering the domestic mode of production*, ed. Richard Wilk, 11–22. Boulder, Colo.: Westview.

Conway, Dennis, and Jeffrey H. Cohen. 1998. Consequences of migration and remittances for Mexican transnational communities. *Economic Geography* 74 (1): 26–44.

Foster, George M. 1965. Peasant society and the image of limited good. *American Anthropologist* 67 (2): 300–323.

Grimes, Kimberly M. 1998. *Crossing borders: Changing social identities in southern Mexico.* Tucson: University of Arizona Press.

Instituto Nacional de Estadística, Geografía e Informática. 1995. *Oaxaca: Conteo de Población y Vivienda 1995: Resultados Definitivos.* Oaxaca, Mexico: Instituto Nacional de Estadística, Geografía e Informática.

Long, Norman. 1968. *Social change and the individual: A study of the social and religious responses to innovation in a Zambian rural community.* Manchester: Manchester University Press.

Massey, Douglass S., Rafael Alarcon, Jorge Durand, and Humberto Gonzales. 1987. *Return to Azatlán: The social process of international migration from western Mexico.* Berkeley: University of California Press.

Montes Mozo, Segundo, and Juan Jose García Vásquez. 1988. *Salvadorian migration to the U.S.: An exploratory study.* Hemispheric Migration Project, Center for Immigration Policy and Refugee Assistance. Washington, D.C.: Georgetown University.

Pahl, Jan. 1980. Patterns of money management within marriage. *Journal of Social Policy* 9 (3):313–35.

Poats, Susan, Hilary Feldstein, and Dianne Rocheleau. 1989. Gender and intra/inter-household analysis in on-farm research and experimentation. In *The household economy: Reconsidering the domestic mode of production*, ed. Richard Wilk, 245–66. Boulder, Colo.: Westview.

Rapp, Rayna, Ellen Ross, and Renate Bridenthal. 1979. Examining family history. *Feminist Studies* 5 (1): 174–99.

Reichart, Joshua S. 1981. The migrant syndrome: Seasonal U.S. wage labor and rural development in central Mexico. *Human Organization* 40 (1): 56–66.

Rempel, Henry, and Richard A. Lobdell. 1978. The role of urban-to-rural remittances in rural development. *Journal of Development Studies* 14:324–41.

Rubenstein, Hymie. 1982. The impact of remittances in the rural English-speaking Caribbean: Notes on the literature. In *Return migration and remittances: Developing a Caribbean perspective*, ed. William Stinner, Klaus de Albuquerque, and Roy S. Bryce-Laporte, 235–65. Washington, D.C.: Smithsonian Institution.

Saul, Mahir. 1989. Separateness and relation: Autonomous income and negotiation among rural Bobo women. In *The household economy: Reconsidering the domestic mode of production*, ed. Richard Wilk, 171–96. Boulder, Colo.: Westview.

Smith, R. 1992. Mixteca in New York; New York in Mixteca. *NACLA Report on the Americas* 26 (1): 39–41

Stark, Oded. 1978. *Economic-demographic interactions in agricultural development: The case of rural to urban migration*. Rome: Food and Agriculture Organization of the United Nations.

———. 1980. On the role of urban-to-rural remittances in rural development. *Journal of Development Studies* 16:369–74.

Tapia, Javier. 1995. Making a living: The microeconomics of U.S. Mexican households. *Urban Anthropology* 24 (3–4): 255–80.

Trager, Lillian. 1984. Migration and remittances: Urban income and rural households in the Philippines. *Journal of Developing Areas* 18:317–40.

———. 1991. *The city connection: Migration and family interdependence in the Philippines*. Ann Arbor: University of Michigan Press.

———. 2001. *Yoruba hometowns: Community, identity, and development in Nigeria*. Boulder, Colo.: Rienner.

Whittaker, William. 1988. Migration, remittances, and the Himalayas. *Pacific Viewpoint* 29 (1): 1–24.

Wilk, Richard. 1989. Decision making and resource flows within the household: Beyond the black box. In *The household economy: Reconsidering the domestic mode of production*, ed. Richard Wilk, 23–52. Boulder, Colo.: Westview.

7

Women Migrants and Hometown Linkages in Nigeria

Status, Economic Roles, and Contributions to Community Development

Lillian Trager

We are just sojourners here, whereas our place of abode is at home; attachment to home is always there.

—*Statement by Lagos-based woman who is a chief in her hometown, June 18, 1992*

In Africa, as elsewhere in the Third World, migration involves not only the movement of individuals from one place to another but also the maintenance of ties between those who move and those who do not. The extent, frequency, and importance of such ties vary considerably, depending on gender, socio-economic status, occupation, and the nature of social networks. In many societies of West Africa, migrants maintain ties not only with family at home but also with the home community itself, by participating in hometown-based organizations and contributing to local development. Return migrants often take on prominent leadership roles in their local communities.

Research on these issues has primarily emphasized the role of men in these processes, with the implication that women participate little in such linkages and development efforts in the African context. In this chapter, I argue to the contrary that the majority of women migrants, of all statuses and occupational groups, maintain some connection with family and kin in their home

225

communities, at least while close kin are resident there. These ties involve visiting; contributions of money and goods, both from migrants to those at home and from those at home to migrants; and participation in organizations based on place of origin.

In this chapter, I examine the interrelationships among women's status, their economic roles, and their participation in local-level community development among women migrants and return migrants in southwestern Nigeria. It is based on in-depth interview and survey data collected among migrants and return migrants in five communities in the Ijesa region of Yorubaland (the urban center of Ilesa, two medium-size towns, and two villages), as well as among migrants from those communities now resident in the large cities of Lagos and Ibadan.[1]

In the first part of the chapter, I briefly review literature on three interrelated issues: women in the migration process, rural-urban linkages, and the economic roles and activities of Nigerian women. I then examine data from the study area and argue that female migrants of high status and in professional occupations, like men of similar background, participate in hometown organizations and make substantial contributions to community development efforts. These activities in turn enhance the status of the migrants, who are seen as nonresident community leaders. On the other hand, women migrants with fewer economic resources who participate in informal sector occupations are less likely to be involved in activities in their own hometowns. They have neither the financial resources necessary nor the requisite status for being seen as community leaders or potential leaders. Return migrants from this group are not likely to be well known locally or to play leading roles in community organizations and development.

This chapter has implications for our understanding of the role of women migrants in the migration process and in local development activities, and it demonstrates the ways in which social status and economic role affect such participation. Female migrants, like male migrants, are seen as part of extensive social and economic networks linking rural and urban areas, with status and role in one place having implications for status and role in the other.

MIGRATION, WOMEN, AND RURAL-URBAN LINKAGES

In considering the involvement of migrant women in their home communities, I assume a complexity to the migration process in which rural and urban places are part of a single social field and in which migrants move among a number of different places and may have social networks and resources in several. The questions addressed here are not simply those of "Who migrates?" and "Do women migrate?" Rather, I address the issue of what happens during and after the migration process both to those immediately involved (the migrants) and to others with whom they have ties. I incorporate an understanding that women involved in migration, like men, may differ in their characteristics and that some may participate in a range of activities in their home communities and others may not. In addressing these issues, I focus on three interrelated themes: women and migration, rural-urban linkages, and the economic roles and activities of women. Earlier research on these themes provides the background and context for the present study.

Women and Migration in Nigeria

Most research on migration in Nigeria, as elsewhere in Africa, has focused primarily on men.[2] Perhaps this was due to the assumption that "migration by women until recently [in Nigeria] was primarily to join husbands" (Hollos 1991, 854). For example, P. K. Makinwa's comprehensive study (1981) of migration in Bendel State mentions that female migrants, like their male counterparts, tend to be young, and it includes an analysis of the fertility of female migrants in comparison with women of urban origins, but it provides little data or analysis of other characteristics of those females who migrate.

Those studies that do focus on women in the migration process have been largely concerned with the relationship between migration and women's status as reflected in education and employment characteristics. In his study of female migrants in southwestern Nigeria, Aderanti Adepoju found that urban migrants tend to be younger and better educated and hence to be employed in "diversified economic activities," as compared with rural migrants (1984, 74). Linda Lacey (1986), likewise, investigated the relationship between migration and economic opportunities. She argues that, unlike men, women do not improve their occupational status as a result of migration. She found that few women moved from what she terms "traditional sector activities" (such as trading) into professional, clerical, or skilled occupations and, further, that some women "even experienced downward shifts from the modern economic sector to informal sector activities such as trading" (16). This assumes, of course, that trade represents downward occupational mobility, whereas in fact both men and women in some regions of Nigeria choose self-employment in business and trade after a period of working in the formal sector and see such self-employment as a preferred occupation.

A more complex analysis of the relationship of migration to women's status is that of Marida Hollos (1991), who is concerned not simply with occupational status but also with the status of women in the household, as reflected in decision making and autonomy. She argues that it is not urban migration as such that leads to a change in women's status but rather educational and employment characteristics that determine whether a woman is part of a nuclear family urban household or whether she is part of an urban household similar in structure to rural households. According to her, it is the less-educated woman, usually working in an informal sector occupation, who has greater domestic status and power in contrast to the better-educated woman, whose public status may be higher but whose domestic autonomy is reduced.

Other studies that focus on specific forms of migration also demonstrate the complex ways in which migration may be related to status. Susan J. Watts (1983) shows that marriage migration to the city of Ilorin may improve the opportunities for women to engage in trade and other informal sector occupations, while in a contrasting case, Renee Pittin shows that some young Hausa women who engage in autonomous migration are able to "parlay their earnings into considerable wealth through shrewd investment, careful planning, and a great deal of hard work" (1984, 1308).

Like the study of migration in general, the research on women in the migration process in Nigeria is based largely on survey data and focuses on the individual migrant in her new, urban setting. Yet there is ample evidence to indicate that migration is not a simple one-way process, nor is it a process in which individuals engage on their own. The complexity of migration—involving social networks and connections in a number of different places, as well as moves of individuals and groups among several places over time—needs to be considered for a more complete understanding of the role of women in migration.

Rural-Urban Linkages

As the understanding of the complexity of migration has increased, more attention has been paid to issues such as circular migration and the role of migrants in their communities of origin. In other regions of the Third World, studies have focused on the connections that migrants maintain to families in their places of origin and to the ways in which migration is a part of family strategies of survival and mobility (Chapman and Prothero 1983; Hugo 1982; Trager 1988). I have argued that the migration of women is best understood in the context of such strategies (Trager 1984). Maintenance of ties with rural areas, including the rural community itself, has been recognized as being particularly important in Africa, and a number of studies have shown the ways in which connections with the hometown are maintained and utilized by migrants (e.g., Weisner 1976; Moock 1978–1979; Gugler 1971, 1991; Aronson 1971). Recent research on hometown associations also reflects the importance of the participation of migrants in local-level community development activities in their home areas (Barkan, McNulty, and Ayeni 1991; Honey and Okafor 1998; Trager 1998, 2001).

However, few researchers on rural-urban linkages in Africa consider the participation of women in these networks. As with migration research in general, there seems to be an assumption that women play a less-important role in maintaining the connections with family and community in their places of origin. Josef Gugler and Gudrun Ludwar-Ene argue that evidence from a number of countries indicates that women show "weaker attachment to the rural area" (1990, 10). On the other hand, a study of return migrants in southern Nigeria shows that both men and women tend to return to their hometowns before retirement (Peil, Ekpenyong, and Oyeneye 1988). LaRay Denzer and Nkechi Mbanefoh (1998) focus on the women's wings of hometown organizations run by men, arguing that women play relatively unimportant roles in these associations.

The type and extent of contact maintained seems to vary considerably, depending both on the specific context and the socioeconomic circumstances of the migrants. In Zimbabwe, for example, Ann Schlyter (1990) found that low-income urban women drew on contacts in the rural areas in times of crisis. On the other hand, in Bamako, Mali, both men and women send money back to their families in the village, and those who have lived longer in the city tend to send gifts to the village (Vaa, Findley, and Diallo 1989).

Further consideration of this issue necessitates examining the specific socioeconomic circumstances of those involved and recognizing that different types of migrants may participate in such networks in varying ways.

Economic Roles of Yoruba Women

The Yoruba of southwestern Nigeria are well known for their entrepreneurial and trade activities. Women's role in trade has been examined in terms of its importance within the local and regional economy (Trager 1976–1977, 1981) and in terms of its relationship to household and family organization (Afonja 1981; Sudarkasa 1973). While Yoruba women in rural communities also participate in farming, they tend to have an independent source of income through trade in both rural and urban areas. Economic change in recent years has affected women's participation in trade and other informal sector activities; in some cases, opportunities have expanded, with access to new sources of income-generating activities (Trager 1985). However, the Structural Adjustment Program of the past few years has increased the burden on rural and urban women (as well as that on men; Dennis 1991a, 1991b). Women, in particular, have fewer opportunities in the informal sector, while greater demands are placed on their income-generating capacities since there is a decrease in formal-sector and wage-labor jobs for men (Dennis 1991a, 100).

One question that arises in the current circumstances is the extent to which rural and urban residents rely on support from kin located elsewhere or, conversely, the extent to which people cut off ties with those elsewhere in order to reduce the demands on their limited incomes. The data that I consider in the following discussion only begins to address that question. By considering women migrants and return migrants in one specific set of communities and by examining their different socioeconomic and class statuses, we can begin to consider the complexity not only of migration itself but also of the continuing links maintained by those resident in different locales.

WOMEN AND MIGRATION IN IJESALAND

In this section of the chapter, I consider results from research begun in the Ijesa area of Yorubaland between October 1991 and July 1992 and continuing over varying periods throughout the 1990s.[3] The Ijesa form a Yoruba subgroup located in the eastern part of Yorubaland, and they include people with allegiance to the city of Ilesa, which is the traditional capital of the Ijesa kingdom, and a number of smaller towns, villages, and hamlets in the surrounding hinterland (see figure 7.1). As J. D. Y. Peel has pointed out, the Ijesa "only came to consider themselves 'Yoruba' in the course of the twentieth century" (1983, 15). The research took place in five Ijesa communities—the city of

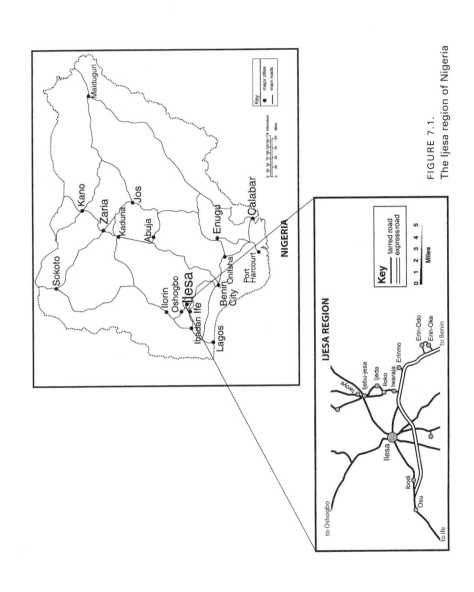

FIGURE 7.1.
The Ijesa region of Nigeria

Ilesa; two medium-sized towns, Osu and Ijebu-jesa; and two villages, Iwoye and Iloko.[4]

For the Ijesa, as for the Yoruba in general, a crucial concept that informs behavior and motivates action is the concept of *ilu*, translated in English as "hometown." The hometown is the place where one has kinship connections, usually the place of origin for one's patrilineage. It is, however, more than the place of origin; it provides a source of social identity and a web of social connections that influence actions regardless of where a person is residing. In general, the Ijesa believe that people with origins in a specific Ijesa town who live elsewhere "should associate themselves with the town, build houses and spend money there, and above all give it effective leadership in the competition of communities for the resources of the state" (Peel 1983, 260). The hometown is not the same as birthplace, and there is no assumption that an individual has actually lived for long periods in his or her hometown; nevertheless, the majority of Ijesa people consider the maintenance of ties with the hometown to be central to identity and action (see Trager 2001, 49–58, for a more extensive discussion of the concept of hometown). The following discussion demonstrates the current importance and dynamics of connections with the hometown.

The Ijesa, like many other Yoruba, have tended to be highly mobile, at least in the twentieth century. Evidence from other Yoruba areas shows that people move in and out of their hometowns, residing there for some period of time, moving to other places (including larger cities), and moving back to the hometown. For example, Sara S. Berry found that in one village over a period of seven years, the total population remained stable but 60 percent of the people counted the first time had left and been replaced by others seven years later (1985, 70; see also Aronson 1978). For the Ijesa in particular, mobility has been influenced by the fact that many people have worked as traders, known as *osomaalo*. Particularly in the first part of the twentieth century, the major reason for men to migrate out of Ijesaland was to work as *osomaalo*, meaning that they traded in cloth in small towns around Nigeria (Peel 1983, 148–59) and lived for extended periods in other regions of the country, usually returning home only for major holidays. Although few people today claim to be *osomaalo*, many of those interviewed in the current research had relatives who were. Although the term most frequently applies to men who worked as traders, many women are also involved in trade, and they too have been mobile in connection with their trading activities.[5]

Mobility for the Ijesa, as for the Yoruba in general, includes migration for a variety of reasons, from movement for jobs and education to following family members to a combination of reasons. It includes movement within the region, from smaller, more rural places to regional cities such as Ilesa; movement from the region to other large cities, such as Lagos and Ibadan; as well as movement to other regions of Nigeria and, in some cases, out of the country. As is clear in the following discussion, individuals move a number of times during the course of their lives; nevertheless, the length of time they stay in any one locale is relatively long, with the majority staying between two and five years (see Trager 2001, 59–72 for discussion of historical and contemporary dimensions of migration in Ijesaland). As is true in much of West Africa (see Koenig, this volume, chapter 2, for another example), migration takes place in a cultural context where mobility is more the expectation than the exception; however, such mobility is less common among women in other regions of West Africa.

The following discussion is based both on survey data collected in the five communities under study in May–June 1992 and on extended interviews carried out throughout the research period. While the survey focused on people who were currently residing in the communities under study, therefore including migrants, return migrants, and nonmigrants, the interviews provide case study material on people who are from the Ijesa region but who were not currently residing there. Furthermore, the survey was designed to provide information on a variety of characteristics of current residents in the communities, whereas the case study and interview material focused on people who were identified as being actively involved in their hometowns.

Women Migrants and Return Migrants in Ijesa Communities

A survey was carried out in five Ijesa communities in May–June 1992. In each community, sections of the town or city were delineated to include all types of housing and residences.[6] The survey includes data not only on the individual interviewed but also on other household members and on nonresident members of the family. However, the following analysis focuses on the individual data. A total of 281 people were interviewed in the five towns studied.

The following analysis is based on a portion of the survey data—that from the two medium-sized towns of Osu and Ijebu-jesa.[7] There were 119 respondents in those communities, of whom 66 are women. The 66 female respondents ranged in reported age from 18 to 105; the mean age was 47. Overall, 47 percent had no formal education; 29 percent had some primary school; and the rest were people who had at least some middle or secondary school. There is one university graduate in the sample. Of the total, 71 percent were married, while 22 percent were widowed. In terms of occupation, these respondents reflected the occupations typical of women in small- and medium-sized Yoruba towns: 59 percent were traders, and 21 percent were in other informal sector occupations, such as seamstressing and hairdressing. The remainder included farmers (8 percent) and women with no occupation, including a student, someone looking for work, one who termed herself a "housewife," and several others who either were retired or reported no occupation.

Most significant for the present discussion is that of these sixty-six respondents, only nine (14 percent) reported having lived in only one place during the course of their lives. The other fifty-seven—86 percent—have lived in more than one locale. They were either women who had been migrants and returned to live in their hometowns, or they were currently migrants who had moved to Osu and Ijebu-jesa from somewhere else. In other words, nearly every woman in the sample was involved in the migration process at some time in her life.

The rest of the discussion focuses on these fifty-seven respondents, thirty of whom were return migrants and twenty-seven of whom were current migrants. In the first part of this discussion, I consider both return migrants and current migrants as one group. I then consider whether there are differences between migrants and return migrants in terms of involvement in hometown affairs.

Of the fifty-seven women who were current migrants or return migrants, 72 percent were under sixty, and 28 percent were over sixty. Overall, 40 percent of the migrants and return migrants had no education; 32 percent had some primary school; and 28 percent had middle school or above, including six with secondary school certification and one university graduate. Of the total, 75 percent were married and 18 percent widowed. In terms of occupation, 58 percent were traders, and 25 percent were in other informal sector occupations; 7 percent were farmers, and 11 percent had no occupation.

In how many places have women migrants lived, and what kind of places are they? The majority lived in either three or four different places or, in other words, moved two or three times: 42 percent lived in three places and 28 percent in four places;[8] 12 percent lived in two places, and 18 percent reported having lived in five or more different places. The places in which respondents lived are spread throughout Nigeria and even beyond, but for most, their moves were to centers that were close to their current residences. Of the fifty-one who reported the location of their first move, seven (13 percent) moved to other towns in Ijesaland, and twenty-three (45 percent) moved to places in what was formerly Oyo State (now divided between Oyo State and Osun State); the latter include ten who moved to the city of Ibadan. Interestingly, only five respondents reported moving to Lagos, the capital of Nigeria, for their first move, but another five reported it as the place of their second move. Other moves include several locations in eastern and northern Nigeria, as well as Ghana (see figure 7.1.).

The most common type of reason that respondents gave for moving was family: 25 percent reported that their first move was to join or accompany their spouse, and 10 percent gave that as the reason for their second move as well. Other family reasons were for movers to go with their parents or to stay with other relatives and, for those who were older, to stay with their children; in all, 62 percent of first moves and 66 percent of second moves were due to such reasons. Overall, 18 percent of first moves and 22 percent of second moves were for work or trade, and 16 percent of first moves and 11 percent of second moves were to study or learn a trade. Similar responses were given by those who moved to Osu and Ijebu-jesa for the reasons why they left their hometowns and the reasons for their move to their current residence.

On the other hand, for those who were living in their hometowns (return migrants), the reasons given for their return home are more varied. While 9 percent stated that they came with their spouses, another 10 percent simply stated that it was time to return or settle at home. Still others reported financial problems or illness, and several reported that they returned because of specific problems where they were living, including being expelled from Ghana (two respondents) and religious conflict in northern Nigeria (two respondents).

In sum, in the two medium-sized towns of Osu and Ijebu-jesa, a large majority of the women surveyed have been involved in the migration process; most have lived in several different communities for varying lengths of time. Although their reasons for moving are largely based on family considerations, all have been involved in some type of occupation (including those who were currently not working) and, like Yoruba women in general, have earned income and participated in economic activities separately from the activities of their spouses. In fact, although they stated that they had moved for family reasons, the majority carried out their economic activities, especially trade, in whatever locale they were living and were not likely to comment on those activities, even when they were part of the context in which mobility took place.

The discussion to this point has included both women who were migrants to Osu and Ijebu-jesa from other places and women who returned to their hometowns after being migrants elsewhere. While all had been or were currently migrants, their current residential situation differed in significant ways, especially for the consideration of linkages with family and community. One might expect that those who had been migrants but were now resident at home would have been more involved in hometown activities than those who were living outside their hometowns. On the other hand, one might also expect those living away from home to have been more involved in visiting and sending things to relations elsewhere. The following section examines these issues by considering current migrants and return migrants separately.

Migration, Linkages, and Hometown Involvement

Among the fifty-seven women who participated or were currently participating in the migration process, thirty are women whose hometown is either Osu or Ijebu-jesa and who were now residing in one of those towns after having moved elsewhere. The other twenty-seven are women whose hometown is elswhere and who had moved to Osu or Ijebu-jesa from somewhere else.[9] The hometowns of those who are not from Osu or Ijebu-jesa are primarily located in the Ijesa region or nearby, eight (29 percent) are from other Ijesa towns, and seventeen (63 percent) are from Osun State or a neighboring state in southwestern Nigeria. Only two had come from places that are farther away, one from Kwara State and one from eastern Nigeria; in other words, there are no major ethnic or cultural differences within this group.

Table 7.1 examines data on the extent to which migrants and return migrants were involved in maintaining ties with family members residing elsewhere. For those who were return migrants, the issue considered here is whether they visited family members who did not reside in the hometown; whether those family members visited them; and whether they sent things to family elsewhere in addition to, or instead of, visiting them. For those who were current migrants, the question is whether they visited family who resided in the hometown, received visits from them, or sent things to them. As is clear from table 7.1, visiting was much more common than sending. Overall, 76 percent of return migrants and 100 percent of current migrants reported that they visited family, while 100 percent of return migrants and 93 percent of current migrants reported that they got visits from family elsewhere. In addition, 59 percent of current migrants reported sending things to relatives at home, but only 23 percent of return migrants sent things to relatives who lived elsewhere. The majority also brought things with them—usually money or goods—when they visited.[10]

It is clear from table 7.1 that both current migrants and return migrants maintain relationships with relatives elsewhere, with whom they exchange visits and goods. Women migrants, like men reported on in earlier studies, are clearly involved in visiting their hometowns and maintaining contact with family not only in the hometown but elsewhere as well.

Table 7.2 illustrates participation in hometown activities and ownership of property in the hometown. Among return migrants currently living in their hometowns, 50 percent were members of hometown organizations, compared to 41 percent of current migrants not resident in their hometowns. While 20 percent of return migrants had a house, only 4 percent of current migrants had built a house in their hometown. There are somewhat higher numbers regarding those who owned farms, and some had property elsewhere (including land). Finally, 23 percent of return migrants and 15 percent of current migrants reported having contributed to an activity in

Table 7.1. Contact with Family Among Women Migrants

	Return migrants[a] (n = 30)		Current migrants[b] (n = 27)	
	n	%	n	%
Visit family elsewhere	23	76		
Visit hometown			27	100
Family visit respondent	30	100	25	93
Send to family elsewhere	7	23		
Send to family in hometown			16	59

[a]Return migrants are women who had lived outside the hometown but returned to the hometown later.
[b]Current migrants are women whose hometown is outside the survey community and who had moved to the survey site from somewhere else.

Table 7.2. Participation in Hometown Activities by Women Migrants

	Return migrants (n = 30)		Current migrants (n = 27)	
	n	%	n	%
Belongs to hometown organization(s)	15	50	11	41
Has house in hometown	6	20	1	4
Has farm in hometown	8	27	5	19
Has other property in hometown	13	43	4	15
Has property elsewhere	3	10	5	1
Contributes to hometown activities	7	23	4	15

their hometown, primarily by donating money for a project, such as the building of a school, town hall, or palace.

Given the data presented here, it appears that women participate to a limited degree in hometown activities. Relatively few have built their own houses or contributed to local projects; on the other hand, 50 percent of return migrants belonged to at least one hometown organization (and some belonged to several). However, this data must be viewed in light of who the women in the sample were: they had relatively low levels of education, and they worked in occupations, primarily trade, that although potentially lucrative, most often were not. For the most part, then, these were not women who were likely to have money available for acquiring property or for contributing extensively to hometown activities. That they did participate in some ways—by joining hometown organizations, for example—is therefore significant.

Lagos-Based Ijesa Migrants

At this point, it seems that while women are involved in migration in the Ijesa area and that many maintain ties with family and relatives living elsewhere, fewer are involved in community-based activities in their hometowns, whether they are living in those communities or not. However, broadening the set of people studied to include those who are based outside of the hometown and readily identified as being active in it provides a different view of the situation.

I turn now to consider data from case studies of women who migrated from the Ijesa area to Lagos; all had been living outside Ijesaland for long periods but had retained connections with their home communities. Unlike the people considered in the preceding section, those discussed here were selected through network sampling. During the course of interviews in the communities under study, I asked for names of individuals from Ijesaland and of Ijesa organizations in Lagos and other large cities.[11] Initially, I was primarily referred to men and men's organizations. However, after some time, I was given names of a number of key women as well as introductions to several women's organizations. I followed two procedures in obtaining data on these women: I carried out extended interviews with those identified as leaders, and I circulated written questionnaires through the organizations to reach a wider number of respondents. I also attended meetings of several organizations in Lagos and met some of these same individuals at events in Ijesaland. The following discussion is based on the information obtained from eight women.

All of those considered here were already identified as being involved in some way in Ijesa activities. The characteristics of these women are considered later. It is clear that they differ in significant ways from most of those in the samples taken in the hometowns. These differences not only derive from the simple fact that the women were currently living in Lagos but involve a variety of socioeconomic characteristics. Overall, the women form a set of women who, like many men of similar status and background, were involved in Ijesa affairs in multiple ways and for whom the connection to their hometown remained important despite the fact that they had long lived elsewhere and may never actually return to live in Ijesaland.

Of the eight women considered here, six regard the city of Ilesa as their hometown, while one is from Osu. One other is not from the Ijesa area at all; rather, her husband is from Ilesa, while she is from Lagos. However, she is active in Ijesa activities, viewing her husband's hometown as her "home," along with the city of Lagos. Only four were actually born in Ilesa, and two others spent part of their childhood there, returning when their parents decided to do so. One has never lived in Ilesa, having been born in Lagos and living there essentially all her life, except for a period when she studied overseas. The oldest of these women, who was in her late seventies, first came to Lagos in 1926, although she later spent some time working back in Ilesa before returning again to Lagos. The woman whose husband is from there also lived and worked there briefly before her marriage.

Six of the women under consideration are between the ages of forty-five and sixty, and the other two are over seventy. They had all lived in Lagos for long periods of time. One woman, now forty-six, had lived there for twenty-two years, while those who were in their fifties and sixties had all lived there more than thirty years. Like the two in their seventies—the one who came to Lagos in 1926 and the other, who had always lived in Lagos—these women had essentially spent their entire adult lives in Lagos. Further, they had left Ilesa even earlier, having traveled out of their hometowns both for education and for work before their marriages. All except the oldest had lived elsewhere in Nigeria, and three, including one of those in her seventies, had studied in England.

The educational and occupational backgrounds of these women are remarkably similar. Of those who were between forty-five and sixty, all but one had specialized postsecondary education in teacher training; the other finished secondary school but did not receive additional education. However, she, like the others, worked for some time in a formal sector occupation; the woman with only secondary school worked as a secretary, while the others worked as teachers. Likewise, the woman in her late seventies received specialized training in nursing and worked for a short time at a hospital in Ilesa when she was young. The other woman in her seventies is more highly educated, having received medical training and having then worked for many years in government as a doctor. While all had worked in formal sector occupations, only one, a teacher, continued to do so. The doctor was retired but involved in numerous organizations, including ones that drew on her medical experience. The other women were all in business, with several stating their current occupation as "trading" and others in catering and book selling. One, a widow, took over her husband's business when he died, about twenty-five years ago. Although their occupations may be termed informal sector occupations, they are different in crucial ways from the informal sector occupations of those women who were traders in the medium-sized towns of Osu and Ijebu-jesa, involving greater capital investment and leading to considerably better incomes (see Trager 1987).

It should be clear from the description that the set of women considered here are people who were established in Lagos and who had been, in broad terms, successful there. Given their long residence in Lagos and their educational and occupational backgrounds, one might well expect that they would have little reason or motivation to remain in contact with their hometowns. However, the reverse was the case.[12] All of these women visited Ijesaland regularly. With the exception of the doctor, who went only occasionally and mainly for special events, the others reported that they went to Ilesa at least several times a year, with three stating that they went monthly and one stating that she went every two weeks. All, including the ones who did not go frequently, had actually been in Ilesa at some time in the previous three months, and most had visited during the month when they provided the data (June or July 1992). Despite the fact that their own immediate families (i.e., children) were largely resident in Lagos and that their parents are dead, all reported visiting home to see relatives and to attend a variety of events, including weddings and funerals. One woman pointed out that she had made a policy of visiting her father every two weeks for the five years before he died, because she "didn't want to wait until he died and then just go home to bury him."

But their involvement in Ijesaland was not limited to visiting relatives there and attending social events. Four of the women had houses in Ilesa, and a fifth was building one. This includes the woman in her late seventies who has lived in Lagos since 1926, as well as the woman whose husband died a number of years ago. None reported having their own farm there, but two referred to their fathers' farmland; further, four reported having land there, including the woman who had lived her entire life in Lagos, who stated that she had bought land in Ilesa and was thinking about establishing a farm on it.

Even more significant is these women's involvement in hometown organizations and activities. All were members of at least one Ijesa organization, and several were members of more than one. For example, one woman was active in a woman's organization, which she had helped to form in the early 1970s; she was a member of a recently formed organization that included both men and women and was based both inside and outside Ijesaland itself; and she was a representative to the Council of Ijesa Societies in Lagos. In addition, she had recently been installed as a chief, having taken a traditional chieftaincy title. While she is no doubt one of the most active, the others tend to have multiple involvement in organizations, including social and service organizations, church organizations, and chieftaincy organizations. Three of these women have been given traditional chieftaincy titles and are therefore members of the Ijesa Council of Chiefs in Lagos, which includes all Ilesa chiefs—both men and women—who are based in Lagos. The oldest woman in this set is the head of an organization of Ilesa women in Lagos; a member of several church organizations, including ones in Lagos and Ilesa; and a chief.

With their organizational commitments, these women were frequently called on to contribute to activities in Ilesa and Ijesaland. All had made monetary contributions in the recent past. For example, two reported contributing to a development fund, and others said that they have contributed at various fund-raising and launching ceremonies. Still others had made even more substantial financial contributions, including one woman who was helping to pay the salary of teachers in an adult education program organized by one of the churches in Ilesa.

Their efforts tended to go beyond monetary contributions to involvement, both formally through their organizations and informally through their personal social networks, in a variety of other issues in the Ijesa area. During the period of the research, there were many meetings and discussions in Ijesaland concerning disputes among various chiefs; women's organizations, like men's organizations, sent delegations as part of efforts to settle these disputes. Women were also involved in efforts at community development in Ilesa and the Ijesa area more generally. Two of the women's organizations had purchased land in Ilesa with the intention of establishing something for children and students. As individuals, several had been involved in discussions with other people from Ijesaland to try to find ways to promote economic development there. In general, the women interviewed focused on the importance of assisting women in their hometown; one emphasized the importance of education, another stated that she would like to see more "industrial development involving women."

Like many men of similar status and backgrounds, the women discussed here were involved in hometown affairs in multiple ways and at many levels. They shared a personal commitment to the place, which is in part an emotional tie; as the oldest stated, "No matter where you are, you have to continue to maintain contact with home." For the most part, they continued to have relatives in Ijesaland, even though their immediate families were not there, and they felt an obligation to maintain ties with those relatives. Even though they had long lived outside, most had built houses at home or invested in other ways, such as through the purchase of land. They belonged to hometown organizations and contributed financially and in other ways to hometown activities. The participation of women, like that of men, has important implications for both the migration process and local development.

DISCUSSION

In recognizing the complexity of migration, scholars have increasingly sought conceptual and methodological tools for helping to understand that complexity. One crucial aspect of this development has been to consider individual migrants within broader contexts of family and community and to examine the ways in which migrants continue to be tied to, and maintain connections with, people and institutions in a variety of locales. Emerging out of much of the research in recent years is a sense that, in many situations, individual migrants form a part of a nexus of relationships that span rural and urban areas. We need to understand that nexus in order to comprehend the actions and motivations of many of the people involved in the migration process and to consider the implications of those actions for other societal processes. For example, we too often consider the "rural" and the "urban" to be entirely separate, with developments in one type of locale bearing little relation to those in the other. How, then, are we to understand what is immediately apparent to anyone traveling the roads of southwestern Nigeria on a Friday afternoon or a Saturday morning—the long lines of cars leaving Lagos traveling to smaller cities and towns of the region? And, even more significant, how do we understand the contribution of large sums of money at a launching in a small rural community made by visitors from Lagos who spent four hours traveling on a weekend during a fuel shortage and were not sure whether they had sufficient fuel to return?

The data considered in this chapter contribute to our understanding of the migration process and to our considering some of the broader implications of that process in one particular setting and among one set of people. In this discussion, I want to briefly examine the following issues: the role of women in the migration process; the importance and extent of maintenance of hometown ties; and the relationship of migration, multilocality, and women's status.

Women and Migration

This study moved beyond much of the earlier literature on women and migration in Nigeria in demonstrating that there was high mobility among the women studied in the Ijesa area. Of those surveyed in the two medium-sized towns of Osu and Ijebu-jesa, 86 percent had moved at some point in their lives, and the majority had moved more than once. These include women who had returned to their hometowns after having lived elsewhere, as well as women who had migrated to the towns from other places. While it is not surprising that women had returned to their hometowns to live, it is noteworthy that this occurred at a number of different points in the life cycle; some had returned when they were elderly, but many were still quite young, and it was quite possible that at least some of them would move again at some stage in their lives. It is also interesting that there were considerable numbers of in-migrants to the towns studied, making clear that migration among the Yoruba did not simply involve movement to big cities but also included smaller cities and medium-sized towns.

The data also indicate that women involved in the migration process in southwestern Nigeria had come from a variety of socioeconomic backgrounds. Most of those in the sample in the two towns had little or no education, and nearly all worked in informal sector occupations, with trade as the dominant occupation. On the other hand, elite women were also involved in migration, as is clear from the network sample of Ijesa women based in Lagos, who were highly educated and who had worked at some point in formal sector occupations, although most were now engaged in small business.

While most of the women included in the survey data moved for family reasons, education and work were important motivations for migration, especially among those who were better off. However, given the economic independence of Yoruba women, it would be misleading to assume that they moved simply because they had to follow their spouses; in fact, older women frequently lived apart from their spouses, and some of those interviewed were return migrants who had come back to their hometowns while their spouses remained elsewhere.

Overall, it is evident that migration is a common process for Yoruba women in general, as it is for Yoruba men. It is perhaps the rare woman who has not lived for some period of her life in a community other than her hometown; in fact, in the sample, it is only among the oldest women that one finds some who had never lived anywhere else.

Women and Attachment to Home

The simple fact of migration, however, tells us little about the extent to which women migrants maintain ties with people elsewhere. Is there a "weaker attachment" to home among women than among men, as Josef Gugler and Gudrun Ludwar-Ene (1990) have suggested? Do women participate in hometown organizations primarily because of their connections through men, with their main involvement in women's wings of men's organizations, as proposed by LaRay Denzer and Nkechi Mbanefoh (1998)?

The data considered here indicate that "attachment" is quite strong. Among those in the survey who were migrants currently living outside their hometowns, all reported that they visited their hometowns, as did all of the Lagos-based women in the network sample. Likewise, most of those who had returned home to live reported that they visited family elsewhere, and all stated that family members currently residing elsewhere had come to visit them.

There are many different types and degrees of attachment. The women in the sample survey were less involved in a variety of hometown activities than might be expected. As we have seen, among both those who had returned home to live and those who were still living outside their hometowns, there were varying rates of participation and involvement. While it is true that 50 percent of return migrants were members of hometown organizations, only 23 percent reported contributing to hometown activities. Likewise, 40 percent of current migrants belonged to hometown organizations, and 14 percent contributed to an activity at home.[13]

On the other hand, those in the network sample participated in a variety of activities in their hometowns. They owned houses and land, belonged to organizations, made financial contributions, and were engaged in efforts to improve the home community. Three have taken chieftaincy titles.

What was the basis for the range in participation and "attachment" to home among those studied, including both those in the survey sample and those in the network sample? For the Lagos-based women in the network sample, their own view of attachment to home was expressed in the statement quoted at the beginning of this chapter: "We are just sojourners here, whereas our place of abode is at home; attachment to home is always there." This may seem to be an emotional expression of an attachment to a place that they left long ago. And certainly that is one element of the connection. But the degree to which people travel back and forth and contribute in substantive ways suggests that it is not simply an emotional and symbolic link. Rather, for these women, as for men of similar status, their involvement in hometown affairs is an important aspect of their overall status. I would argue that while some degree of attachment and involvement is important for just about everyone, the extent of that attachment varies with socioeconomic status; it is much more crucial for those of higher status to be visibly involved at home. This issue is discussed further in the next section.

Multilocality and the Status of Women

The notion of attachment to home makes clear that there are a variety of connections that span location. For the Yoruba women considered here, the locales in which people were involved included not just "rural" and "urban" (i.e., large city) but a range of places in between—smaller cities such as Ilesa as well as medium-sized towns like Osu and Ijebu-jesa. People participated in social activities and organizations in more than one place and moved regularly between these places. In this discussion, I emphasize the ties with hometown, but those currently resident in urban areas such as Lagos were also incorporated into activities and institutions there as well. For example, women in the network sample described Lagos-based church organizations in which they participated. The point here is simply that we cannot fully understand the social organization and behavior of migrants by focusing on what they did only in the place to which they have moved. Nor can we understand the impact of migration by focusing only on the social structure of the city.

In other words, we need to examine this population in terms of its *multilocality*, that is, the attachment to and participation in social and economic activities in a number of places.[14] I would argue that multilocality, and the interaction among activities in a number of different places, is significant in considering the question of the status of women.

Among the women considered in this study, the process of migration per se had little effect on their status. This is not surprising, considering that nearly all women in the communities studied participated in migration at some point. Therefore, the act of migrating does not, in general, lead to a change in status.

Rather, what is interesting and important about migration and the resulting multilocality of women is that there is a relationship between status in one locale and status in other locales and that those of high status in particular can enhance that status through their participation in hometown activities. I would argue that for the women in the network sample, involvement in hometown affairs was an important aspect of their overall status. As for many men of similar socioeconomic background, recognition of their success requires that they are seen as playing a role in their hometowns. To be a person of importance means that one's status is recognized at home, and part of the process of achieving that recognition is carried out by engaging in activities that are seen as having significance to the home community. This includes participation in a range of activities: membership in organizations, giving contributions for special events, assistance in settling disputes, and so on.

It is significant that three of the women in this sample had been given chieftaincy titles and are clearly proud of those titles—especially given that these are "traditional" titles, not just honorary ones. As one woman explained to me, these positions are still important "at the grassroots," so she therefore decided that it was worthwhile to become involved in the chieftaincy institution. Not everyone shared this view; there were many elite men and women who avoided being given chieftaincy titles and who stated that they would not accept them if they were offered. However, as this woman indicates, it is an institution that is still viewed with considerable importance by many and one that has considerable status.

For these women, then, their success and status achieved through migration enhanced their status and recognition in their hometown and led to participation in a variety of hometown activities. In this, they are like many men of similar backgrounds, although it is probably the case that more men than women are engaged in such activities and that the participation of men is seen as being, in general, more important than that of women. For example, one elite woman who returned to live in Ilesa with her husband explained to me that she stayed in the background so that her husband could play an active role in hometown affairs and so that they were seen as speaking with one voice; she viewed her role as a supportive one played behind the scenes.

On the other hand, women with fewer financial resources are less likely to participate in hometown activities while they are still migrants, and when they return home, they participate in more limited ways than do those who are elite. They have neither the financial resources nor the requisite status for being seen as community leaders, although in some cases they do take on leadership roles in the organizations to which they belong, and in some cases, they take traditional chieftaincy titles, as in the case of one woman in the survey. Nevertheless, they maintain their status in family and kinship settings by engaging in exchange with family and kin elsewhere, and they make at least token contributions to community activities as well.

In a society such as Nigeria, and elsewhere in Africa, where the commitment to the hometown remains strong, the linkages to place and those among people in different places form the crucial web of connections that influence individuals' actions and behavior. Hence, all those cars leaving Lagos on Fridays and Saturdays: they carry people going to visit relatives at home, people attending ceremonies at home, and people going to the ceremonies of friends in the friends' hometown. There are strongly felt obligations to participate in such activities; one can hear discussions among Lagos residents about how they met a variety of often-conflicting obligations on a given weekend, in some cases by traveling to a number of different places.

These obligations probably affect members of the elite most, in that they are the ones who are expected to appear and participate in a range of social events and for whom it is most important to do so. But they affect everyone to some degree, as is clear by the fact that all of the current migrants in the survey in Osu and Ijebu-jesa reported visiting their hometowns. The participation of elite in hometown social networks is not just a matter of attending a variety of ceremonial events. Rather, both men and women in this set of people are contributing in substantial ways to local development activities in their hometowns. They do so primarily by contributing money to development funds and at launchings, as described by the women in the network sample. Some go further than this and contribute to a specific project that they have organized, usually as part of the activities of an organization to which they belong. One result of this scenario is that "local development" is in fact heavily dependent on the contributions of those who reside outside the local area (see Trager 1998, 2001, for further discussion of this issue). In other words, what is crucial for local development activities is the ability to mobilize externally generated resources through a variety of local and external social connections.

How have changing economic circumstances affected people's willingness and ability to continue to fulfill these obligations and hence the continued maintenance of linkages? During the 1990s, Nigeria went through a period of severe political and economic crises to which individuals and communities responded in a variety of ways (see Trager 1997, 2001). For the elite, there were an increasing number of demands on their resources. A key question became whether they would reach a point where they had to cut back on the ties maintained, declining to visit their own or others' hometowns or declining to attend ceremonial events, in order to conserve their resources. For the majority of others, who were not well off and whose lives became increasingly difficult during those years, the situation was much more serious; were such individuals making fewer visits home, sending less to kin elsewhere, and in general cutting back on their involvement in social networks? Or, conversely, did they contribute more because of the greater need?

These issues are discussed at some length elsewhere, especially in my consideration of the impact of structural adjustment on migrants and their local development activities (Trager 1997). However, in that discussion I do not consider the impact on women specifically. Among those considered in the present chapter, they demonstrated, if anything, more involvement rather than less. Women in the network sample, particularly those who had become chiefs, not only continued to travel home to Ijesaland but did so even more frequently. All were aware of the difficulties of the period and commented on them but did not change the basic patterns of activity as a result. Those who were less well-off also continued to contribute, at least in small ways, to their communities as well as to other family members.[15]

Most research on migration and on rural-urban linkages in the migration process focuses on those who are low-income urban migrants, who make up the majority of migrants throughout the Third World. In my research on migrants in the Philippines, for example, I have stressed the way in which rural-urban linkages are crucial in the survival and maintenance of low-income families, and I have demonstrated the key role played by young women in those linkages (Trager 1984, 1988). However, that is just part of the picture. By including migrants who are elite and relatively well off, the present research indicates the importance of rural-urban linkages for communities as well as for individuals and families. The nexus of connections that span place plays a role not only in family support and maintenance but also in the support of local community development activities.

Migration is a complex process involving people and institutions in different locales interacting in a variety of ways over time. Rather than focus on those in a single place, in this chapter I focus on the connections between people and places—specifically, the connections with hometown. For women as well as men, such connections are crucial and continue to influence behavior and actions long after the specific act of moving takes place. The maintenance of connections across place has implications not simply for what individuals do but also for the larger community of which they are a part. Our understanding both of what happens in the places to which migrants move and in the hometowns from which they come necessitates further research from such a perspective.

NOTES

This chapter is republished with permission from the International Union for the Scientific Study of Population. It was originally presented at the IUSSP seminar Women and Demographic Change in Sub-Saharan Africa, held in Dakar, Senegal, March 3–6, 1993, and published in the volume *Women's Position and Demographic Change in Sub-Saharan Africa*, ed. Paulina Makinwa and An-Magritt Jensen (Liege, Belgium: IUSSP, 1995). References and some of the content have been updated to reflect later research and publications.

1. The research reported here was supported by the National Science Foundation (award no. BNS-9120584) and the University of Wisconsin–Parkside Committee on Research and Creative Activity. During the initial period of the field research, I was a visiting professor in the Department of Sociology and Anthropology at Obafemi Awolowo Universty, Ile-Ife, Nigeria.

2. Migration in Nigeria, as elsewhere in West Africa, includes not only labor migration but also movement to new locales for trade and other informal economic activities; for education (even secondary school attendance may require moving to a regional urban center); and for family reasons, including marriage, returning home in old age, and so on. As shown here, nearly all women are economically active; economic activity is often not the sole or major reason to move but nevertheless is part of the context in which there is overall high mobility of both women and men.

3. Later research periods include those of one to three months in every year from 1993 through 1998; I have continued to make observations in the region during subsequent years, including the 2000–2001 period, while a Fulbright Senior Scholar at Obafemi Awolowo University.

4. In the 1963 census, Ilesa had a population of about 160,000; Osu and Ijebu-jesa were in the range of 5,000 to 10,000. The provisional results of the 1991 Nigerian census, which were never released in final form, showed Ilesa as having a population of 138,321 but did not give figures for other towns in the region (Federal Republic of Nigeria 1992).

5. J. D. Y. Peel's discussion (1983) of *osomaalo* trade focuses on only male heads of households.

6. In Yoruba towns and cities, there is a range of housing, from large modern houses to Brazilian-style two-story houses to compounds and small houses. Each type may be occupied by members of more than one household. Efforts were made to include the full range of residences in the survey. Likewise, the interview schedule includes questions designed to find out about nonfamily members living in the house or compound. In the city of Ilesa and the two medium-sized towns of Ijebu-jesa and Osu, samples were selected in several of the delineated sections; in the two small towns, the sample was taken from the entire town. Preliminary mapping identified residences and compounds; a 10 percent sample was taken by selecting every tenth household or compound for interviews. Interviewers were instructed to interview one adult male or female in each of the residences or compounds selected.

7. I have discussed other data from the survey elsewhere (Trager 2001, as well as in other publications that resulted from the research); however, none of the other publications focuses specifically on women.

8. The places referred to here are distinct communities, including small towns (reflecting rural-to-rural migration) as well as regional cities and large urban centers. I consider movement to all of these types of places to be migration. Movement within the region is not commuting, nor is it circular migration, considering the length of time people reside in each locale.

9. There is one woman in the sample who reported that she moves back and forth between her residence in her hometown and a residence elsewhere.

10. The data also include considerable detail on the frequency of visits and the types of gifts and remittances (Trager 2001, 83–86).

11. There are numerous hometown organizations of Ijesa people in Lagos. Some are single-sex organizations; others include both men and women. Some are social clubs; others are service organizations—while some also take on lobbying and community-development activities. Elsewhere, I provide detailed discussion of the range and complexity of hometown organizations (Trager 2001).

12. Certainly there may be comparable individuals who do not retain strong connections with their hometown; they, of course, are much more difficult to identify in a city such as Lagos. However, there is a clear cultural expectation that both men and women should retain ties with the hometown.

13. Later surveys considered specific types of contributions (see Trager 2001, 189–92, for discussion of the results of those surveys). That discussion, however, considers the contributions of both men and women rather than examine those of women separately.

14. In his comments at the International Union for the Scientific Study of Population seminar where this material was first presented, John Clarke used this term, which seems to me particularly appropriate for the situation I am describing. Therese Locoh (1991) has suggested a similar term, *multipolarity*. I discuss the idea of multilocality more generally in the introduction to this volume. Dolores Koenig's contribution in this volume (chapter 2) also applies this concept to the patterns she studied in Mali.

15. I have continued to interact with some of those who were part of the network sample in the years since the major portion of the research was completed. One woman in that sample made clear to me in early 2003 that, for her, the connection with Ijesaland is as strong as ever. Whether this is a function of her own individual circumstances or whether this represents a more general pattern is difficult to say. It does seem, however, that for both men and women, the difficulties of the 1990s did not lead to a cutting of ties or to significant reduction in involvement in hometown activities.

REFERENCES

Adepoju, Aderanti. 1984. Migration and female employment in southwestern Nigeria. *African Urban Studies* 18:59–75.

Afonja, S. A. 1981. Changing modes of production and the sexual division of labour among the Yoruba. *Signs* 7:299–313.

Aronson, Dan R. 1971. Ijebu Yoruba urban-rural relationships and class formation. *Canadian Journal of African Studies* 5:263–79.

———. 1978. *The city is our farm: Seven migrant Ijebu Yoruba families.* Cambridge: Schenkman.

Barkan, Joel D., Michael L. McNulty, and M. A. O. Ayeni. 1991. "Hometown" voluntary associations, local development, and the emergence of civil society in western Nigeria. *Journal of Modern African Studies* 29:457–80.

Berry, Sara S. 1985. *Fathers work for their sons: Accumulation, mobility, and class formation in an extended Yoruba community.* Berkeley: University of California.

Chapman, Murray, and R. Mansell Prothero. 1983. Themes on circulation in the Third World. *International Migration Review* 17:597–632.

Dennis, Carolyne. 1991a. Constructing a "career" under conditions of economic crisis and structural adjustment: The survival strategies of Nigerian women. In *Women, development, and survival in the Third World*, ed. H. Afshar. London: Longman.

———. 1991b. The limits to women's independent careers: Gender in the formal and informal sectors in Nigeria. In *Male bias in the development process*, ed. D. Elson. Manchester: Manchester University Press.

Denzer, LaRay, and Nkechi Mbanefoh. 1998. Women's participation in hometown associations. In *Hometown associations: Indigenous knowledge and development in Nigeria*, ed. Rex Honey and Stanley Okafor, 135–41. London: Intermediate Technology.

Federal Republic of Nigeria. 1992. 1991, population census (provisional results). *Official Gazette* 79, no. 56 (November 30, 1992).

Gugler, Josef. 1971. Life in a dual system: Eastern Nigerians in town, 1961. *Cahiers d'Etudes Africaines* 11:400–421.

———. 1991. Life in a dual system revisited: Urban-rural ties in Enugu, Nigeria 1967–87. *World Development* 19:399–409.

Gugler, Josef, and Gudrun Ludwar-Ene. 1990. Many roads lead women to town in sub-Saharan Africa. Paper presented at the World Congress of Sociology, Madrid, July.

Hollos, Marida. 1991. Migration, education, and the status of women in southern Nigeria. *American Anthropologist* 93:852–70.

Honey, Rex, and Stanley Okafor, eds. 1998. *Hometown associations: Indigenous knowledge and development in Nigeria*. London: Intermediate Technology.

Hugo, Graeme. 1982. Circular migration in Indonesia. *Population and Development Review* 8:59–83.

Lacey, Linda. 1986. Women in the development process: Occupational mobility of female migrants in cities in Nigeria. *Journal of Comparative Family Studies* 17:1–18.

Locoh, Therese. 1991. Structure Familiales D'accueil des Migrants et Developpement des Structures Familiales Multipolaires en Afrique. In *Migration, Changements*

Sociaux et Developpement, ed. P. Vimard et A. Quesnel. Paris: Colloques et Seminaires de l'ORSTOM.

Makinwa, P. K. 1981. *Internal migration and rural development in Nigeria: Lessons from Bendel State.* Ibadan, Nigeria: Heinemann Educational Books.

Moock, Joyce L. 1978–1979. The content and maintenance of social ties between urban migrants and their home-based support groups: The Maragoli case. *African Urban Studies* 3:15–31.

Peel, J. D. Y. 1983. *Ijeshas and Nigerians: The incorporation of a Yoruba kingdom, 1890s–1970s.* Cambridge: Cambridge University Press.

Peil, Margaret, S. K. Ekpenyong, and O. Y. Oyeneye. 1988. Going home: Migration careers of southern Nigerians. *International Migration Review* 22:563–85.

Pittin, Renee. 1984. Migration of women in Nigeria: The Hausa case. *International Migration Review* 18:1293–1314.

Schlyter, Ann. 1990. Women in Harare: Gender aspects of urban-rural interaction. In *Small town Africa: Studies in rural-urban interaction,* ed. J. Baker. Uppsala, Sweden: Scandinavian Institute of African Studies.

Sudarkasa, N. 1973. *Where women work: A study of Yoruba women in the market place and in the home.* Ann Arbor: Museum of Anthropology, University of Michigan.

Trager, Lillian. 1976–1977. Market women in the urban economy: The role of Yoruba intermediaries in a medium-sized city. *African Urban Notes* 2 (part 2): 1–9.

———. 1981. Customers and creditors: Variations in economic personalism in a Nigerian marketing system. *Ethnology* 20:133–46.

———. 1984. Family strategies and the migration of women: Migrants to Dagupan City, Philippines. *International Migration Review* 18:1264–77.

———. 1985. From yams to beer in a Nigerian city: Expansion and change in informal sector trade activity. In *Markets and Marketing,* ed. S. Plattner. Monographs in Economic Anthropology 4. Lanham, Md.: University Press of America.

———. 1987. A Re-examination of the urban informal sector in West Africa. *Canadian Journal of African Studies* 2:238–55.

———. 1988. *The city connection: Migration and family interdependence in the Philippines.* Ann Arbor: University of Michigan Press.

———. 1997. Structural adjustment, hometowns, and local development in Nigeria. In *Economic analysis beyond the local system*, ed. Richard E. Blanton et al., 255–90. Lanham, Md.: University Press of America for the Society for Economic Anthropology.

———. 1998. Hometown linkages and local development in southwestern Nigeria: Whose agenda? What impact? *Africa* 68 (3): 360–82.

———. 2001. *Yoruba hometowns: Community, identity, and development in Nigeria.* Boulder, Colo.: Rienner.

Vaa, Mariken, Sally E. Findley, and Assitan Diallo. 1989. The gift economy: A study of women migrants' survival strategies in a low-income Bamako neighborhood. *Labour, Capital, and Society* 22:234–60.

Watts, Susan J. 1983. Marriage migration, a neglected form of long-term mobility: A case study from Ilorin, Nigeria. *International Migration Review* 27:682–98.

Weisner, T. 1976. The structure of sociability: Urban migration and urban-rural ties in Kenya. *Urban Anthropology* 5:199–223.

8

The Moral Economy of Nonreturn among Socially Diverted Labor Migrants from Portugal and Mozambique

Stephen C. Lubkemann

FOUR VIGNETTES AND AN INTRIGUING PROBLEM

For several years during the early and mid-1990s, I was a graduate student in Providence, Rhode Island—long a destination for Portuguese migrant laborers and the location of one of the most established and long-standing Portuguese American communities in North America. Every spring, during his annual yard sale, I crossed paths with a man who had emigrated to the United States from Aveiro (central Portugal). He had left his home almost thirty years ago to work "temporarily" in the United States, where he ultimately raised his family and now had kids with kids of their own. Every year he told me that this was his "final yard sale" because "he was just about to go home" to Portugal, where his sister and other extended relatives still lived. He explained that there were just a few things that needed taking care of and then he'd be off. In the meantime, he planned to add the yard sale proceeds to the funds he remitted to his sister, who "looked out for his interests back home" in Portugal. Throughout my entire eight-year tenure as a resident of Providence, I came across this "final yard sale" every year in the same place at about the same time. Every year I had roughly the same conversation with this man about his imminent return "in a matter of months," and every year he un-self-consciously, and with expression entirely devoid of irony or aware of any contradiction, ended our conversation with the following words: "Adeus—até para o ano que vem [Goodbye—I will see you next year]." *I will see you next year!*

Shift the scene to another fieldsite: the townships of South Africa, where many migrants from neighboring Mozambique are illegally working in the industries of the Vaal region. In the course of conducting migrant life-history interviews among these Mozambicans in 1997, I interviewed one man in his home in Sharpeville, who had first arrived as a migrant laborer in South Africa in 1956. He had retired from a factory job, though he ran a highly successful welding business that supplemented what, by local standards, was a fairly robust pension. He lived in one of the better houses in the township, with internal plumbing, five rooms, a stereo, refrigerator, and a color television. He received additional income from his son whom he described as working in Johannesburg as a medical technician. We discussed in some detail the best way to purchase a new car on the black market since he had two parked outside his home. In the course of our interview, however, he claimed that much as he would love to return to Mozambique immediately and planned to do so eventually, he simply was too poor to return. Shortly thereafter, he terminated the interview because he had a regularly scheduled appointment—what I later found out to be an appointment to go buy his daily lottery tickets!

A third shift to a new setting: The early 1990s in Olival, a rural town in the central coastal plain of Portugal where the casual observer passing through the region would probably have been struck by the large number houses seemingly frozen in various stages of construction, the majority apparently benefiting from very little, if any, actual construction activity. Equally noticeable would have been the homes that were locked and shuttered up, showing no signs of current residence . . . that is, except in August when a good number of these houses suddenly bustled with activity. Cars with French, German, and Swiss license plates suddenly crowded in the driveways. New walls might have appeared on the formerly silent facades of half-built houses. But by mid-September the houses were shuttered up again, likely to lay eerily quiet for at least another eleven months.

A fourth and final scene takes us to the district of Machaze, in rural Mozambique, where in 1998 I interviewed the brother of the aforementioned lottery player living in South Africa. We sat in his small "tuck shop" (little more than a roofed stand where general merchandise was sold) that at the time was devoid of anything to sell, discussing the difficulties of running a small business in the postwar environment. He established the shop with money he earned while working in South Africa. However, the shop ultimately failed—a fairly common occurrence, as testified to by the many empty and sometimes semicollapsed stalls in the immediate vicinity. His shop had seemed destined to a similar fate until his brother in South Africa agreed to send him merchandise to sell.

"Are you waiting for him to reinvest the profits from what you have sold in order to have more things to sell?" I asked, looking around at the barren shelves.

"Oh no," he replied, "that money was all eaten," a metaphor meaning it had all been spent by him.

"So how will you get more things to sell?"

"My brother will send it—it should arrive soon," he answered with confidence.

"And will you pay for it after you sell it?" I ventured.

"No," he said. I was quiet. It was hot.

"Perhaps your brother will not be able to send much," I proposed.

"No, he will send many things to sell," he responded. "It is how he marks presence."

These four little vignettes tell two sides of a common story about the links between migrants and their communities in two very different migration streams. In both the United States (among Portuguese emigrants) and in South Africa (among Mozambican ones), we find migrant workers who may publicly claim that they intend to return home but in fact never actually seem to do so. Originally participants in a labor migration system that involved their chronic circulation between community of origin and employment destinations, such individuals have become, in essence, permanent emigrants who reside abroad.

This chapter focuses on such individuals whom I designate as "socially diverted migrants." I use the phrase "socially diverted" to refer to migrants who no longer plan an eventual return and permanent resettlement in their communities of origin and whose social investments are no longer primarily oriented toward that original home community. Rather, they have begun to plot, invest in, and realize total social lives in the areas of migrant destination even as they remain enmeshed in material and symbolic circuits of exchange that link them with their communities of origin and to those who are still circular migrants. By "total social lives," I refer to the possibility for (1) pursuing a culturally prescribed life course in its entirety, including marriage, having children, and retirement; (2) maintaining social networks that provide a subjectively determined "appropriate" sense of community or "social world" (Marx 1990); and (3) pursuing the economic activities necessary for living out this life course (Lubkemann 2000d).

In juxtaposition, the opening vignettes raise a rather simple but interesting question that motivates this ethnological study: why do socially diverted migrants who have little if any intention of actually returning to settle in their communities of origin continue nevertheless to invest in those communities? If they are unlikely to live in these houses or are steadily losing money in these businesses back in their communities of origin, what is it they are actually investing in? What role do these investments in their areas of origin play in their strategies for constituting total social lives?

LABOR MIGRATION IN PORTUGUESE AND MOZAMBICAN RURAL SOCIETIES

International labor migration has long been a central factor in the organization of social life and subsistence strategies in both of the two contexts addressed in this chapter: rural Portugal (from the central region south of Aveiro) and rural Mozambique (the south-central district of Machaze). Temporary labor migration has shaped rural Portuguese society and identity for at least four centuries (Brettell 1986, 1990; Serrão 1977; Rocha-Trindade 1981, 1990; Higgs 1990; Baganha 1999; Silva et al. 1984). Migration patterns have varied considerably over time, though this chapter focuses primarily on migration behavior since World War II. Throughout the 1950s, 1960s, and 1970s in particular the importance of emigrant remittances to local Portuguese rural economies grew substantially (Graham 1990). During these decades different areas of Portugal tended to specialize in migration to particular international destinations. Those from the Azores were disproportionately drawn to North America and those from Madeira to South Africa (Baganha 1999). Likewise, continental Portugal provided the majority of migrants to European destinations such as France (Brettell 1981, 1986; Baganha 1999), Germany (Klimt 1989, 2000b), and Switzerland (Baganha 1999) while contributing to North American, South African, and Australian (Noivo 1997,

2002) streams. Venezuela also became an important destination during the 1970s and 1980s, only to diminish in significance during the 1990s (Baganha 1999).

Brettell has described emigration from Portugal as primarily a strategy focused on improving and reproducing peasant life in rural areas of origin rather than as a way of leaving Portuguese society altogether (Brettell 1990). Thus, migrants in all of the aforementioned streams regularly remitted significant sums of money to immediate family members. Visits back to communities of origin were typically undertaken on an annual or biannual basis, giving rise to the institutionalization of the annual "Festivals of the Emigrant" every August, in what arguably became the major social event in many rural communities throughout Portugal.

These celebrated visits "home" by those working abroad brought an influx of money and gifts for relatives and provided an opportunity for those working abroad to deal with social affairs and extended family business. During these visits, many emigrants worked on the construction and furnishing of their houses in their towns of origin. As has been the case in other communities worldwide that have been shaped by circular labor migration (see Grigolini, this volume, chapter 6), homes were one of the principal investments in Portugal for earnings from abroad and in many cases provided a major reason to temporarily emigrate in the first place. The general features of this pattern—temporary emigration, regular remittance, periodic visits and investment back home, and the maintainence of strong social ties with family and community of origin—that I observed in the central-plains region south of Aveiro during fieldwork in the early 1990s have long been fairly typical of other rural Portuguese communities in the north (Brettell 1986, 1990; Klimt 1989, 2000b) and to a lesser extent in the southern Alentejo region (Arroteia 1984; Boura et al. 1984; Silva et al. 1984) and in the Azores (Baganha 1999).

In a very different setting—the south-central district of Machaze, in Mozambique, where I have conducted fieldwork since 1995—international migration has played a central role in the organization of social life and subsistence strategies for over a century, albeit under significantly different economic and political circumstances. Labor migration from the Machaze region to South Africa and to present-day Zimbabwe (formerly Rhodesia) has occurred since at least the last quarter of the nineteenth century (Lubkemann 2000b). Early on, under the Portuguese colonial regime, migration developed as both a strategy for social reproduction and a form of resistance against specific colonial state policies, such as forced labor recruitment. A severely understaffed colonial administration prevented the Portuguese district administrators from effectively enforcing forced labor contracts that would have prevented Machazian men from working abroad, where they consistently could earn anywhere from twice to ten times the wages offered within the Portuguese colony. Machazian men much preferred employment abroad since it allowed them to earn the money necessary for paying annual taxes in a much shorter period. Local colonial administrators also recognized that policies opposing illegal labor migration to South Africa threatened their one secure stream of revenue—the payment of these taxes. The administrators thus tended to turn a blind eye to this massive "illegal" migration stream, making only feeble and periodic attempts to improve their forced labor recruitment (Lubkemann 2000b). In this context, migration developed as a powerful "weapon of the weak" (Scott 1985).

At the same time that labor migration to South Africa provided a way to avoid the most onerous of the colonial government's policies (forced labor) and more easily fulfill its minimal demands (taxes), it also became a central factor in the organization of local social relations, identities, and subsistence strategies at the community, family, and individual level. By the middle of the century, male labor migration to South Africa was virtually universal and followed a predictable life cycle. Young men would first undertake one or two trips to nearby Rhodesia to work on the tea and coffee plantations. These trips would range from several months to a couple years and would afford them with experience and the money they needed to subsequently undertake the longer, more arduous, and more expensive trip to South Africa. Machazian men who arrived in South Africa easily found employment in the rapidly developing and labor-starved mining industry. Typically after one to three years of work, these men would return to Machaze, where they would remain for at least six months before returning to work again in South Africa. This pattern of circular labor migration was repeated in some cases dozens of times before these men eventually retired and settled permanently back in Machaze (Lubkemann 2000b).

In this context circular labor migration became a particularly central force in the organization of local social relations. The money that young men earned in South Africa not only allowed them to pay taxes but also provided them with a way to pay *lobola* (bride-price) necessary for marriage. Circular migration also played a key role in effecting gradual yet fundamental transformations in household and kin-based social relations throughout the twentieth century. Migrant earnings allowed young men to achieve greater personal autonomy by reducing their dependence upon elder kinsmen for the payment of *lobola*. Circular labor migration also dramatically increased the degree and visibility of socioeconomic differentiation between households, as a result of the differential success of labor migrants in terms of the employment they were able to procure and the savings they were able to bring home. Intragenerational conflict among brothers caused by this socioeconomic differentiation and intergenerational conflict caused by the autonomy of younger migrants both contributed to the nuclearization of coresidence, as large compounds of multiple generations of related married men and their families gave way to smaller households, comprising only a man and his wife or wives (Lubkemann 2000b).

Ultimately, in both rural Mozambique and in rural Portugal, forms of temporary international labor migration became central factors in the organization of social relations and subsistence strategies in the migrants' communities of rural origin. In both cases, large numbers of men (and in the Portuguese case, a significant number of women) entered international migration streams and pursued what were often long careers as laborers abroad. In both cases migration was conceived as a strategy for pursuing social reproduction in the area of origin (Mozambique or Portugal), and in both cases migration was dominated by a strong ideology that valued continuous connection and ultimate return to the area of origin.

THE MONITORING FACTORS OF SOCIAL REPRODUCTION IN MORAL ECONOMIES OF LABOR MIGRANCY

Both of the aforementioned forms of temporary labor migration posed specific threats and challenges to social reproduction, which home communities in both Portugal and Mozambique responded to in structurally similar, yet culturally particular, ways. Home communities that depend heavily on circular migration always face the risk that migrants may choose to redirect their investments in factors of social reproduction elsewhere and eventually opt to pursue total social lives in the communities in which they sojourn rather than in their home areas of origin. In short, circular migrants may become permanent emigrants and jeopardize their home communities by ceasing to invest economically or socially in them.

In Mozambican and Portuguese home communities, kin and neighbors who were left behind developed strategies for confronting this challenge and mitigating its threat. Two features of these strategies are particularly noteworthy. The first of these features is the continuous social monitoring by home community members of the specific types of investments made by kin who are working abroad. The specific types of investments in question are those that are made in strategic or key factors of social reproduction—such as marriage, housing, land, and businesses that can generate long-term or permanent income. The second feature is the way in which this investment behavior of emigrants is assigned "moral value" by home community members.

In rural communities throughout Portugal, such as Olival, kinsfolk and home community members long evaluated whether labor migrants abroad proved themselves willing and able to perform what can be thought of as an idealized "emigrant script" (Lubkemann 2002a, 2003). This script idealized a migrant who did not wish to lose connections with the community of origin in Portugal and whose commitment to home, hearth, and kin was continuously manifest through a specific set of activities, investments, and public performances. Thus, those who remained behind closely monitored how an emigrant's extended family fared in his or her absence, using their well-being as a gauge with which to measure that emigrant's willingness to fulfill the moral obligation to remit. Similarly, they paid close attention to the frequency and timing of visits by those working abroad, particularly on marked life occasions, such as the death of close relatives. Emigrants were also expected to be major contributors to community projects, such as the building of local sports facilities, and in supporting local civic associations and clubs.

Kin and community members also monitored the way in which emigrants plotted out and fulfilled their own individual life strategies, seeking clues and signs of continued connection and intention of ultimate return. Thus, a consistently raised question in casual conversations with visiting emigrants or their family members would be "How is the construction of so-and-so's house coming?" (with "so-and-so" being an emigrant member of the family in question and with "house" meaning the local house, in the community of origin). Throughout the 1980s and into the early 1990s, partially built houses in all stages of construction dotted the landscapes of many rural communities throughout Portugal.

Particularly close attention was also paid to what those working abroad did with inherited family land. Plans to build homes or start businesses back in Portuguese communities of origin received approval. Conversely, the sale of family land was considered anathema. Family members remained particularly concerned with the marriage choices made by those who emigrated to work abroad, approving in particular the choice of a "home girl" or "home boy" as a spouse and frowning on the choice of a non-Portuguese spouse from the countries in which migrants sought employment. The raising of children provided another arena of strategic social surveillance. Were the children brought back for visits? Were they learning Portuguese? How well did they speak it? Were they familiar with local customs and food?

In rural Mozambique, even greater attention was paid to the timing and choice of marriage partners by migrants working abroad in South Africa. Fathers, mothers, and other senior kin paid close attention to whether migrants continued to make bride-price payments (often an affair that was drawn out over many years and sometimes indefinitely). Sojourns abroad that stretched beyond two or three years were likely to generate letters from senior kin to migrants about how their wives' dissatisfaction from being left waiting behind was creating tension within the extended household, thus raising the specter of possible witchcraft—commonly seen as a by-product of social strife in Ndau belief systems (Lubkemann 2002b).

Thus, in both rural Portugal and rural Mozambique, kinfolk and community members carefully monitored specific types of migrant investments back home—most particularly, investments in key factors of social reproduction. This investment behavior was assigned what might be termed *moral value* in the sense that it was measured against a socially prescribed, idealized script of "what that behavior should be." In these societies that remain so dependent on the continued investment and ultimate return of circular migrants, moral value is ultimately determined as a measure of one's commitment to pursuing a total social life in the home community itself. Therefore, when migrants make material and social investments back home, they are not only making economic decisions but also performing moral scripts. Such investments are thus simultaneous transactions in both a material and a moral economy.

Introduced by E. P. Thompson (1963, 1971), the idea of "moral economy" has been variously retheorized, sometimes in mutually contradictory ways (Hyden 1980; Scott 1985). Without plunging too deeply into the hornet's nest that surrounds this term, this chapter takes as its point of departure Harry Englund's definition of moral economy as "a continuous argument about the specific meaning and imputation of morality itself" and in which "the focus is not on the material process of livelihood, but rather on certain qualities of relationships which may, of course, secure access to livelihood as a concomitant" (1995, 25). Developing more specifically on this definition, I characterize moral economies as follows:

1. They are systems of symbolic transaction in which different values are assigned to behavior.
2. Value is a measurement of conformity to socially prescribed ideal scripts.
3. The determination of each measurement is a socially contested and negotiated process.
4. The assignment of value is consequential to social actors, either enabling or constraining their possibilities for social interaction and to command resources—whether social or material.
5. Thus, social actors are highly responsive to this system of transaction in formulating their strategies and realizing their actions.

In both Portugal and in Mozambique, the evaluation of migrant investment behavior by kin and home community did have considerable social and material consequences for the circular migrant. For example, in Mozambique, where extended kin played a significant role in the determination of appropriate marriage partners and the negotiation of bride-price payments, a migrant whose investment behavior back home was seen as wanting often faced a more limited pool of willing marriage partners. Migrants whose connection and commitment to home were seen as questionable were likely to confront the prospect of higher bride-price rates or less-favorable terms of payment. In such cases, migrants might be asked to front large sums immediately rather than be allowed to make small payments over many years. Similarly, in rural Portugal determinations about property inheritance (land and businesses in particular) could be significantly influenced by histories of remittance support and other forms of demonstrated commitment and investment back home. In short the evaluation of the moral value of investments was highly consequential in both Mozambique and Portugal, in that it ultimately influenced the distribution and costs of critical material and social resources that could significantly influence life chances and opportunities.

Consequently, when those who migrated and worked abroad made investments back home, they were as keenly aware of and responsive to the value and returns on these investments in the moral economy as they were to their material returns. Migrant behavior was thus responsive not only to the dynamics of material economies but to the terms of value in moral economies as well.

FROM LABOR MIGRANTS TO PERMANENT EMIGRANTS: TWO COMPARATIVE HISTORICAL TRAJECTORIES OF TRANSFORMATION

While the responsiveness of migration behavior to moral economies may serve the purposes of home communities by reinforcing ideologies of return, it is a well-documented fact that a significant number of labor migrants from both rural Portugal and rural Mozambique were eventually "socially diverted" over time. In both of the home origins compared in this study—Olival in Portugal and Machaze in Mozambique—a minority of labor migrants eventually chose to concentrate the bulk of their social and economic investments and build new lives in what had initially been merely employment destinations. These locations abroad became places of permanent resettlement—new homes in which were realized life strategies devoid of any actual intention to return permanently to areas and countries of origin.

In the Portuguese case, large transgenerational communities in Canada (Brettell 1981; Noivo 1997; Teixeira and Da Rosa 2000; Giles 2002), the United States (Baganha 1999), Australia (Noivo 2002), France (Brettell 1986, 1993), and Germany (Klimt 2000a, 2000b) attest to the fact that not all those who enter circular migration flows ultimately return home. Half-built shells of houses that have stood unfinished for decades render starkly apparent the absence of many of these self-styled members of a "Portuguese diaspora" (Klimt and Lubkemann 2002).

It has only been since the 1970s that any similar form of social diversion has occurred among Mozambican labor migrants to South Africa—the result of a very different set of historical circumstances that can only be briefly outlined here. My own survey of two hundred Machazian men working in South

Africa in 1997 showed a small but growing minority of Mozambican migrant laborers (11 percent) who claimed no intention of ever returning to Mozambique and planned to remain permanently in South Africa (Lubkemann 2000d).

Yet even those who do claim that they intend to return to Mozambique make key social and economic investments in South Africa that belie their stated intention. Thus, of the two hundred Machazian men whom I surveyed in South Africa in 1997, 65 percent were involved in ongoing conjugal relationships in South Africa with South African women. Over one-third of those involved in these conjugal relations had no marital ties with anyone back in Mozambique. Over 40 percent of those men involved with South African women reported paying *lobola* or having held a church ceremony. Of the total sample of two hundred men, 72 percent planned to keep a house in South Africa and 79 percent a business, despite their stated intention to eventually return to Mozambique (Lubkemann 2000d).

In both the Portuguese case and the Mozambican case, economic factors such as employment opportunity, higher wages, and higher standards of living in countries of destination provided important motivators that led some labor migrants to exit the labor migration stream abroad and permanently eschew a return home. Yet, in neither case did economic factors come close to fully explaining why some migrants ultimately made such a choice. In the Portuguese case, economic development that occurred after the end of the country's dictatorship in 1975 had drastic effects that significantly transformed rural Portuguese economies. In the central and northern regions of Portugal, the smallholder agriculture, in which the majority of the population participated in 1975, rapidly gave way to what in essence became a manufacturing and increasingly service-sector economy closely tied to regional and national urban centers. Throughout the 1980s, wage differentials between Portugal and important destinations such as Germany and France narrowed considerably; however, the availability of secure, well-remunerated employment in these countries so characteristic of the 1960s and 1970s was by the late 1980s clearly a thing of the past (Baganha 1999; Klimt 2000a, 2000b).

Researchers working throughout the Portuguese diaspora have therefore identified other, "noneconomic" reasons that played a role in encouraging labor migrants to opt for permanent resettlement abroad rather than return home. In the Portuguese case, one of the most interesting factors identified has been a perceptible shift since the end of the 1980s in the way emigrants are imagined and portrayed broadly throughout the Portuguese public. Whereas emigrants were once widely regarded with a mixture of admiration and envy as symbols of upward mobility and socioeconomic success, they are increasingly portrayed as rural hicks who may have money but are far from being socially *au courant* or sophisticated. Edite Noivo (2002) has pointed to the ways in which cultural differences such as dress, idiomatic speech, and taste in clothing and music have been increasingly emphasized by residents of Portugal as markers for attaching stigma to visiting emigrants. She has also documented an emergent tide of perplexed resentment among many of these emigrants, sentiments that underlie a dawning realization that they are more comfortable in, and identify more strongly with, their diasporic communities abroad than they do with their communities of origin in Portugal.

Similarly, among those Portuguese emigrants studied by Andrea Klimt (1989, 2000a, 2000b) in Germany, many have found the rapid social and economic changes in Portugal distressing. Their comments are often similar to those made to me in 1997 by one elderly emigrant in Providence: "I found a Portugal that I no longer recognize. The Portugal I know is more visible here than back home." And, indeed, within the Portuguese community in Providence, you can still find the small *mercearias* (grocery shops) that were once such an established feature of Portuguese life but by the mid-1980s had begun to give way to the jumbo hypermarkets and discount megastores that increasingly dominated the evermore urbanized Portugal of the new millennium.

The historical process by which the social diversion of circular migrants has developed and grown among Mozambicans labor migrants in South Africa is both more sudden and traumatic. Machazian men were originally participants in a system of mine labor migration tightly regulated by a South African regime that depended on a racial division of labor and colluded with the Portuguese colonial administration. As such, Machazian men fulfilled eighteen-month contracts, during which they lived in guarded compounds and after which they were returned to Mozambique for required periods of stay (and to pay taxes to the colonial government). A draconian pass system that regulated the settlement options of black South Africans to a number of "independent homelands" (the notorious *bantustans*) provided further obstacles and disincentives of significance to Mozambican miners who might have contemplated a more permanent stay.

South Africa's rapid transformation into an industrial society after World War II brought about significant economic and demographic transformations that began to make the possibility of permanent resettlement in South Africa feasible for Mozambican labor migrants. Between 1950 and 1975, the industry and service sectors experienced spectacular growth,[1] creating a huge demand for labor and driving up manufacturing wages at such a rate that by 1951 they doubled mine labor wages and by 1970 tripled them.[2] Responding to the expansion in manufacturing employment opportunities and better wages, many Mozambican mine migrants followed the lead of the general South African population and increasingly eschewed mine labor in favor of employment in industrial or service positions. The fact that these jobs were located in the peri-urban regions of the Vaal and the Rand produced a massive growth in informal peri-urban settlement.

Ultimately, the apartheid regime's housing policies and labor legislation failed thoroughly in preventing black urbanization—not only because the impossibility of subsistence agriculture and widespread poverty on the Bantustans provided a powerful push factor but also because labor-starved manufacturing firms were generally willing to collude with migrants who sought to circumvent the ponderous legal and bureaucratic procedures for acquiring legal pass documentation. The growth of informal peri-urban units from 1966 to 1979 was estimated in different parts of the country's urban areas to range between 137 percent and 458 percent (Schlemmer 1985, 168–69). Bearing in mind that manufacturing jobs did not generally provide compound housing, Machazian migrants, much like their South African counterparts, began to acquire informal housing in the peri-urban townships. As early as the mid-1950s, a number of Machazians were able to obtain housing in Sharpeville and in Evaton near the manufacturing center of Veereneeging. By the mid-1950s, Machazians had developed several means for obtaining documentation that allowed them to present themselves as "South Africans."

These changes created new opportunities for a more "total social life" (Lubkemann 2000d) in South Africa for Machazian labor migrants. The move into the townships established the potential for long-term conjugal unions with South African women. Meanwhile, the greater influx of South African women into the urban areas during this period increasingly improved the "marriage market" in terms of potential partners for men from Machaze.[3] As

I have explored elsewhere (Lubkemann 2000a, 2000d, 2002b), by the mid-1970s a small but highly visible minority of Machazian men had begun to experiment with new strategies of social reproduction, organized around the transnationalization of polygyny (having wives and raising families in both Mozambique and in South Africa simultaneously) and involving significant investment in key factors of social reproduction in both countries.

While the aforementioned changes made permanent resettlement in South Africa more possible for Mozambican labor migrants, it would be Mozambique's devastating civil war that made this option particularly desirable. Armed conflict arrived in Machaze in 1977 and persisted for almost fifteen years, until the negotiation of peace in 1992. Machaze was one of the hardest-hit areas of the country. Almost 90 percent of the population was displaced, either internally or across international borders.

The distribution of displacement was, however, highly gendered. Responding to the forced recruitment efforts of both sides in the conflict much as they had to attempts by colonial governments at forced labor recruitment, adult men were much more likely than women to flee the country, often using established labor migration routes to South Africa. As the war intensified and became prolonged, women, children, and the elderly generally relocated internally or immediately across the border in Zimbabwe, where they sought relief in the United Nations High Commissioner for Refugees camps that were established there in the mid-1980s (Lubkemann 2000c).

As the war dragged on for many years, a growing number of the Machazian men in South Africa began to contemplate the possibility that they might not be able to return to Mozambique. The war partially or completely disrupted the contact of some with family members back in Mozambique. Conjugal relationships with South African women became increasingly attractive.

The termination of hostilities in 1992 immediately lead to widespread return by those resettled in South Africa. Fewer than 20 percent of the estimated quarter-million self-settled Mozambicans in South Africa ultimately availed themselves of UNHCR assistance to return permanently (Lubkemann 2000c). The wartime devastation of Mozambique and the inherent uncertainties about its postwar political situation reinforced the importance of economic options in South Africa. Even those who did return remained concerned with keeping options in South Africa open.

WHY SOCIALLY DIVERTED MIGRANTS CONTINUE
TO INVEST BACK HOME

These historical particularities that transformed labor migrants into permanent emigrants in the Mozambican and Portuguese cases are interesting. Yet for purposes of this chapter, the phenomenon of greatest interest is not the social diversion of these migrants. Rather, it is the fact that in both cases these emigrants continue to make what are often quite costly investments in their communities of origin despite never intending to actually returning to settle there.

An illustrative case is that of one Machazian migrant I interviewed in 1998 who briefly left behind his house, extended family, and pension in South Africa to return to his "home" in Machaze in order to take a Mozambican wife, build three huts (one for his mother, one for himself, and one for his new wife), clear two fields (one for the wife and one for the mother), and then returned immediately to continue to live with his South African wife in the township of Sebokeng. Despite his private admission to me that he had no intention of ever returning to live for any significant amount of time in Machaze (much less retire there permanently), he regularly sends letters along with his remittances that promise precisely such a return! In the seven years since he had reestablished his homestead and took a new Mozambican wife, he has visited her and his mother twice. Such cases are absolutely typical, as attested by the many well-kept, if empty, migrant rondavels (round thatched houses) in homesteads throughout Machaze district and by the frequent complaints of mothers, wives, and senior relatives commenting on the long years of delay between what had become much shorter visits (weeks) than what used to be the case (months or years).

Similarly, throughout rural Portugal, in small communities such as Olival, many emigrant houses were often found stalled in a partially finished state. Yet they were still being built, even if at a painfully slow rate of years or even decades. Remittances continued to flow "home"; visits during the festival of the emigrant still occurred; and children who were born abroad and spoke thickly accented and grammatically convoluted Portuguese were still brought or sent for short visits with relatives. Often they were sent home repeatedly in the hopes that they just might find "a nice Portuguese boy/girl" to marry.

However, it is necessary to ask, why would socially diverted migrants who had left labor migration streams and chosen to permanently resettle abroad continue to invest resources—time and money—in building houses they rarely if ever used, in business ventures from which they gained marginal (or even negative) returns, and in marriages or other social relationships that seemed to contribute little to the life strategies they pursued in their new homes abroad? Put another way, why did socially diverted migrants continue to make investments in moral capital?[4] Why might they still attempt to transact in the moral economies that originally informed their migratory practice?

A comparison between the Mozambican and Portuguese cases highlights at least three common reasons why socially diverted migrants continued to transact in these moral economies. The first and most obvious of these is that it was often useful to retain the option of going back "home" even if there was no intention of actually doing so. It is probably fairly safe to make a generalization that the usefulness of retaining such an option is likely to be closely related to the legal, social, and economic vulnerabilities that diverted migrants confront in the settings where they have resettled and now concentrate the bulk of their social and economic investments. The case of the Mozambicans who resettled in South Africa is particularly illustrative of the usefulness of pursuing risk-diversifications strategies by retaining viable options back home, even while pursuing new opportunities abroad.

While the postwar Mozambican economic picture remained bleak and the political situation unsavory to many Machazian men resettled in South Africa, they also confronted other daunting challenges in postapartheid South Africa that generated different forms of apprehension and uncertainty. Throughout the 1980s and 1990s, the economic situation in South Africa deteriorated considerably. After 1992, the large secondary industries such as ISCOR (the state-run steel monopoly under the apartheid regime) that dominated the economic landscape experienced the pressure of international competition from which they were protected throughout the 1980s. Some of the largest employers, such as VECOR (one of the major steel-related industries in the Vaal region), closed their doors in the early 1990s. Whereas unemployment was a rarity for Mozambican migrants who arrived in South Africa before 1975, the majority of Machazians of all ages in South Africa that were surveyed in 1997 and 2001 were unemployed—some for months or years at a time (Lubkemann 2000b, 2000d).

Like many South Africans, Machazians increasingly turned to activities in the informal sector. In the late 1990s, many Machazians opened up "tuck shops," where they sold oil, bread, canned goods, matches, cookies, paraffin, eggs—bought in town at the hypermarkets for resale in the townships at miniscule profit. Relatively easy to start because of the low capital required, most of these enterprises eventually failed because of low profit margins, stiff competition, and frequent burglaries.

By the late 1990s, crime had also become a prominent concern among Machazians in South Africa. Virtually all Machazian interviewees listed crime as the greatest problem they had to confront in South Africa. Foreigners were particularly vulnerable because they were known by thieves to be unlikely to report crime to the police. In fact, the authorities themselves often targeted Machazian migrants with criminal abuse—in the 1997 survey of two hundred Machazian men in one township in South Africa, 88 percent reported that they had paid at least one bribe to a South African police officer in order to avoid deportation (Lubkemann 2000b, 2000d).

Similarly, in conjugal disputes or in the case of separations, South African women often use the illegal status of their husbands to their advantage. In several cases that were recounted to me, the illegal status of the Mozambican husband allowed a South African wife and her male relatives to refuse to repay *lobola* payments after a divorce since the husband was reluctant to press his claims with authorities. The South African government's own public endorsements of xenophobic sentiment and its massive deportation campaigns have clearly provided an environment conducive to a whole new mode of criminality that targets foreigners and is complicitous of petty official abuse.

In the Portuguese case, legal status has been less of an issue, although over the last three years there has been a growing rate of deportation of illegal Portuguese emigrants in New England, particularly emigrants from the Azores (Moniz 2004). In the wake of September 11, these policies have intensified. Economic vulnerability in areas of permanent resettlement has been most evident in the growing stream of those who had permanently emigrated to Venezuela in the 1970s and early 1980s but have since returned in the wake of that country's political and economic downturn (Baganha 1999). Similarly, Klimt (2000a, 200b) has identified economic pressures and growing anti-immigrant sentiment in Germany resulting from the country's reunification that have encouraged its long-term Portuguese emigrants to revive their interest in maintaining an option of return to Portugal.

A second reason why socially diverted migrants may continue to make investments in moral capital back home is that they need to maintain and participate in a community of compatriots that includes those who are still in the labor migration track. Such "ethnic enclave" communities may serve critical purposes and enable emigrants to respond to specific pressures, opportunities, and problems confronted in societies of permanent resettlement.

During the late 1990s, many of the men who opted to settle permanently in South Africa sought to counter their vulnerability to South African spouses by "importing" wives from Machaze to live with them in South Africa. These wives rarely had legal documentation of any kind and thus were more legally vulnerable than their husbands. However, the possibility of obtaining wives from Machaze required that connections and appropriate social relations be maintained with those in Machaze who were the source of possible partners.

These men were also concerned with protecting Machazian norms of gender and generational interaction that they perceived as being threatened by a very different South African social environment. Many were concerned that Machazian women might aspire to the less-asymmetrical gender norms that characterized conjugal relationships in South Africa. Other men feared that their wives might become "smart at trade" and gain a form of economic independence unavailable to them back in Machaze, where women are primarily practitioners of subsistence agriculture. These men also expressed concern with losing parental authority over their children who had been born and raised in South Africa.

These men therefore urged their children and wives to interact primarily with other Machazians in South Africa in an attempt to foster a sense of identity prescribed in moral terms. They constructed this identity by essentializing difference and making moral markers part of the definition of "Machazianess." This moral discourse drew a sharp line between Machazian and South African identity. The churches in particular served as the most important forums for fostering this sense of Machazian community and seperateness in South Africa. These men also attempted to influence the marriage partners of their children so that they would marry other Machazians. Ironically, they often even encouraged children to visit Machaze despite the fact that they themselves expressed no intention of establishing permanent residence there anymore.

The function of Machazian community and identity for these men was thus not merely that of an economic network that connected Machaze and South Africa as it always has done. Nor could it be reduced to a form of social capital that enabled Machazians to find work, employment, and identity papers in South Africa. For those socially diverted male migrants who decided to stay permanently in South Africa, Machazian identity was a way to mark social identity in ways that promoted desired behavior among their wives and children (Lubkemann 2000d).

Finally, there is a third set of reasons why socially diverted migrants continue to invest heavily in moral capital. Culturally specific beliefs about the ways in which moral universes work and about cause and effect can significantly influence how socially diverted migrants construct their senses of self and evaluate both that self and the likely consequences of their morally consequential choices. This is most clearly illustrated by Machazian beliefs. Machazians believed that the social world encompassed not only the living but also the spirits of the dead. Foremost among these spirits were the *vadzimu*: one's own deceased ancestors. The *vadzimu* were believed to intervene in the lives of the living in order to correct moral failings or to not be forgotten, usually by causing minor illnesses (rather than grievous harm). Such admonishment was believed to occur if the living neglected to perform rituals of respect—for example, if they neglected an ancestor's grave.

Machazians also believed that ancestral reproach could easily be "triggered" by contentious relationships among the living. *Vadzimu* were believed to act particularly in defense of the rights of older and senior kin, whose age and social rank ascribed them with a status that makes them in some sense "closer to the ancestors." Within this belief system, social duties and obligations toward others were often fulfilled in order to avoid provoking ancestral resentment and not only out of fear that the living offended party might exercise material sanctions directly. The prolonged absences of Machazian men and the weakening of their ties with extended kin back in Machaze were regarded as a major cause of problems with ancestral spirits among migrants abroad in South Africa (Lubkemann 2002b).

This belief system provided an independent motivation for migrants to continue to remit and invest in factors of social reproduction back in Machaze that were keyed with particular value in the moral economy, even as they actively planned not to return. By way of example, one Machazian man in

Sharpeville that I interviewed in 1997 had not been back to Machaze since 1954. As one of the most powerful Machazian job brokers in the area, he was highly respected and relatively well off. Yet despite his extended absence, he had long felt compelled to visit his area of origin in order to appease his ancestral spirits, to whom he attributed his troubled health. In 1996, he finally visited Machaze for two weeks. However, he then recently fell ill again, and a *nyanga* (diviner) interpreted this as a resurgence of pressure by his grandfather's spirit that he return to Machaze. Consequently, he felt that he had to at least establish a homestead to mark his presence in Machaze. In the meantime, he paid a considerable sum to a church *profeta* (prophet) to negotiate with his ancestors an acceptable delay for that investment. Similar beliefs have been widely documented to exert similar pressure in favor of migrant return and continued investment in areas of origin throughout sub-Saharan Africa (Gugler 1975; Gugler and Geschiere 1998; Piot 1999; Ferguson 1999).

HOW MEANING IS MANAGED:
THE STRUCTURE OF NARRATIVES OF NONRETURN

In the last part of this analysis, I want to turn from the question of why investment continues even after return is no longer a preferred option to an even more intriguing question—namely, how exactly do migrants who do not intend to return nevertheless manage the meanings of their investments back home so that these are still taken as valid statements of a commitment to return?

To summarize the argument so far, positive moral value is assigned to the behavior of migrants by those who remain at home to the degree that the behavior is seen to signify an intent of ultimate return. Investments in specific key factors of social reproduction are the behaviors monitored for this type of evaluation. In this final section, I argue that investment in these key factors are not always clear and self-evident signifiers. The meaning of these investments is vulnerable to reinterpretation that can jeopardize their validity or potency as signs of commitment to original home and hearth. As a concrete example, the unfinished emigrant's house in Olival may eventually cease to suggest that the labor migrant is investing in an eventual return home and may begin to tell a different story—one of neglect rather than eventual return—if construction drags out too long.

Here we confront a paradox: socially diverted migrants are making investments in moral capital to avoid having to return, yet in the terms of the moral economy, positive value is a function of commitment to return. The challenge for socially diverted migrants is thus to devise strategies to ensure that their investments are accepted as legitimate signifiers of homeward orientation, without however actually requiring them to disinvest in factors of social reproduction in their new homes abroad where they have chosen to resettle.

This is accomplished through a carefully crafted public discourse that (1) explains investments in factors of social reproduction in new areas of origin as means for contributing to ultimate return home and (2) recasts return as a process that is subject to forms of conditionality whose interpretation can be easily manipulated by the migrant.

Thus, in what I have identified elsewhere as "narratives of intended return" (Lubkemann 2000d), Machazian men in South Africa tended to publicly represent their long absences from Machaze and their considerable social and material investments in South Africa not as evidence of their never returning but rather as necessary to ensure the quality and success of that return. These men frequently explained that their children had become accustomed to certain amenities in South Africa. They explained that their delayed return allowed them not only to acquire sufficient amenities for their immediate families but also for other, extended kin—a justifiable explanation in light of the widely held belief that witchcraft could easily be provoked by the jealousy of poorer relatives exposed to the relative material wealth of returning migrants. Such narratives were structured to emphasize the inevitability and desirability of "return" as an end while simultaneously emphasizing conditionality and indeterminacy in defining means to that end.

Klimt (2000) discusses her surprise at finding virtually all of the Portuguese emigrants that she interviewed in Germany in 1984 still residing in Hamburg in 1992, given that they had adamantly affirmed their imminent return. Similarly to the Mozambicans in South Africa, they explained that they would have enough to return and "finish the house," "start the business," and "help the family" "in a few little years." Finding virtually the same group in the same place and still claiming "just a few more little years . . . when the kids finish their education" was a little less surprising when she returned in 1998.

In social encounters among Mozambican men in South Africa, highly detailed and concrete plans for future postreturn life in Machaze are always a favorite topic of conversation, along with romanticized and stereotyped contrasts between Machaze and South Africa that favorably depict the former. Yet the concreteness of the activity depicted in these plans—constructing houses, starting a grinding mill or a chicken-raising business, drilling a well— tend to sharply and starkly contrast with vagueness about when exactly return might occur. Though stated as an inevitable and imperative outcome, return generally tends to be presented as being subject to particular conditionalities governing its timing. To quote from various interviews conducted with Machazian men discussing their as yet unrealized plans to return, "Of course I must return . . . but I must make sure I have enough money for the trip and for drilling [the well]"; "I will go soon . . . but my son must first be well established in his work so all is well here"; "When the political situation is stable, it will be safe to take my wife and children back." Similarly, among Portuguese emigrants prolonged absences are always portrayed in letters home as being "undesired" and "regrettable" with a return home as a "future inevitable" . . . though also one projected into an indeterminate future.

The conditions that govern timing in these narratives are ones that are "selectively structural." They are structural in that they tend to remove the agency of the migrants themselves from the timing-determination equation. Return is not portrayed as a decision the migrant makes but as a condition that larger forces allow. The specific conditions tend to be ones that are subjective and can only be identified by the migrant. After all, how much money is enough for any particular migrant to return home and live "comfortably"? When is a child "established"?

It is thus not only continued investment in culturally keyed factors of social reproduction back home that allows nonreturnees to translate their investments into moral capital but also this continuously and carefully constructed public discourse that maintains and reproduces a particular frame for interpreting the meaning of these investments. "Narratives of intended return" are framing devices that paradoxically recast social investments abroad as means to ensure ultimate return while explaining ongoing absence as a conditionally deferred return rather than permanent departure.

CONCLUSION: GENERALIZATIONS IN THE
THEORIZING OF "ATTACHED NONRETURN"

In conclusion I want to venture a few generalizations about moral economies of migrancy. These testable generalizations may help theorize how and why socially diverted migrants continue to invest in their communities of origin despite never intending to definitively return.

A first generalization is that moral economy transactions are explicitly and necessarily public transactions. Investments in moral capital are ultimately forms of "presentation of self" to others and claims about one's behavior that only gain moral value through the legitimization of others.

A second and related generalization is that the terms of value and exchange in moral economies will necessarily be culturally idiomatic. If at a structural level we can identify key factors of social reproduction as privileged sites for measuring value in moral economies (or at least moral economies of migration), we must recognize that strategies of social reproduction also operate with a high degree of cultural specificity. The social world that Machazians perceive and react to is thus in many ways a sociospiritual world, peopled with ancestors unlike anything in the Portuguese case. Similarly, interesting and illustrative contrasts can be drawn between the "moral value" generated by specific migrant behavior in the cases discussed here and the meaning of, and moral capital generated by, similar behavior discussed in this volume—such as house building (Grigolini, chapter 6) and return visits (Trager, chapter 7; Newell, chapter 5).

A third generalization is that transactions in a moral economy retain an inherent degree of ambiguity—as, in a sense, do all symbolic transactions. The meanings of investments in key factors of social reproduction (and even arguably what factors are considered "key") are not simply, straightforwardly, or uncontestedly "given." Neither are they historically static. Such investments potentially have variable meanings and are thus subject to continuous contestation over which meanings are applied. Inasmuch as they are subject to contestation, they are also subject to social power.

A final and fourth generalization is that moral capital requires continuous reinvestment to maintain value; otherwise, it has a peculiar tendency to depreciate over time. What renders any narrative of intended return a credible claim about one's intention to eventually return (despite significant historical rates of de facto attrition)? In part, that such performances are managed from abroad means that motives for nonreturn remain inscrutable (*Is he really not well? Did the car really break down and cost them too much to repair?*)—a fact that plays a critical role in legitimizing narratives of intended, postponed, and deferred return.

But perhaps even more critically, the credibility of such claims rests on the credibility and unbroken continuity of previous performances. This is a process that starts with the performance of the initial leaving. Caroline Brettell describes just such a performance in *Men Who Migrate, Women Who Wait* (1986) as a young labor migrant to France attempts to assuage his mother's tears not just with vague or abstract promises of return but by talking in detail about his concrete plans for what will happen back home once he returns. These are plans that orient the whole migration enterprise back to home and hearth—a new house on that plot of adjacent land, a restaurant to be built in the yard, and so forth.

Such performances of departure establish frames within which to interpret future action in particular ways. The moral capital generated through the beginning performance plays a critical role in imputing moral value to later performances. It is the accumulation of moral capital through continuous prior investment that allows a missed visit by a migrant son to be interpreted as evidence of his or her desire to save more money for a successful and more-rapid ultimate return rather than as evidence that he or she is becoming social invested elsewhere (and may never return). Ultimately, to maintain its potency for signifying potential return and thus positive moral value, the house under construction in Olival must visibly denote progress in the performance of the idealized script. Such signs signify positive moral value only if they evidence progression, even if ever so slowly.

NOTES

1. Between 1945 and 1955 the total number of manufacturing establishments in South Africa rose by 47 percent and the total employment of nonwhites in the manufacturing sector rose by 88 percent (Jones and Muller 1992, 175). During a time of significant state-led industrial expansion, the total numbers of private manufacturing establishments rose from 13,789 in 1949 to 16,838 in 1958 (Posel 1993, 416). The industrial sector continued to grow at an even more spectacular pace during the 1960s and early 1970s. In 1961 the types of economic activity forming the South African gross domestic product were as follows: agriculture, 12.4 percent; mining, 13.4 percent; manufacturing, 19.3 percent; commerce, 12.7 percent. In 1976, agriculture and mining had diminished to 7.8 percent and 11.9 percent, respectively, while manufacturing and commerce had increased to 24.0 percent and 14.3 percent,

respectively. During this same time, the gross domestic product multiplied almost sixfold (Jones and Muller 1992, 230).

2. This growth had a significant effect on wages. From 1937 and 1950, mine wages remained virtually the same, while wages in manufacturing for blacks almost doubled (Crush, Jeeves, and Yudelman 1991, 67; Jones and Muller 1992, 128–31). By 1951 manufacturing wages were twice as high as mine wages (Crush, Jeeves, and Yudelman 1991, 63). The need to contain costs in a world market with lower demands for gold and coal meant that the wages offered in the mining industry could keep pace with the rising wages in the manufacturing and service occupations during this period. By 1970 mine wages stood at approximately one-third of those paid in these secondary sector activities (Crankshaw 1997, 98–100).

3. In 1950 women were estimated to form less than 30 percent of the peri-urban population. By 1980 they were estimated to compose 45 percent of that population (Smits 1985, 116–17).

4. I introduce the term *moral capital* to denote an intangible asset that has generative capacity—that is, it is capable of generating additional value. As I explain throughout this chapter, the value that moral capital generates is that of legitimizing interpretations of events in ways that are favorable to the claim maker when in fact other interpretations that would have less-positive consequences for him or her are possible. Credibility and legitimacy are thus the first-order value generated by moral capital. As I explain further, such first-order value, though largely intangible, can significantly affect access to tangible resources—whether these be social (say, a wife or kinship assistance) or material (inheritance of property). Such tangible resources thus constitute a second-order value that is generated by moral capital. I use this term in contradistinction to the more widespread but highly problematic term *social capital*. Although variously deployed by different theorists (Bourdieu 1984, 1986; Coleman 1994; Putnam 1994; Portes 1998; Lin 2000), they all tend to share the notion that social capital is a function of the density and breadth of social relations. Yet as critics such as Paul Durrenberger (2002) and especially John Field (2003) have pointed out, it is not in anyway clear what form of value social relations necessarily generate. Thus, being more enmeshed in denser or more-extensive social networks may or may not provide an individual with more resources to draw on, inasmuch as relations of hierarchy and power may equally result in such social relations restricting options and making claims on one's own resources. It thus seems analytically useful to me to separate out a notion of reputation and credibility (i.e., moral capital) as a source of value generation from any a priori relationship with particular structural characteristics of social relations—such as density and extent of

networks (i.e., what might still arguably be called "social capital"). At the very least, such a move fruitfully problematizes the relationship between social relations and social reputation or credibility and allows us to empirically investigate the effect of each on the other.

REFERENCES

Arroteia, Jorge. 1984. Ilhavo e Murtosa: Dois Casos da Emigracao Portuguesa. In *Emigracao e Rotorno na Regiao Centro*, ed. Commissao de Coordenacao da Regiao Centro, 123–48. Coimbra, Portugal: Commissao de Coordenacao da Regiao Centro.

Baganha, Maria I. 1999. Migracoes Internacionais de e para Portugal: O que sabemos e para onde vamos? *Revista Critica de Ciencias Socias* 52/53:229–80.

Boura, Isabel M., et al. 1984. *The economic impact of returned emigrants: Evidence from Leiria, Mangualde, and Sabugal*. Coimbra, Portugal: Commissao de Coordenacao da Regiao Centro.

Bourdieu, Pierre. 1984. *Distinction: A social critique of the judgement of taste*. London: Routledge.

———. 1986. The forms of capital. In *Handbook of theory and research for the sociology of education*, ed. J. G. Richardson, 241–58. New York: Greenwood Press.

Brettell, Caroline. 1981. Is the ethnic community inevitable? A comparison of the settlement patterns of Portuguese immigrants in Toronto and Paris. *Journal of Ethnic Studies* 9 (3): 1–17.

———. 1986. *Men who migrate, women who wait*. Princeton, N.J.: Princeton University Press.

———. 1990. Leaving, remaining, and returning: Some thoughts on the multi-faceted Portuguese migratory system. In *Portuguese migration in global perspective*, ed. D. Higgs, 61–80. Toronto: Multicultural History Society of Ontario.

———. 1993. The emigrant, the nation, and the state in nineteenth and twentieth century Portugal: An anthropological approach. *Portuguese Studies Review* 2 (2): 51–65.

Coleman, J. S. 1994. *Foundations of social theory*. Cambridge, Mass.: Belknap Press.

Crankshaw, O. 1997. *Race, class, and the changing division of labour under apartheid*. New York: Routledge.

Crush, Jonathan, A. Jeeves, and D. Yudelman. 1991. *South Africa's labor empire: A history of black migrancy to the gold mines.* Boulder, Colo.: Westview.

Durrenberger, Paul. 2002. Why the idea of social capital is a bad idea. *Anthropology News* 43 (9): 5.

Englund, Harry. 1995. Brother against brother: The moral economy of war and displacement in the Malawi-Mozambique borderland. Ph.D. diss., Department of Social Anthropology, University of Manchester.

Ferguson, James. 1999. *Expectations of modernity: Myths and meanings of urban life on the Zambian copperbelt.* Berkeley: University of California Press.

Field, John. 2003. *Social capital.* London: Routledge.

Giles, Wenona. 2002. *Portuguese women in Toronto: Gender, immigration, and nationalism.* Toronto: University of Toronto Press.

Graham, Helen. 1990. Money and migration in modern Portugal: An economist's view. In *Portuguese migration in global perspective,* ed. David Higgs, 81–98. Toronto: Multicultural History Society of Ontario.

Gugler, Josef. 1975. Migration and ethnicity in sub-Saharan Africa: Affinity, rural interests, and urban alignments. In *Migration and development: Implications for ethnic identity and political conflict,* ed. Helen Safa and Brian M. du Toit, 295–309. The Hague: Mouton.

Gugler, Josef, and Peter Geschiere. 1998. The urban-rural connection: Changing issues of belonging and identification. *Africa* 68 (3): 309–19.

Higgs, David. 1990. Portuguese migration before 1800. In *Portuguese migration in global perspective,* ed. David Higgs, 7–29. Toronto: Multicultural History Society of Ontario.

Hyden, Goran. 1980. *Beyond Ujamaa in Tanzania: Underdevelopment and an uncaptured peasantry.* Berkeley: University of California Press.

Jones, S., and A. Muller. 1992. *The South African economy, 1910–1990.* New York: St. Martin's Press.

Klimt, Andrea. 1989. Returning "home": Portuguese migrant notions of temporariness, permanence, and commitment. *New German Critique* 46:47–70.

———. 2000a. Enacting national selves: Authenticity, adventure, and disaffection in the Portuguese diaspora. *Identities* 4 (4): 513–50.

———. 2000b. European spaces: Portuguese migrants' notions of home and belonging. *Diaspora* 9 (2): 259–85.

Klimt, Andrea, and Stephen Lubkemann. 2002. Argument across the Portuguese-speaking world: A discursive approach to diaspora. *Diaspora* 11 (2): 145–62.

Lin, Nan. 2000. *Social capital: A theory of social structure and action.* Cambridge: Cambridge University Press.

Lubkemann, Stephen. 2000a. Other motives, other struggles: Gender politics and the shaping of wartime migration in Mozambique. In *Rethinking refuge and displacement: Selected papers on refugees and immigrants,* vol. 8, ed. Elbieta Godziak and D. J. Shandy, 343–68. Arlington, Va.: American Anthropological Association.

———. 2000b. Situating wartime migration in central Mozambique: Gendered social struggle and the transnationalization of polygyny. Ph.D. diss., Department of Anthropology, Brown University, Providence, Rhode Island.

———. 2000c. Sociocultural factors shaping the Mozambican repatriation process. In *Humanitarian action: Social science connections,* ed. Stephen Lubkemann, Larry Minear, and Thomas Weiss, 91–126. Providence, R.I.: Thomas Watson Jr. Institute for International Studies.

———. 2000d. The transformation of transnationality among Mozambican migrants in South Africa. *Canadian Journal of African Studies* 34 (1): 41–63.

———. 2002a. The moral economy of Portuguese postcolonial return. *Diaspora* 11 (2): 189–214.

———. 2002b. Where to be an ancestor? Reconstituting socio-spiritual worlds and post-conflict settlement decision-making among displaced Mozambicans. *Journal of Refugee Studies* 15 (2): 189–212.

———. 2003. Race, class, and kin in the negotiation of "internal strangerhood" among Portuguese retornados, 1975–2000. In *Europe's invisible migrants,* ed. Andrea Smith, 75–94. Amsterdam: University of Amsterdam Press.

Marx, Emmanuel. 1990. The social world of the refugee: A conceptual framework. *Journal of Refugee Studies* 3 (3): 189–203.

Moniz, Miguel. 2004. Strangers in their own land: Criminal deportee forced return migrants and transnational identity: The Azorean case. PhD. diss., Department of Anthropology, Brown University, Providence, R.I.

Noivo, Edite. 1997. *Inside ethnic families: Three generations of Portuguese Canadians.* Montreal: McGill-Queens University Press.

———. 2002. Towards a cartography of Portugueseness: Challenging the hegemonic center. *Diaspora* 11 (2): 255–75.

Piot, Charles. 1999. *Remotely global: Village modernity in West Africa.* Chicago: University of Chicago Press.

Portes, Alejandro. 1998. "Social capital": Its origins and applications in modern sociology. *Annual Review in Sociology* 24:1–24.

Posel, D. 1993. Influx control and urban labour markets in the 1950s. In *Apartheid's genesis, 1935–1962,* ed. P. Bonner, P. Delius, and D. Posel, 411–30. Johannesburg, So. Africa: Witwatersrand University Press.

Putnam, Robert. 1994. *Bowling alone: The collapse and revival of American community.* New York: Simon and Shuster.

Rocha-Trindade, M. B. 1981. *Estudos Sobre a Emigracao Portuguesa.* Lisbon, Portugal: Sa da Costa.

———. 1990. Portuguese migration to Brazil in the nineteenth and twentieth centuries. In *Portuguese migration in global perspective,* ed. D. Higgs, 29–42. Toronto: Multicultural History Society of Ontario.

Schlemmer, Lawrence. 1985. Squatter communities: Safety valves in the rural-urban nexus. In *Up against the fences,* ed. Hermann Gilomee and Lawrence Schlemmer, 167–92. New York: St. Martin's Press.

Scott, James. 1976. *The moral economy of the peasant: Rebellion and subsistence in Southeast Asia.* New Haven, Conn.: Yale University Press.

———. 1985. *Weapons of the weak: Everyday forms of peasant resistance.* New Haven, Conn.: Yale University Press.

Serrão, Joel. 1977. *A Emigracao Portuguesa-Sondagem Historica.* Lisbon, Portugal: Horizonte.

Silva, Manuela, Rogerio R. Amaro, G. Clausse, C. Conim, M. Matos, M. Pisco, and L. M. Seuya. 1984. *Retorno, Emigracao, E Desenvolvimento Regional em Portugal.* Lisbon, Portugal: Instituto de Estudos Para o Desenvolvimento.

Smits, Philip. 1985. The process of black urbanization. In *Up against the Fences,* ed. Hermann Gilomee and Lawrence Schlemmer, 114–25. New York: St. Martin's Press.

Teixeira, Carlos, and Victor M. P. Da Rosa. 2000. Introduction: A historical and geographical perspective. In *The Portuguese in Canada*, ed. Carlos Teixeira and Victor Da Rosa. Toronto: University of Toronto Press.

Thompson, E. P. 1963. *The making of the English working class.* London: Victor Gollancz.

———. 1971. The moral economy of the English crowd in the eighteenth century. *Past and Present* 50:76–136.

9

"Direct to the Poor" Revisited

Migrant Remittances and Development Assistance

Robyn Eversole

Despite huge philosophical and political fissures around defining what *development* is, what it should look like, and how to accomplish it, an encouraging consensus has formed in recent years around "pro-poor" or "antipoverty" development policies. Such policies focus on the importance of prioritizing human well-being and reducing inequities. In the year 2000, the Organisation for Economic Cooperation and Development (OECD) set millennium development goals that included halving the incidence of extreme economic poverty worldwide; increasing access to schooling; reducing maternal, infant, and child mortality; improving access to reproductive health services; and reversing the loss of environmental resources (OECD 2000). These development goals represent an international commitment to "the world's poorest and most vulnerable"—such as the estimated 1.2 billion people around the world who live on less than one U.S. dollar a day (OECD 2000).

The OECD's development goals characterize much of the current vision behind international development policymaking. Antipoverty goals are regularly articulated in mainstream agencies. Economic growth is no longer understood to be sufficient to address poverty without taking into account the distribution of the fruits and costs of growth. Growth-led development has thus been retooled into the concept of "pro-poor growth" (Department for

International Development 1997, 8). Poverty is also recognized as being "multidimensional," involving not only economic deprivation but other forms of social and political deprivation as well. Simon Maxwell of the Overseas Development Institute has observed the encouraging trend that, with the World Bank's taking on part of the United Nations Development Programme's antipoverty agenda, an international consensus on reducing poverty is closer than ever before (Maxwell 2003, 9).

Nevertheless, many poverty-creating and poverty-solving processes are still falling outside the sights of international development policy. In this chapter, I consider migrant remittances, a phenomenon generally excluded from mainstream international development discussions. In the following sections, I refer to data and cases from around the world in order to explore the role of migrant remittances in achieving antipoverty development goals. In this chapter, I approach antipoverty debates from the perspective of what "poor people" themselves actually do about poverty. Doing so thus provides us with an opportunity for thinking outside the development box. If migration is a relevant strategy, then what are the larger implications for development policy?

From a background in international development work, my interest in migrant remittances came through the fieldwork of a geographer colleague, James Keese. Keese was studying the impact of agriculture development projects in highland Ecuador over a period of six years. He did an initial study in 1995, with a follow-up in 2001, and found that a group of development projects implemented with local grassroots organizations had not been very successful in reducing poverty. The reasons varied, but one was particularly notable: the lack of labor power to maintain projects over time. This was a direct response to a much more significant economic opportunity—migration to the United States:

> International migration is having a dramatic impact. . . . Migrant families with US incomes have the means to acquire resources and improve their standard of living. Formerly poor indigenous farmers now have new two-story houses and own cars. (Remittances are sometimes used to buy land and dairy cattle as well.) . . . The income from remittances can make the returns from an NGO project seem insignificant. (Keese 2003, 23, 25)

Ecuadorians living in the United States send home approximately US$1.4 billion dollars each year in remittances (Keese 2003, 5). This is many times the value of the US$147 million that Ecuador receives in a year in official development assistance.[1] Houses, cars, cows, and land for the poor—such were the benefits of remittances, while development projects in Keese's study region, costing about $300,000 per year, had left only some overgrown trout ponds, a few guinea pig runs and pigpens, nonfunctioning greenhouses and sprinkler systems, and some trees. If the idea is to channel resources to poor people and empower them, what is working? One begins to wonder, are we looking for development policy in the wrong places?

I take as my starting point in this chapter the international development field's commitment to combating poverty. I assume that this commitment is genuine: that the issue is not whether to make resources available for closing equity gaps but how to do so most effectively. A key challenge is how to ensure that disadvantaged people actually receive the resources intended for them—a challenge sometimes referred to as "reaching the poor." The following section provides a brief overview of the grassroots and participatory development perspectives that inform current understandings about how development resources can best reach the poor. From there, I move on to explore data on migrant remittances, and I place these in the context of the international development field's own articulated antipoverty goals. International remittances, which parallel international aid and development funds as forms of wealth transfer between countries, are the main focus of this chapter. Nevertheless, many of the uses of international remittances also hold true for internal remittances—that is, remittances from people who migrate within the borders of their home country; these similarities are also noted. I conclude this chapter by suggesting that migrant remittances are a significant and often-overlooked source of funding for a range of development activities: activities that are generally instigated and managed by poor people themselves. This in turn has important implications for the way we think about development policies to fight poverty.

REACHING THE POOR: DEVELOPMENT AND EMPOWERMENT

The concept of grassroots development is a key hinge for this discussion of migrant remittances and international development. In theory, grassroots development is the emic perspective on development. It posits that local people know best what their own needs are, and if given access to the appropriate resources, they can achieve their own development goals (see e.g. Inter-American

Foundation 1977). "Community development" and "community economic de-velopment" are similar approaches, their core proposition being that commu-nities decide what development will look like for them (Kenny 1999; Ife 2002; Coirolo et al. 2001). Grassroots and community-based approaches have often reacted against top-down development models, not only on efficiency grounds (local people know their local contexts best), but also on philosophical ones (who controls development?).

In Sheldon Annis and Peter Hakim's well-known work on grassroots devel-opment in Latin America, *Direct to the Poor* (1988), the authors argue that "the best way to help poor people is to give money to the organisations that they themselves create and control." Such direct resource transfer to poor people would avoid the "strings," "baggage," "politics," "waste," and "diversion" often involved in channeling resources through public agencies (1). This approach reflects the common concern that, as Amartya Sen once wrote, "official aid does not go to poor people . . . it goes instead to their rulers" (Sen 1981, 111, quoted in David 1997, 210). Grassroots development approaches have aimed to remedy this situation. They have also recognized people's own knowledge and analytical capabilities and the value of local resources of all kinds (Annis and Hakim 1988, 1; Chambers 1994)—things that economic anthropologists find it quite easy to notice but are often invisible to faraway policymakers.

In a growing trend through the 1980s and 1990s to support grassroots civil-society organizations and nongovernmental organizations (NGOs), the grassroots development approach has entered mainstream development discussions—albeit with some important caveats. The concept of empower-ing disadvantaged groups has become fashionable, based somewhat on Freirian ideas of consciousness raising and encouraged by the current focus on "democratization" and "good governance" in much current international development policy. Mainstream antipoverty policies focus on encouraging organizations and activities that are participative, inclusive, and empowering of "the poor" themselves (World Bank 2000; United Nations Development Programme 2000; United Nations Educational, Scientific, and Cultural Or-ganization 2000; Coirolo et al. 2001). Nevertheless, outside funders who sup-port grassroots groups have their own goals, which may or may not agree with those at the grassroots. Outside funders may also fail to realize or ac-knowledge the complexity of local interests. Thus, it is important to realize that even when outsiders' work is couched in the language of participation, it may still be an attempt to direct social change from the outside (see, e.g., Simonelli and Earle 2003; White 1996).

As an international development practitioner, one almost inevitably ends up party to conversations about how best to "reach poor people," especially "the poorest," with programs, services, and support of all kinds. Development organizations often have a mandate to provide benefits to the disadvantaged and want to ensure that their work is reaching those who need it most. Some attempt to "poverty-target" their programs in order to reach needy people, communities, and regions. There is also a stated desire for greater participation from local people in development activities (see, e.g., Simanowitz 2000; Davis and Whittington 1998). Behind this lies an understanding that people must be part of the processes meant to benefit them. Yet there is also an awareness that people are often reluctant to join development processes—which are often led in the first instance by outsiders and may be seen to offer costly, uncertain, or inappropriate solutions.

Given the general interest in "reaching" and including poor people in the process of planned social change that we call development, the political climate seems right to take a closer look at these people's own development strategies. While antipoverty rhetoric does place under a deceptively simple umbrella a huge swathe of the world's population ("the poor"), it is nevertheless a useful shorthand signaling a desire for change. Current international understandings of development articulate that its criteria must reach beyond mere economic growth or well-being for the few into serious concerns about equity and social justice. Yet "reaching" poor people is not a one-way street in which those with needs sit passively and await assistance. Grassroots and participatory development philosophies have recognized this, yet they have not gone far enough toward seeing and supporting people's own strategies for solving their economic and social ills. This chapter focuses on one such strategy: labor migration and the funding of a range of development activities via migrant remittances. This is certainly a grassroots strategy, and despite its disadvantages, it is one that does allow resources from wealthier countries and regions to flow "direct to the poor."

THE POOR REACH OUT: MIGRATION AND MIGRANT REMITTANCES

Economic anthropologists are skilled at seeing the way real economies in real places work. Among people categorized by outsiders—and sometimes, by themselves—as "the poor," economic anthropologists have documented production strategies and exchange systems; ways of controlling labor and accessing resources; and strategies for survival, reproduction, and wealth generation. This sort of information is key to understanding how to decrease poverty; it offers insight into the sorts of issues that Amartya Sen (1985, 1999) and other development theorists have raised: the rights and the institutions, formal and informal, that determine what resources people can access in specific places (Gore 1993). Once we learn how "poor people" access resources of all kinds, then we can understand how pro-poor policies can make access easier for them.

Migration is one key economic strategy employed by many people from disadvantaged parts of the world. It is certainly not new: migration for trade, conquest, and gathering or cultivation of resources in different local environments has long been characteristic of human societies. Nor is migration by any means limited to poor or disadvantaged populations: many kinds of people migrate, for many different reasons. Furthermore, many poor people do not migrate. Yet, migration is one important way in which people access new sets of resources. In the contemporary world, we see less migration to seasonal fishing grounds or lowland agricultural plots and more migration from rural areas to the city, from countries of the geopolitical "South" to those of the "North," and from stagnant economies to dynamic economies. A common migration pattern is movement from areas of economic disadvantage to areas of economic advantage, whether comparative or perceived—for instance, to places where there are jobs (see, e.g., in this volume, Koenig, chapter 2; Pérez, chapter 1). Such migration may be temporary, cyclical, or permanent. It may take place within the borders of a single nation (internal migration) or across national borders (international migration).

The purpose of this chapter is to draw attention to a significant subset of the migration literature—the literature on migrant remittances—and to explore its relevance to antipoverty international development policy. Remittances are the economic transfers that migrants make to their places of origin, most often to their own family members but also to organizations, communities, and (for international migrants) their national economies. Remittances can be in the form of currency or goods. The term refers exclusively to direct economic contributions; it does not include other contributions migrants can make to their places of origin, such as innovative ideas, political clout, or access to information and networks in other places.[2] These, though they may have significant development impact, are much more difficult to identify and measure.

Not all migrants remit, of course, and an extensive literature explores the extent of and reasons for remitting. Motivations include altruistic support for family members, the felt obligation to repay families' investments in education and establishment costs, the desire to ensure eventual family inheritances, and a way to secure a comfortable return at retirement (see Brown and Ahlburg 1999; Regmi and Tisdell 2002). As for the many attempts to define who exactly remits (and how much), it appears that generalizations are difficult to make. Lindsay Lowell (2001) has observed that more-educated international migrants are less likely to remit than those with less education. In another international study, Shivani Puri and Tineke Ritzema (1999) have indicated that migrants with higher salaries remit a smaller portion of their total earnings, though they may remit more in absolute terms.[3]

Ultimately, the specific personal and family situation of each migrant (amount saved, amount earned, the number of dependents back home, and so forth) influences the decision whether, and how much, to remit (International Organization for Migration [IOM] 2002, 3). Other factors, such as the security and cost of the various channels of money transfer, also play a role in migrants' remittance decision making (IOM 2002, 5; Lianos 1997, 77). Most remittances are sent and received by members of the same family (see, e.g., Lowell and de la Garza 2000, 21; IOM 2002, 5). In some cases, local or transnational organizations are important receivers of remittances.

The following discussion draws on literature on migrant remittances from various parts of the world. While some areas of debate exist and specific contexts do vary, these studies present a remarkably coherent picture about the development impact of remittances:

1. Migrant remittances are a significant source of resource transfer from rich areas to poor areas.
2. Migrant remittances arrive not just to poor areas but often to poor families.
3. In sheer numbers, the total income represented by international migrant remittances is greater than official development assistance (though this varies from country to country).

4. Migrant remittances are a source of development finance that poor people can control themselves.

THE DEVELOPMENT IMPACT OF MIGRANT REMITTANCES: A REVIEW OF THE DATA

This section draws on a range of recent studies of migrant remittances to illustrate the validity of the four points proposed here. As noted, the focus is on international migration, with references to the literature on internal migration to highlight similarities. In the following subsections, I examine each of these points in turn.

Migrant remittances are a significant source of resource transfer from rich areas to poor areas. The value of international remittances worldwide has been estimated in excess of US$100 billion per year and growing, with more than 60 percent going to developing countries (Martin 2001). Worldwide, India has had the greatest volume and growth of remittances over the past two decades, followed by Mexico (Orozco 2000, 15). India alone received over US$11 billion in remittances in 1999 (Economic and Social Commission for Asia and the Pacific [ESCAP] 2002, 5). And migrants from Mexico to the United States send home more than $22 million a day, providing "basic support" for nearly 1.2 million, or about 5 percent, of Mexican households (Smith 2001). Such figures generally exclude remittances that are not transferred through official channels—such as those hand carried in the form of money or goods. Nor do they consider the internal remittance flows within countries—for example, those from urban dwellers to their rural relatives, which can be significant (see, e.g., Bryceson 2000).

Countries in the Asian and Pacific region that rely significantly on remittances from migrant workers abroad are the Philippines, India, Pakistan, Bangladesh, and Sri Lanka (Skeldon 2002, 76–77); other important labor-sending countries are Thailand, Indonesia, and Vietnam. In 1999, total recorded remittances to these eight countries exceeded US$20 billion (ESCAP 2002, 5). The Philippines alone, with nearly a tenth of its population living or working overseas, received over US$6 billion in the year 2000 (Go 2002, quoted in Skeldon 2002, 76–77). Some small countries such as Samoa and Tonga also rely heavily on remittances, with 90 percent of Tongalese households being remittance recipients according to a 1984 national survey (Brown and Ahlburg 1999).

In Latin America, the major migrant-sending countries include Mexico, Colombia, the Dominican Republic, El Salvador, and Guatemala; these countries together receive an estimated total of US$8 billion per year in international remittances (Lowell and de la Garza 2000, 1). Other Latin American countries, such as Ecuador and Brazil, also receive significant remittances. In Africa, combined international remittances to fifteen countries were estimated in 1999 to be about US$8.2 billion (IOM 2002, 2). Egypt is the largest receiver of remittances in Africa, with over US$3.7 billion dollars worth in 1999. However, for much of Africa, international remittances are of comparatively small significance. According to World Bank development indicators, Western African countries tended to receive international remittances ranging between US$30 million and US$90 million in 1999; these also varied considerably from year to year (2). However, if money transferred via informal channels were included, these figures might be expected to double or even triple, given the low development of banking systems in many African countries (2).

The movement of migrant remittances internationally is clearly a flow from wealthier countries toward poorer countries—though not the poorest. It is difficult to generalize about the characteristics of countries that are major labor exporters and thus significant receivers of remittances. However, none of the major remittance-receiving countries listed here has a "high" human development index, according to the *Human Development Report 2003*—with the exception of Mexico (where internal inequality is a major issue). Labor-exporting countries are mostly ranked as having "medium" human development (see United Nations Development Programme 2003). This suggests that a certain level of economic resources and human development may be necessary in a country before its citizens can take advantage of international migration opportunities.

Similarly, while remittances reach many poor households and poor regions within countries, they may not necessarily reach the poorest (a point discussed further in the following section). There is, however, evidence to support that remittances do reach disadvantaged regions within countries, such as rural regions of Mexico, thereby creating opportunities for social and economic change (Orozco 2003, 9–12). Similarly, Richard C. Jones's household survey data (1998) for Mexico's central Zacatecas state show that remittances from international migration have contributed toward decreasing inequalities between Mexico's urban and rural areas.

Where do international remittances come from? Significant sources include the United States, Canada, European countries, and wealthy areas of the Middle East, reflecting the destination choices of international migrants. International migrants from Western Africa tend to go to neighboring countries (for instance, from Mali to Côte d'Ivoire or Zaire) or to France, as well as increasingly to other European countries and the United States (de Haan 1999; see also, in this volume, Koenig, chapter 2; Newell, chapter 5; and Trager, chapter 7). Mexicans and Central Americans tend to seek jobs in the United States or Canada; migrants from the South Pacific often look to the United States, Australia, or New Zealand (Brown and Ahlburg 1999); those from the Philippines gravitate largely to the Middle East and Asia (ESCAP 2002, 2); and migrants from South Asia go mostly to the Middle East (1).

Not only does the research reflect the significance of the sheer size of the resource transfers represented by international remittances, thus having "profound effects of local and national economies" (Lowell, de la Garza, and Hogg 2000, 17), but data from many parts of the world indicate that remittances and the number of international migrant workers have been growing over time. Overall growth in remittances to Colombia, the Dominican Republic, El Salvador, Guatemala, and Mexico, for instance, has been estimated at 26 percent annually (Lowell and de la Garza 2000, 1). During the 1990–2000 period, Bangladesh's number of migrant workers more than doubled, Indonesia's quadrupled, and immigrants from the Philippines (excluding seafarers) nearly doubled as well (ESCAP 2002, 2). Such a rapid expansion in international labor migration can be attributed to "widening disparities in the level of economic development between countries of origin and countries of destination" as well as demographic and institutional shifts (1).[4] Migrants are attracted to more economically "successful" areas; their remittances are one way that they can capture the resources of wealthy areas and channel them toward their own places of origin.

On the surface, significant resource transfer is clearly happening through international migrants' remittances. Yet at the same time as remittances are flowing in, labor is flowing out. Is the net effect a benefit to the labor-sending countries? This has been a long-standing debate, as summarized by Jose Itzigsohn (1995). On the positive side, remittances are seen as a source of foreign currency for developing countries. They assist with the balance of payments and help cover the cost of imports. They also provide an incentive for the local production of goods and services—overall, creating net positive effects on the labor-sending area. On the other hand, some scholars have linked migration and remittances with increasing social inequalities back home, dependence on labor-receiving countries, and increased demand for imported goods (634–35). The long-term absence of family and community members can cause disruption and stress for spouses, children, and other community members, as well as for migrants themselves.[5] It is important when discussing the benefits of migration to acknowledge its costs as well.

Finally, resource transfer from rich areas to poor areas happens not only as a result of international migration but also through the remittances of internal migrants. Migration to areas of comparative economic advantage does not necessarily involve crossing borders. Therefore, it is possible to witness relationships between poorer and wealthier regions of the same country that reflect relationships between poorer and wealthier countries on the international scene. Some areas, such as rural villages, are senders of labor and receivers of remittances; other areas, such as cities, major agricultural plantation areas, and mines, are receivers of labor (see, e.g., Regmi and Tisdell 2002, for Nepal; de Haan 2002, for India; Trager 1998, for Nigeria; Francis 2002, for South Africa). The value of internal migrants' remittances is even more difficult to estimate than international remittances (see de Haan 1999, 23), yet it is important to recognize that they can also represent significant sources of resource transfer.

Migrant remittances arrive not just to poor areas but often to poor families. While migrant remittances provide a form of resource transfer from wealthier to poorer areas, this leaves open the question of who within those areas actually benefits. Do migrant remittances—particularly, international migrant remittances—actually reach poor families, or are they concentrated among the wealthy households? Do they lessen or increase inequality among households in migrant-sending areas? Given the available data, it is clear that the benefits of migrant remittances do reach poor families, directly or indirectly, in a range of ways. Their impact on inequality is less clear; in some settings, the presence of remittances has been shown to increase inequality and, in others, to decrease it.

The international evidence suggests that poor people certainly benefit from remittances, but it is less certain whether the poorest benefit. In general, the poorest people in an area cannot afford the costs of migration (ESCAP 2002, 8), particularly international migration. Thus, data from Richard H. Adams Jr.'s study of households (1998, 161) in the poorest district of each of three Pakistani provinces indicate that international remittances tend to go to upper-income households in those districts because of the high cost of travel and permits for migrants. Similarly, Dolores Koenig (this volume, chapter 2) found that very poor Malian households were not benefiting much from remittances as compared with wealthier households, because the former had fewer people able to migrate. And Jeffrey H. Cohen (this volume, chapter 3) found that in Mexico, some very poor households did not send migrants at all, because they found migration too costly.

Nevertheless, wealth is not necessarily a prerequisite to migration, as many migrants around the world do borrow heavily, particularly from family members, to finance the cost of their travel and establishment abroad. Thus, it is a mistake to assume that international migrants are always simply those who are wealthy enough to make the trip. Various studies confirm that poor households do receive international remittances. Data from a Thai study by Osaki indicate that both poor and wealthier households receive remittances, and while the amount remitted to poor households tends to be less, it has a much greater relative impact (cited in Skeldon 2002, 78). In a study in Guatemala and Haiti, it was the better off among the poor (though not the poorest) who received remittances (Itzigsohn 1995, 645). Similarly, Manuel Orozco (2003) presents data indicating that half of remittance recipients in Mexico have no other source of income. Finally, remittances do reach the poorest in some areas; for instance, Massey and colleagues (1987) found that Mexican urban households that relied on remittances are those with the lowest income and the worst labor-market prospects (cited in Itzigsohn 1995, 645).

International migration can be a way for families facing unemployment and unstable income streams to capture needed income. In the Caribbean, for instance, the economic crisis of 1980s, with deteriorated domestic labor-market conditions, led people from lower socioeconomic strata to migrate and send remittances; there, "remittances have become a fundamental source of income for lifting households out of poverty" (Itzigsohn 1995, 636). Similarly, Dennis Conway and Jeffrey H. Cohen (1998) describe international migration by Zapotec people in Santa Ana, Mexico, to the United States as "a widely used survival and subsistence strategy" in response to the protracted economic crisis of the mid-1980s. Even without crisis, international migration and remittances can be an ongoing strategy to meet basic needs in places with few indigenous income-generating opportunities. This is the case, for instance, for some Pacific islands; Geoff Bertram (1999) observes that "remittances from citizens living abroad are crucial for the sustainability of many island economies," allowing them to have higher standards of living than what the gross domestic product would indicate possible. And Connell's 1983 South Pacific study (cited in Brown and Ahlburg 1999) shows that "remittances have enabled basic needs to be met on the outer islands of Tonga especially where income-earning opportunities are otherwise few."

Remittances are often used to meet basic needs and day-to-day expenditures of recipients. Lindsay Lowell and Rodolfo O. de la Garza, in a study of Mexican migrants, for instance, found that most remittance monies are "solidly earmarked for basic needs" such as health care (2000, 22). Itzigsohn (1995) quotes a range of studies that demonstrate how "remittances are spent mostly on basic subsistence needs, and after those are fulfilled, on housing improvement and eventually land purchase." Research in the South Pacific indicates that remittances are often directed into the purchase of consumer goods, most importantly food: "hence . . . remittances play an important role in maintaining households" (Brown and Ahlburg 1999). The emphasis on covering basic needs suggests that households receiving remittances are often poor. A Greek study showed that remittances from workers abroad are used primarily for consumption and that they raised the standard of living of recipient families in the study region from only 72 percent of average rural expenditures to 160 percent (Glystos 1993, 144).

Migration can help diversify households' economies, which can help alleviate poverty caused by dependence on a single resource at one location (Skeldon 2002, 75). This is true for both internal and international migration. In a study of migration in the African Sahel, for instance, David (1995) found that while remittances were low, they were nevertheless vital to food security as a way to diversify risks (cited in de Haan 1999, 24). Migrant remittances may also allow sending households to move beyond meeting basic needs and toward achieving a certain level of social mobility. Various studies on migrants from Tonga and Samoa, for instance, have shown that remittances raise living standards and contribute to employment, especially in the service and construction sectors (Brown and Ahlburg 1999). In Bangladesh, a village study by Islam (1991) on remittances from migrants to the Gulf indicates that remittances are spent in a variety of ways, from basic needs to luxury consumption, including buying social status and land (cited in de Haan 1999, 25). This suggests opportunities for social mobility for poor households.

Remittances are clearly reaching poor families in poor areas and making some poor households better off. But what is the impact on households that do not receive remittances? Is inequality among households—the gap between wealthy (or newly wealthy) and poor—increased or reduced? The evidence from studies in different countries is contradictory (see Skeldon 2002, 78; Rodriguez 1998, 329–30). The effect seems to depend on a complex variety of contextual factors, such as when and where migration takes place and the social networks and social capital of those who are involved (see, e.g., Itzigsohn 1995, 635). Studies in Tonga and Samoa, where many families receive remittances, show that remittances tend to decrease, or else have no impact on, income inequality among households (Brown and Ahlburg 1999). In the Indian Punjab, Oberai and Singh (1980) also found that remittances improved the distribution of income (cited in de Haan 1999, 24). Yet Edgard R. Rodriguez (1998), using data from the 1991 Family Income and Expenditure Survey in the Philippines, argues that international migrants' remittances may raise incomes but worsen income distribution. He does observe, however, that much depends on how evenly dispersed are the opportunities for international migration (346). This point is also made by Oded Stark, J. Edward Taylor, and Shlomo Yitzhaki (1986) in their study of the effect of migrant remittances in two Mexican villages—that is, it matters how migration opportunities are diffused across households. The accessibility of opportunities to migrate is thus an important factor influencing the inequality question.

Another important factor is whether the multiplier effects of remittances are captured locally or if they exit the area. The question here is, to what extent can nonrecipients of remittances benefit from remittance income? If migrants' families buy local products, this can have a positive impact on multipliers, creating more economic opportunities locally. However, if these families buy imported goods, demand for local goods may actually decrease, exacerbating interhousehold inequalities (IOM 2002, 6). A report on international development and migration in Asia and the Pacific states, "Remittances and savings from international labour migration help not only the families of migrants but also others in the community because of spending on housing, labour, goods and services" (ESCAP 2002, 9). One important use of remittances in many parts of the world is housing, which tends to have reasonably high multipliers, as it generally uses local labor and often local materials. If remittances in Tonga and Samoa are indeed contributing to local employment in construction and services, as Richard P. C. Brown and Dennis A. Ahlburg state, then it is easy to see why they are not exacerbating interhousehold inequalities.

Overall, evidence from a range of studies shows that migrant remittances often—though not always—reach poor households. Remittances may even, in some cases, reach the poorest. And, given the right conditions (such as encouragement for remittance recipients to spend and invest locally), the remittances of international migrants can even benefit local people who do not migrate. Thus, migration and the transfer of migrant remittances can create benefits that are not necessarily limited to the households of migrants themselves.

In sheer numbers, the income represented by international migrant remittances is greater than official development assistance. The World Bank estimated in the early nineties that recorded international remittances alone were 50 percent higher than total official development assistance (Taylor and Wyatt 1996, 899). By 1999, official development assistance from OECD countries stood at US$56.4 billion (Development Assistance Committee [DAC] 2000, table 2), while the worldwide flow of remittances, according to the International Monetary Fund's *Balance of Payments* report, was over US$100 billion (cited in Martin 2001).[6] Not only are remittances much higher than official development assistance, and have remained so over time, but they are also greater than foreign investment from OECD countries to developing countries, which in 1999 totaled only US$89.4 billion (DAC 2000, table 2). Susan F. Martin's description (2001) of reconstruction efforts in El Salvador is telling: "The President of El Salvador, Francisco Flores Perez, recently used a visit with President George W. Bush to request work permits for Salvadorans in the United States. The increased earnings that legally authorized workers could remit would far outweigh the likely foreign aid that would be forthcoming."

The more than $8 billion in remittances now sent annually to Mexico and Central America are, as Linday Lowell, Rodolfo O. de la Garza, and Mike Hogg (2000, 14) observe, "an amount much greater than U.S. foreign aid and as great as foreign direct investment in some countries." Douglas S. Massey and Emilio A. Parrado's 1994 study found that "migradollars" entering Mexico in 1990 nearly equaled its earnings from export agriculture and "would constitute 78 percent of its direct foreign investment, 59 percent of its tourist revenues, and 56 percent of its earnings from maquila production" (quoted in Durand, Parrado, and Massey 1996, 424). Using both quantitative data and examples from ethnographic fieldwork, Durand and colleagues conclude that the inflow of around $2 billion in migradollars annually into Mexico as a result of labor migration to the United States stimulates economic activity and leads to significantly higher levels of employment, investment, and income.

For many African countries, such as Senegal, Burkina Faso, and Mali, overseas development assistance is a larger source of financial inflows than that from remittances; nevertheless, in these and many other cases, remittances are still significant and are also larger than foreign direct investment in many cases (IOM 2002, 2–3). For instance, from 1980 to 1999, remittances represented on average 4.5 percent of Benin's gross domestic product and 5.8 percent of Burkina Faso's; foreign direct investment over the same period was negligible (2–3). Nigeria received about $1.3 billion in official remittances from abroad in 1999 (2) but only $152 million in official development assistance that same year (DAC 2000, table 25), though it did receive significant foreign direct investment (IOM 2002, 3).

A review of Asian countries that receive significant remittances from international migrants shows that these remittances play a significant role when compared with that of overseas development assistance.[7] Bangladesh, for instance, received US$1.8 billion in remittances in 1999, as compared with $1.2 billion in overseas development assistance. That same year, the Philippines received nearly the same amount of remittances as it did official overseas development assistance: US$6.8 billion in remittances and $6.9 billion in development assistance. Sri Lanka received over US$1 billion in remittances and only $251 million in development assistance; Thailand received $1.6 billion in remittances and $1 billion in development assistance; and India received $11.1 billion in remittances and only $1.5 billion in development assistance.

These data demonstrate that remittances are a significant source of financial inflows for many countries around the world, considerably exceeding what they can hope to receive via official development assistance. When considering countries' ability to capture external resources, remittances should not be overlooked—particularly given Jones's argument (1998) that remittances are more likely to reach poor regions and poor families than financial inflows such as overseas development assistance or foreign direct investment. While international development assistance still has an important role to play, and foreign direct investment as well as export development are key ways for countries to capture external resources, it is a mistake to overlook the importance of remittances as a source of development finance. These figures indicate the impact that increased openness to migration could have on the overall quantity of resources channeled to poor countries. One OECD paper has argued that if the European Union, Canada, Japan, and the United States allowed migrants to make up just 4 percent of their labor force, the returns to migrants' places of origin would be an estimated US$180 billion per year (Skeldon 2002, 79).

Migrant remittances are a source of development finance that poor people can control themselves. Migration and migrant remittances are, ultimately, a strategy by individuals and households to improve their well-being. They are thus a "development" strategy and one that people themselves pursue: placing money back in the hands of their own families, organizations, and home communities. Writing about the migradollars that Mexican immigrants to the United States send home, Durand and colleagues (1996, 441) have observed that "unlike other sources of foreign exchange, migradollars flow directly to the people who need them the most, without being filtered through intervening social and economic structures. . . . Virtually all of the money goes to the poorest segments of Mexican society." In other places around the world as well, we have seen that remittances arrive to poor regions and poor households and in significant quantities.

A growing number of voices are calling attention to the volume and reach of the resource transfers represented by migrant remittances. These remittances can be important development resources. Yet, what sort of "development" do migrant remittances finance? There is, after all, considerable agreement in the literature that most remittances are used for "consumption" rather than "productive investment" (see various studies cited in Durand et al. 1996; Conway and Cohen 1998; see also Basok 2000, 79, 85). In some quarters, this has led remittances to be dismissed as being irrelevant for development. Many other authors, however, have emphasized that there is more to development than merely productive investment; that investments in consumption can lead indirectly to productive investment and employment (see, e.g., Grigolini, this volume, chapter 6); and that in some areas and at some periods in the migration stream, remittances are used directly for productive invest-ment. Thus, remittances do play an important role in financing development goals.

Arguably, many of the consumption investments that remittances finance make positive contributions toward human development in poor areas, helping to counteract deprivation (Conway and Cohen 1998, 28). "Consumption" gen-erally includes spending on nutrition, health, and education, which not only contribute toward human development goals but are in many ways investments for the future. In Indonesia, one study identified children's educations as a main goal of international migration and migrant remittances (Hugo 1995, quoted in ESCAP 2002, 10). Tanya Basok's study (2000, 85–86) of Mexican migrants to Canada also found that children's schooling was one important use of their re-mittances, as was buying land and building a house. Similarly, in Ecuador, Brad Jokisch (2002) found that many rural families, after paying off debts, used re-mittances to build homes as well as purchase agricultural land. And Elizabeth Francis (2002) found that internal migrants' remittances in Kenya were used for school fees, as well as for clothing, paying taxes, bridewealth, and buying cattle. Analyzing Mexican Migration Project data, Lowell and de la Garza found that three-quarters of workers in the United States who remit funds to Mexico stated that at least some portion of these funds are used for health care. And re-cipients of remittances in Tonga, in a study by Tongamoa, were of the opinion that "nothing is more productive than to be able to provide for their daily sub-sistence and to have the economic power to fulfil their family and social re-sponsibilities" (cited in Brown and Ahlburg 1999).

As Orozco (2000, 2) aptly observes, "Recipients (of remittances) become agents of development when their money creates new markets or improves the welfare of the household through education and health care." It is clear that remittances are often directed to improving household welfare. But what about the creation of markets? A key argument is that even consumption ex-penditure can create new economic and employment opportunities. Durand and colleagues (1996) make the case that consumption stimulates economic activity. For instance, remittances spent on family maintenance—48 percent of the US$2 billion in annual remittances to Mexico (Massey and Parrado 1994)—create additional demand for a range of clothing and food items, which are widely produced in Mexico, thereby leading to more production and employment (Durand et al. 1996, 425). Adelman and Taylor's social accounting matrix (1990) has estimated that, as a result of such effects, each migradollar entering Mexico from the United States raised output by US$3.20 (cited in Durand et al. 1996, 425). As Edward Taylor has stated, consumer use of remittances stimulates economic development, particularly when households spend their remittances locally (cited in Martin 2001; see Taylor 1999). Meanwhile, individuals may use consumption of items such as houses to open up economic opportunities (as Grigolini shows in this volume, chapter 6).

Finally, some remittances are used directly for "productive investments," such as small businesses, although the volume of remittances that go to such investments internationally is rather small. Several studies have suggested that remittances in the South Pacific are used as start-up money for shopkeepers, stores and transport businesses, and other business and farm investment (Brown and Ahlburg 1999). Considering Mexican Migration Project data from 1982 to 1996, Louis DeSipio (2000) found that investment in land, tools, and farm animals, though only reported by a minority of respondents, was the second-largest category of use for both remittances and migrants' savings. Remittances may help compensate for market imperfections, such as missing or incomplete rural credit or insurance markets, and so help poor families to accumulate assets (Taylor and Wyatt 1996, 900–901). For instance, Jokisch (2002, 537, 540) found that although international remittances to Ecuador were not being invested in agricultural improvements, longer-term migrants often purchased pasture land in their places of origin and stocked it with cattle. Also, Adams (1998), in his Pakistani study, found that over time remittances from abroad were invested in both irrigated and rainfed land and thus led to rural asset accumulation.

Remittances, therefore, are resources that are used in a range of ways. Most of these uses have direct or indirect development impacts. Usually, remittances are sent and received by members of the same family, and thus the direct impact of a remittance is on a single household. Nevertheless, an increasing number of studies are pointing to examples of migrant remittances that are not just directed at individuals and households but that finance development for entire communities. The scale of such activities is not huge and is generally much smaller than that for private remittances (Lowell and de la Garza 2000, 16). Nevertheless, they can be significant investments in community and "social capital" (Conway and Cohen 1998, 33) as well as in infrastructure and economic development for migrants' places of origin.

Examples of community-level remittances include those by "hometown associations" established by Latin American migrants in the United States (Orozco 2003, 13–14) or by African rural-urban migrants (e.g., Trager 2001). Such organizations invest in their home areas via collective remittances, generated primarily through fund-raising and donations. Migrants may also remit funds to a range of local organizations in their home communities, thus providing another form of community support. In the South Pacific, for instance, a proportion of remittances—in one Samoan study, 41 percent—is used to support community organizations, such as churches and church schools, local development projects, and other local groups and associations, thereby generating wider social welfare gains (Brown and Ahlburg 1999).

The role of Latin American hometown associations in the social and economic development of their places of origin is attracting increasing attention, as is their role as transnational political actors (see, e.g., Goldring 2002). Using fund-raising events and contributions from members resident elsewhere, such organizations build schools, improve roads, open kindergartens, install septic tanks and clinics in their villages of origin, and even establish microenterprises back home to provide jobs (Martin 2001; Kanaiaupuni and Donato 1999, 340; Lowell and de la Garza 2000). Lowell and de la Garza (2000, 14–15) give the example of the Salvadoran United Community of Chinameca, which rebuilt the infrastructure of its war-ravaged hometown in the 1990s, including a school, septic tank, clinic, church, and children's park. They also describe how hometown associations from Zacatecas committed up to $600,000 for fifty-six projects in 1995 (2). Martin (2001) observes, "These are truly grassroots initiatives that involve community-to-community development." Funds provided by hometown associations may be matched by nongovernmental development organizations (Runsten 2003) or by government programs, such as the Two for One program in Zacatecas (García Zamora 2003; Goldring 2002) or the My Community program, which was designed to launch garment factories in Guanajuato (Lowell and de la Garza 2000, 13).

In Africa, there is a similar pattern of hometown development financing via remittances, but here, these remittances often come from internal migration. Josef Gugler (1991) and, more recently, Lillian Trager (1998, 2001) have written about the close ties between Nigerians living in urban areas and their places of origin: ties maintained over time and often manifested in participation in "ethnic associations" (Gugler 1991, 404) or hometown "improvement associations" (Trager 1998, 364–65). J. O. Oucho (1996) has written on similar associations in Kenya. Among the objectives of such organizations are to "council on village developments and finance a major part of such developments," including roads, bridges, schools, and maternity clinics, and to lobby the government on behalf of their home villages; they may also include economic development efforts (Gugler 1991, 404; Trager 1998, 368–69). In such settings, the remittance picture grows more complex: people may "remit" funds to support a hometown even if they have never actually been resident in that town (Trager 2001).

Remittances to organizations and projects in migrants' home communities are a way that migrants channel resources to support a range of development goals. Like transfers among family members, these community-level remittances take place at the grassroots, among those who have some level of personal connection and commitment to the people, organizations, and towns that their funds support. Of course, this does not mean that remittances to local organizations or communities are exempt from political uses; development decisions may still be controlled largely by nonresident elites (Trager 1998, 369), or the funds may be used to further migrants' own political agendas (Fitzgerald 2003). "Grassroots" certainly does not imply the absence of interest groups and agendas. These are always present, for communities are never homogenous. Nevertheless, remittances offer one of the most direct mechanisms of development resource transfer in which both senders and receivers are among those who know local needs best.

THE INSTITUTIONAL TRAP: RETHINKING DEVELOPMENT

So persuasive is the power of the institutions we have created, that they shape not only our preferences, but actually our sense of possibilities.

—*Ivan Illich*

Pro-poor international development, aiming toward the millennium development goals, tends to run on rather narrow institutional tracks. National-level antipoverty plans, empowerment of poor people and their organizations, deepening of democracy, microfinance lending for economic development— these are all comfortable terms with which to think about the development process. Discussion of migration seems almost an antithesis, problematic terrain; it appears to imply abandonment of disadvantaged places and communities rather than their successful development. Yet the literature discussed here clearly indicates that migration and, specifically, migrant remittances play an important development role.

The role of remittances in development is best understood from the perspective of "poor people" themselves, not how development institutions conceptualize development for them, but how these people themselves actually implement, and succeed in achieving, development—the pursuit of improved well-being—given the opportunities within their reach. Both international and internal migration are important ways that people who are categorized as "the poor" act to obtain resources. And remittances represent one important way that such resources are channeled back to their places of origin. While the specific impact of remittances varies, depending on who receives them and how they are used, it is inarguable that they represent significant resource transfer from wealthier to poorer areas. In addition, remittances are a resource that poor people control directly and successfully use to meet development goals such as improved nutrition, education, and housing. In some cases, remittances lead to increased productivity and employment, as well as to risk diversification and asset accumulation for poor families.

Improving the positive development impact of remittances requires looking seriously at migrant remittances as a development resource. On the international front, one key question is how to facilitate the efficient, low-cost transfer of remittance funds. Migrant-friendly fund-transfer alternatives within the formal banking sector include, for instance, three banks in Paris that are focused on Senegalese, Malians, and Ivorians, respectively, and offer low-fee international transfers (IOM 2002, 7). Related questions include how to increase the inflow of financial resources from migrants abroad and how to leverage these funds for maximum development impact? These include not only direct remittances to family members and those made to community organizations but also savings returned to the home country or investments of various kinds back home.

That migrants decide to save or invest their earnings back home "is not only dependent on objective criteria (such as economic returns) but also on subjective factors such as prestige as well as the sheer wish to contribute to the development of their home country" (IOM 2002, 4). Governments of many, though not all, migrant-sending countries are recognizing the importance of fund transfers from their citizens abroad; some are establishing schemes to attempt to increase their amount and development impact. These schemes include repatriable foreign exchange accounts, foreign currency bonds, and other sorts of financial incentives to stimulate investment (Brown and Ahlburg 1999) as well as to encourage collective remittances, such as those by hometown associations, by offering matching funding for community projects (Lowell and de la Garza 2000; García Zamora 2003; Goldring 2002). One Mexican scheme encourages savings in a state-operated bank account in return for the right to purchase agricultural and other inputs at cost (see Kanaiaupuni and Donato 1999, 351). Most such government schemes do expand the options available to migrants and their families and communities. They differ markedly, however, from mandatory programs to capture remittances for development—for instance, that in North Korea (see Lowell and de la Garza 2000)—where funds that arrive direct to the poor are rerouted direct to government bureaucracies.

Understanding migrant remittances as a development resource also involves taking a serious look at the issue of labor migration. Migration, whether within or between countries, is clearly a development strategy that many poor people are choosing. International labor migration in particular is clearly a growing trend. Legal immigration to the United States alone has gone from an average of 330,000 per year in the 1960s to over 1 million per year during the 1990s. Meanwhile, undocumented migrant apprehensions grew from an average of 830,000 annually during the 1970s to around 1.3 million annually in the 1990s (U.S. Immigration and Naturalization Service 1997, quoted in Massey 1999). Yet, despite the choices people are making to migrate, international migrants are increasingly viewed with suspicion and seen as a threat to national sovereignty and identity in receiving countries (Martiniello 2002, 594).

Security concerns and domestic politics in OECD countries since the 1980s have led to ongoing attempts by wealthier nations to exclude the increasing number of migrants from developing countries desiring entry (Massey 1999). At the same time, markets function globally, and both goods and capital are permitted increasingly free movement across borders (Martiniello 2002, 594; Seabrook 1998; Faux 2003). A scenario in which goods and capital are permitted free movement while people are not is both ethically problematic and inconsistent with the free market rhetoric used to justify globalizing economic practices. Free markets would presume free movement of all production inputs, including labor (Seabrook 1998, 27), yet the "tensions between states and markets . . . in a globalizing world" sustain an essential contradiction in which labor is not free (Martiniello 2002).

The result of this contradiction is not the cessation of immigration to areas of economic advantage—such immigration is clearly growing—but rather the increasingly dangerous conditions for people who migrate. Tougher immigration restrictions simply tend to lead to more risk taking by immigrants, such as those that die while attempting to cross the U.S.–Mexican border: sixteen hundred in the past five years (Faux 2003, 36). Douglas S. Massey (2002, 359) cites a tripling of the rate of border deaths between Mexico and the United States in recent years, as a result of government policies. Elsewhere, boats sink, and a range of other dangers face those who migrate illegally (see Seabrook 1998). We now face a world with "large numbers of immigrant workers bereft of legal status and political rights" (Freeman 2002). Yet despite the dangers, huge numbers of people are still choosing to migrate.

At the same time, with international rhetoric running to equity and the empowerment of the poor, migration policies are kept conveniently out of the debate—as if they were a separate issue altogether. However, this chapter indicates that migration and international migration policies are clearly not a separate issue from international development. If the international community is to talk seriously about development, reducing poverty, and empowering the poor, then it must take into account the development strategies that poor people actually use. And this, for large numbers of people internationally, involves migration: cyclical or permanent, short term or long term, internal or international, to places with better economic opportunities. Not only are these strategies being left unfacilitated by the promoters of antipoverty development, but they are also being actively blocked by immigration policies in the world's wealthiest countries.

A consideration of the importance of migrant remittances assures us that migrants, whether internal or international, are not merely abandoning their places and communities of origin. Rather, migrants are making significant investments in the economic and social development of sending areas— investments that in many cases arrive "direct to the poor." Migrants also benefit receiving areas. Mexican president Vincente Fox once observed, "Migrant labor bolsters the American economy, while migrant remittances fuel the Mexican economy" (Jones 2001, 4). Certainly, on the U.S. front, the presence of a seasonal workforce, many of whom are Mexican and Central American migrants, is important to the survival of many of the United States' agricultural industries (4). Even trade unions, traditional opponents of immigration, may be beginning to see the advantage of having immigrant workers join their unions (Freeman 2002) rather than have to compete with foreign workers who may have no unions at all.

In many ways, migrant remittances reflect the international development field's own best-practice visions: resources in local control being used to meet local needs by empowered local actors in disadvantaged parts of the world. At the same time, migration and remittances are far from the ideal answer to global inequities. As a strategy, migration undoubtedly places stress on sending families and communities. It also places stress on migrants themselves; as Martin (2001, np) writes, "Latin American migrants tend to have low incomes, often living in poverty, yet they remit thousands of millions of dollars to their home countries." Consider the figures for Mexican immigrants to the United States: they remit an average of $240 monthly— that's $2,880 per year—and they have an average annual income of $7,455 (Lowell and de la Garza 2000, 2). And the world is full of stories of exploitation faced by migrant workers. That some of the most targeted development finance reaching poor areas around the world is coming from the hands of underpaid and exploited workers should give us food for thought—particularly those of us who have labored internationally as highly paid development consultants. It seems clear that the area of workers' rights, whether in their home countries or abroad, is one where a great deal of work needs to be done.

In conclusion, real antipoverty commitment can be found on the part of migrant workers, who often make considerable sacrifices not to address a concept called poverty but to help out their own family, friends, and neighbors— people with whom they have a contact, a relationship. Through these relationships, resources are channeled, helping create change. Migrants' commitment, resources, knowledge, and contacts can complement a range of development activities, from building social infrastructure with remittances from hometown associations to improving the consumption and investment opportunities for disadvantaged households to helping to start local nonprofit organizations or microenterprises using contacts and knowledge acquired abroad.[8] These activities and their impact cannot stand indefinitely outside international development policymaking. They must be invited in. The questions must be asked about the benefits and the costs of migration to poor people and poor regions and how policies—including international migration policies—can facilitate poor people's own solutions to poverty. Given the current international commitment to decreasing poverty, now is the time to ask those questions and to push our desires for change through to their logical conclusions.

NOTES

1. United Nations Development Programme (2002) data for 2000.

2. As one example, David Runsten (2003, 11) gives the case of a Oaxacan village women's production cooperative that "had gotten the idea of preserving nopales in jars from a migrant who had seen this at work in Salinas, California." See also Sasha Newell (this volume, chapter 5) on the symbolic importance of migration in Côte d'Ivoire and how successful migrant experiences are a source of prestige (and thus social resources) for migrants' families.

3. See also, the studies on Pakistan, Kenya, and Botswana cited in Theodore P. Lianos (1997, 76–77). Good data on the extent of international migrants' remittances are available from studies in Latin America. These data show that 70 percent of Guatemalans and Salvadorans living in the United States remit funds to their countries of origin; that approximately 60 percent of Colombians and Dominicans do so (DeSipio 2000, based on NALEO Educational Fund and Tomás Rivera Policy Institute 1998); and that 60 percent of temporary or permanent Mexican migrants remit (Lowell and de la Garza 2000, 17).

4. Specifically, the emergence of various migrant deployment agencies run both by government and private enterprises.

5. For instance, Shawn M. Kanaiaupuni and Katharine M. Donato (1999) found that infant mortality increased in the short term when Mexican heads of households migrated internationally. However, in the long term, they found that money from work abroad led to improved living conditions and better health where U.S. migration was common (340).

6. There is some disagreement over this estimate—for instance, one report cites worldwide remittances as being more than US$70 billion per year (ESCAP 2002, 5).

7. Information on remittances from Asia (ESCAP 2002, 5); information on overseas development assistance (DAC 2000, table 25).

8. Conway and Cohen (1998, 35) give the example of conservationist nongovernmental organizations begun by migrants returning to Central America.

REFERENCES

Adams, Richard H., Jr. 1998. Remittances, investment, and rural asset accumulation in Pakistan. *Economic Development and Cultural Change* 47 (1): 155–73.

Adelman, Irma, and J. Edward Taylor. 1990. Is structural adjustment with a human face possible? The case of Mexico. *Journal of Development Studies* 26 (3): 387–407.

Annis, Sheldon, and Peter Hakim. 1988. *Direct to the poor: Grassroots development in Latin America.* Boulder, Colo.: Rienner.

Basok, Tanya. 2000. Migration of Mexican seasonal farm workers to Canada and development: Obstacles to productive investment. *International Migration Review* 34 (1): 79–97.

Bertram, Geoff. 1999. The MIRAB model twelve years on. *Contemporary Pacific* 11 (1): 105–22.

Brown, Richard P. C., and Dennis A. Ahlburg. 1999. Remittances in the South Pacific. *International Journal of Social Economics* 26 (1/2/3): 325–44.

Bryceson, Deborah. 2000. Rural Africa at the crossroads. *Natural Resources Perspectives* 52 (April), www.odi.org.uk/nrp/52.html (Overseas Development Institute; accessed March 10, 2005).

Chambers, Robert. 1994. The origins and practice of participatory rural appraisal. *World Development* 22 (7): 953–69.

Coirolo, Luis, Keith McLean, Mondonga Mokoli, Andrea Ryan, Parmesh Shah, and Melissa Williams. 2001. Community based rural development: Reducing poverty from the ground up. World Bank Rural Strategy Discussion Paper 6, Washington, D.C.

Connell, John. 1983. Migration, employment, and development in the South Pacific. Country Report 18, South Pacific Commission, Noumea, Tonga.

Conway, Dennis, and Jeffrey H. Cohen. 1998. Consequences of migration and remittances for Mexican transnational communities. *Economic Geography* 74 (1): 26–44.

David, Rosalind. 1995. Changing places: Women, resource management, and migration in the Sahel. London: SOS Sahel.

David, Wilfred L. 1997. *The conversation of economic development.* Armonk, N.Y.: Sharpe.

Davis, Jennifer, and Dale Whittington. 1998. "Participatory" research for development projects: A comparison of the community meeting and household survey techniques. *Economic Development and Cultural Change* 47 (1): 73–94.

de Haan, Arjan. 1999. Livelihoods and poverty: The role of migration—a critical review of the migration literature. *Journal of Development Studies* 36 (2): 1–31.

———. 2002. Migration and livelihoods in historical perspective: A case study of Bihar, India. *Journal of Development Studies* 38 (5): 115–42.

Department for International Development. 1997. Eliminating world poverty: A challenge for the 21st century. White paper on international development, www.dfid.gov.uk/Pubs/files/whitepaper1997.pdf (accessed March 10, 2005).

DeSipio, Louis. 2000. Sending money home . . . for now: Remittances and immigrant adaptation in the United States. Working paper, Inter-American Dialogue and the Tomás Rivera Policy Institute, www.thedialogue.org/publications/DeSipio.asp (accessed March 10, 2005).

Development Assistance Committee. 2000. Statistical annex of the 2000 development co-operation report. Paris: Organization for Economic Cooperation and Development (OECD), Development Assistance Committee, http://webnet1.oecd.org/document/9/0,2340,en_2649_33721_1893129_1_1_1_1,0 0.html (accessed August 2003).

Durand, Jorge, Emilio A. Parrado, and Douglas S. Massey. 1996. Migradollars and development: A reconsideration of the Mexican case. *International Migration Review* 30 (2): 423–34.

Economic and Social Commission for Asia and the Pacific. 2002. Migration, urbanization and poverty: International migration and development: Opportunities and challenges for poverty reduction. Paper presented at the Fifth Asian and Pacific Population Conference, Senior Officials Segment, December 11–14, Bangkok, www.unescap.org/pop/5appc/papers/english/prud_sappc_4e.doc (accessed July 2003).

Faux, Jeff. 2003. How NAFTA failed Mexico: Immigration is not a development policy. *American Prospect* 14 (7): 35–37.

Fitzgerald, David. 2003. Clientelism and democracy: Two faces of migrant hometown ties. Paper presented at the Twenty-fourth International Congress of the Latin American Studies Association, March 27–29, Dallas, Texas.

Francis, Elizabeth. 2002. Gender, migration and multiple livelihoods: Cases from Eastern and Southern Africa. *Journal of Development Studies* 38 (5): 167–91.

Freeman, Gary P. 2002. Review of *Immigration policy and the challenge of globalization: Unions and employers in unlikely alliance*, by Julie R. Watts. *International Migration Review* 36 (4): 1222–23.

García Zamora, Rodolfo. 2003. Los Proyectos Productivos con Migrantes en México Hoy. Paper presented at the Twenty-fourth International Congress of the Latin American Studies Association, March 27–29, Dallas, Texas.

Glystos, Nicholas P. 1993. Measuring the income effects of migrant remittances: A methodological approach applied to Greece. *Economic Development and Cultural Change* 42 (1): 131–68.

Go, Stella P. 2002. Recent trends in migration movements and policies: The movement of Filipino professionals and managers. Paper presented at the Workshop on International Migration and Labour Market in Asia, Japan Institute of Labor and Organisation for Economic Cooperation and Development, February 4–5, Tokyo.

Goldring, Luin. 2002. The Mexican state and transmigrant organizations: Negotiating the boundaries of membership and participation. *Latin American Research Review* 37 (3):55–99.

Gore, Charles. 1993. Entitlement relations and "unruly" social practices: A comment on the work of Amartya Sen. *Journal of Development Studies* 29 (3): 429–60.

Gugler, Josef. 1991. Life in a dual system revisited: Urban-rural ties in Enugu, Nigeria, 1961–87. *World Development* 19 (5): 399–409.

Hugo, Graeme. 1995. International labour migration and the family: Some observations from Indonesia. *Asian and Pacific Migration Journal* (Quezon City) 4 (2–3): 273–301.

Ife, Jim. 2002. *Community development: Community-based alternatives in an age of globalisation.* 2nd ed. Frenchs Forest, New South Wales: Pearson.

Illich, Ivan. 1979. Outwitting the "developed" countries. In *The political economy of development and underdevelopment*, 2nd ed., ed. Charles K. Wilber, 436–44. New York: Random House.

Inter-American Foundation. 1977. *They know how . . . : An experiment in development assistance.* Washington, D.C,: Inter-American Foundation.

International Organization for Migration. 2002. *Remittances to Africa and their contribution to development.* Geneva: International Organization for Migration, www.december18.net/paper72IOMRemittancesAfrica.pdf (accessed March 10, 2005).

Islam, M. D. 1991. Labour migration and development: A case study of a rural community in Bangladesh. *Bangladesh Journal of Political Economy* 11 (2B): 570–87.

Itzigsohn, Jose. 1995. Migrant remittances, labor markets, and household strategies: A comparative analysis of low-income household strategies in the Caribbean basin. *Social Forces* 74 (2): 633–55.

Jokisch, Brad D. 2002. Migration and agricultural change: The case of smallholder agriculture in highland Ecuador. *Human Ecology: An Interdisciplinary Journal* 30 (4): 523–50.

Jones, Richard. 2001. Don't bar the door to immigration reform. *American Vegetable Grower*, November, 4.

Jones, Richard C. 1998. Remittances and inequality: A question of migration stages and geographic scale. *Economic Geography* 74 (1): 8–25.

Kanaiaupuni, Shawn M., and Katharine M. Donato. 1999. Migradollars and mortality: The effects of migration on infant survival in Mexico. *Demography* 36 (3): 339–53.

Keese, James. 2003. Smallholder agriculture and poverty alleviation in indigenous communities. In *Here to help: NGOs combating poverty in Latin America*, ed. R. Eversole, 3–27. Armonk, N.Y.: Sharpe.

Kenny, Susan. 1999. *Developing communities for the future: Community development in Australia.* South Melbourne, Australia: Nelson.

Lianos, Theodore P. 1997. Factors determining migrant remittances: The case of Greece. *International Migration Review* 31 (1): 72–87.

Lowell, Lindsay B. 2001. Some developmental effects of the international migration of highly skilled persons. ILO International Migration Paper 46. Geneva, Switzerland: International Labour Organzation.

Lowell, Lindsay, and Rodolfo O. de la Garza. 2000. *The developmental role of remittances in U.S. Latino communities and in Latin American countries.* Washington, D.C.: Inter-American Dialogue and the Tomás Rivera Policy Institute, www.thedialogue.org/publications/pdf/lowell.pdf (accessed March 10, 2005).

Lowell, Lindsay, Rodolfo O. de la Garza, and Mike Hogg. 2000. Remittances, U.S. Latino communities, and development in Latin American countries. *MigrationWorld* 28 (5): 13–17.

Martin, Susan F. 2001. Remittances as a development tool. *Economic Perspectives* (Addressing Global Poverty) 6, no. 3 (September), usinfo.state.gov/journals/ites/0901/ijee/martin.htm (U.S. State Department electronic journal; accessed March 10, 2005).

Martiniello, Marco. 2002. Migration between states and markets. Conference report. Inter-congress meeting, the International Sociological Association, Belgium, May 17–19, 2001. *International Migration Review* 36 (2): 593–96.

Massey, Douglas S. 1999. International migration at the dawn of the twenty-first century: The role of the state. *Population and Development Review* 25 (2): 303–5.

———. 2002. Review of *Thinking the unthinkable: The immigration myth exposed,* by Nigel Harris. *Population and Development Review* 28 (2): 358–60.

Massey, Douglas, Rafael Alarcón, Jorge Durand, and Humberto González. 1987. *Return to Aztlan: The social process of international migration from western Mexico.* Berkeley: University of California Press.

Massey, Douglas S., and Emilio A. Parrado. 1994. Migradollars: The remittances and savings of Mexican migrants to the United States. *Population Research and Policy Review* 13 (1): 3–30.

Maxwell, Simon. 2003. Heaven or hubris: Reflections on the new "new poverty agenda." *Development Policy Review* 21 (1): 5–25.

NALEO Educational Fund and Tomás Rivera Policy Institute. 1998. *America's newest voices: Colombians, Dominicans, Guatemalans, and Salvadorans in the United States examine their public policy needs.* Los Angeles: NALEO Educational Fund and Tomás Rivera Policy Institute.

Oberai, A. S., and H. K. Manmohan Singh. 1980. Migration, remittances, and rural development: Findings of a case study in the Indian Punjab. *International Labour Review* 119 (2): 229–41.

Organisation for Economic Cooperation and Development. 2000. *A better world for all: Progress toward the international development goals.* www.paris21.org/betterworld/pdf/bwa_e.pdf (accessed March 10, 2005).

Orozco, Manuel. 2000. Remittances and markets: New players and practices. Working paper, Inter-American Dialogue and the Tomás Rivera Policy Institute, www.thedialogue.org/publications/Remittances_and_Markets.htm (accessed March 10, 2005).

————. 2003. Remittances, the rural sector, and policy options in Latin America. Paper presented to the World Council of Credit Unions conference "Paving the Way Forward for Rural Finance: An International Conference on Best Practices," Washington, D.C., June 2–4.

Osaki, Keiko. 2002. Internal migration and remittances in Thailand: Economic necessity or social institution? Paper presented at the International Union for the Scientific Study of Population Regional Population Conference, June 11–12, Bangkok.

Oucho, J. O. 1996. *Urban migrants and rural development in Kenya.* Nairobi, Kenya: Nairobi University Press.

Puri, Shivani, and Tineke Ritzema. 1999. Migrant worker remittances, micro-finance, and the informal economy: Prospects and issues. ILO Working Paper 21. Geneva, Switzerland: International Labour Organization.

Regmi, Gopal, and C. Tisdell. 2002. Remitting behaviour of Nepalese rural-to-urban migrants: Implications for theory and policy. *Journal of Development Studies* 38 (3): 76–94.

Rodriguez, Edgard R. 1998. International migration and income distribution in the Philippines. *Economic Development and Cultural Change* 46 (2): 329–50.

Runsten, David. 2003. Migration and rural development: Further notes. Paper presented at the Twenty-fourth International Congress of the Latin American Studies Association, March 27–29, Dallas, Texas.

Seabrook, Jeremy. 1998. A global market for all. *New Statesman,* June 26, 25–27.

Sen, Amartya. 1981. *Poverty and famines.* Oxford: Clarendon.

————. 1985. *Commodities and capabilities.* Amsterdam: Elsevier.

————. 1999. *Development as freedom.* New York: Knopf.

Simanowitz, Anton. 2000. Targeting the poor—comparing visual and participatory methods. *Small Enterprise Development* 11 (1): 29–39.

Simonelli, Jeanne, and Duncan Earle. 2003. Disencumbering development, alleviating poverty through autonomy in Chiapas. In *Here to help: NGOs combating poverty in Latin America*, ed. R. Eversole, 174–98. Armonk, N.Y.: Sharpe.

Skeldon, Ronald. 2002. Migration and poverty. *Asia-Pacific Population Journal* 17 (4): 67–82.

Smith, Elliot Blair. 2001. Migrants flex muscles back home in Mexico: Money, experience earned in USA give them influence. *USA Today*, June 28, A09.

Stark, Oded, J. Edward Taylor, and Shlomo Yitzhaki. 1986. Remittances and inequality. *Economic Journal* 96 (383): 722–40.

Taylor, J. Edward. 1999. The new economics of labour migration and the role of remittances in the development process. *International Migration* 37 (1): 63–88.

Taylor, J. Edward, and T. J. Wyatt. 1996. The shadow value of migrant remittances, income and inequality in a household-farm economy. *Journal of Development Studies* 32 (6): 899–912.

Tongamoa, T. 1987. Migration, remittances, and development: A Tongan perspective. Master's thesis, Department of Geography, University of Sydney.

Trager, Lillian. 1998. Home town linkages and local development in south-western Nigeria: Whose agenda? What impact? *Africa* 68 (3): 360–82.

———. 2001. *Yoruba hometowns: Community, identity and development in Nigeria*. Boulder, Colo.: Rienner.

United Nations Development Programme. 2000. *Overcoming human poverty: UNDP poverty report 2000*. www.undp.org/povertyreport (accessed March 10, 2005).

———. 2002. Human development indicators 2002: Flows of aid, private capital and debt. In *Human development report 2002: Deepening democracy in a fragmented world*. http://hdr.undp.org/reports/global/2002/en (accessed March 10, 2005).

———. 2003. Human development index. In *Human development report 2003: Millennium development goals: A compact among nations to end human poverty*, 237–40. www.undp.org/hdr2003/pdf/hdr03_HDI.pdf (accessed March 10, 2005).

United Nations Educational, Scientific, and Cultural Organization. 2000. *UNESCO's strategy on development and poverty eradication*. Paris: UNESCO, www.unesco.org/

most/160ex13eng.pdf (accessed March 10, 2005).White, Sarah C. 1996. Depoliticising development: The uses and abuses of participation. *Development in Practice* 6 (1): 6–15.

U.S. Immigration and Naturalization Service. 1997. *1996 statistical yearbook of the Immigration and Naturalization Service.* Washington, D.C.: U.S. Government Printing Office.

White, Sarah C. 1996. Depoliticising development: The uses and abuses of participation. *Development in Practice* 6(1): 6–15.

World Bank. 2000. *Attacking poverty: World development report, 2000/2001.* Washington, D.C.: World Bank, http://web.worldbank.org/WBSITE/EXTERNAL/ TOPICS/EXTPOVERTY/0,,contentMDK:20195989~pagePK:148956~piPK:216618 ~theSitePK:336992,00.html (accessed March 10, 2005).

Index

About the Contributors

Jeffrey H. Cohen received his doctorate from Indiana University in 1994 and is a professor of cultural anthropology and demography at the Pennsylvania State University. He has worked on the topics of economics, migration, and development in Oaxaca, Mexico, for over a decade. In 2004 he began a multi-disciplinary investigation of Dominican immigrants relocating to new gateway destinations in the United States. His articles have appeared in several Society for Economic Anthropology publications, *Human Organization*, and the *American Anthropologist*. His most recent ethnography is *The Culture of Migration in Southern Mexico* (2004).

Robyn Eversole is a research fellow at RMIT University, Centre for Regional and Rural Development, Hamilton, Victoria, Australia. Originally from West Virginia, she holds a doctorate in anthropology from McGill University, Montreal, Canada, and has done research on economic and social development issues in South America, Western Australia, and currently in southwestern Victoria. Her publications include the book *Here to Help: NGOs Combating Poverty in Latin America*, a range of articles in international scholarly and practitioner journals, and five books for children.

Peter Finke studied anthropology and Central Asian studies in Munich, Göttingen, and Berlin. He holds a master of arts degree from Free University Berlin (1994) and a doctorate from Köln University (1999). Since 1991, he has conducted field research among Kazak pastoralists in western Mongolia and the effects that the transformation from a socialist to a marketlike economy had on the livelihoods of people. Together with Meltem Sancak, he worked among Kazaks who had migrated from China to Kazakstan after the latter's independence. In 2000, he joined the Max Planck Institute for Social Anthropology, for which he is doing research on collective identity in Uzbekistan. He is also currently a visiting faculty at the Department of Sociology, Middle East Technical University in Ankara, Turkey.

Silvia Grigolini is a doctoral student at Brandeis University, Waltham, Massachusetts. She is currently conducting fieldwork on the management of economic and social resources—including remittances—within migrant-sending households in Oaxaca, Mexico.

Dolores Koenig is professor of anthropology at American University in Washington, D.C. She has worked on various aspects of the anthropology of development in French-speaking West Africa, with special emphasis on the ways in which household labor allocation responds to the changing political economy. With Tiéman Diarra and Moussa Sow, she has authored *Innovation and Individuality in African Development: Changing Production Strategies in Rural Mali* (1998). She has also published articles in the *Journal of Political Ecology, Urban Anthropology and Studies of Cultural Systems* and *World Economic Development*, and the *Women and International Development Annual*.

Stephen C. Lubkemann is assistant professor of anthropology and international affairs at George Washington University and adjunct assistant professor in the Portuguese and Brazilian Studies Department and the Watson Institute at Brown University. His research focuses on displacement, violence, migration, diasporas, and transnationalism. He has completed fieldwork in Mozambique, in South Africa, and with African refugees in Portugal. He is currently pursuing projects on transgenerational displacement and urbanization in Angola and on the political and socioeconomic influence of displacement diasporas in their war-torn countries of origin through a specific study of the

Liberian case. He is also pursuing a critical study of the structure and effects of international humanitarian action. From 1999 to 2001, Steve served on the first Roundtable on Forced Migration of the National Academy of Science's National Research Council. He has published articles in the *Journal of Refugee Studies, Canadian Journal of African Studies, Journal of Peace Research, Anthropological Quarterly*, and *Diaspora*, and he is the author of a number of book chapters, including the chapter on refugees in the award-winning volume *World at Risk: A Global Issues Sourcebook* (2002).

Sasha Newell is a Mellon Fellow at the University of Illinois, Urbana-Champaign. He finished his doctorate at Cornell University in 2003 with a dissertation entitled "Fashioning Modernity: Consumption, Migration, and the Production of Ivoirian Identities." His fieldwork in Côte d'Ivoire was funded by a grant from the Wenner Gren Foundation, and he also conducted research among Congolese immigrants in Paris. His research interests include consumption and value, migration and nationalism, witchcraft, and urban social networks. He is currently at work on a comparative theorization of consumption and magical efficacy, as well as an ethnographic project on the American attic.

Ricardo Pérez is assistant professor of anthropology at Eastern Connecticut State University. In 2000, he obtained a doctorate in cultural anthropology from the University of Connecticut. His teaching and research interests include the analysis of development (and postdevelopment) discourses, representations and discourses of the environment, Caribbean transnational migration, globalization, and the anthropology of the state. His book *Fragments of Memory: State-Sponsored Development and the Spaces of Modernity in Puerto Rico* is due out in 2005. His work has been published in *CENTRO: Journal of the Center for Puerto Rican Studies*, and he contributes book reviews to *CHOICE: Current Reviews for Academic Libraries*.

Meltem Sancak studied sociology and anthropology at the Middle East Technical University, Ankara, Turkey, and at Köln University, Germany, where she earned her master of arts degree in 1999. She conducted field research on life perspectives of second-generation migrants from Turkey in Germany. Together with Peter Finke, she worked among Kazaks who migrated from China to

Kazakstan after the latter's independence. In 2000 she joined the Max Planck Institute for Social Anthropology, for which she is doing research in Uzbekistan on the relationship between economic change and social identities.

Lillian Trager is professor of anthropology and director of the Center for International Studies, University of Wisconsin–Parkside. Her research in Nigeria has focused on market systems, the informal economy, migration and hometown linkages, and local development. She has also conducted research in the Philippines on rural-urban linkages and migration. Her publications include *Yoruba Hometowns: Community, Identity, and Development in Nigeria* (2001) and *The City Connection: Migration and Family Interdependence in the Philippines* (1988). In 2000–2001, she was Fulbright Senior Scholar at Obafemi Awolowo University, Ile-Ife, Nigeria, while doing research on contemporary Nigerian art and artists. She was president of the Society for Economic Anthropology from 2003 to 2005.